Preparing for College

SUNY series
FRONTIERS IN EDUCATION
Philip G. Altbach, Editor

The Frontiers in Education Series draws upon a range of disciplines and approaches in the analysis of contemporary educational issues and concerns. Books in the series help to reinterpret established fields of scholarship in education by encouraging the latest synthesis and research. A special focus highlights educational policy issues from a multidisciplinary perspective. The series is published in cooperation with the School of Education, Boston College. A complete listing of books in the series can be found at the end of this volume.

Preparing for College

Nine Elements of
Effective Outreach

Edited by
William G. Tierney
Zoë B. Corwin
Julia E. Colyar

State University of New York Press

Published by
State University of New York Press, Albany

Printed in the United States of America

For information, address State University of New York Press,
194 Washington Avenue, Suite 305, Albany, NY 12210-2384

Production by Judith Block
Marketing by Anne M. Valentine

Library of Congress Cataloging-in-Publication Data

Preparing for College: Nine Elements of Effective Outreach / edited by
 William G. Tierney, Zoë B. Corwin & Julia E. Colyar.
   p.   cm. — (SUNY series, frontiers in education)
 Includes bibliographical references and index.
 ISBN 0-7914-6275-7 (alk. paper) — ISBN 0-7914-6276-5 (pbk. : alk.
 paper)
   1. Educational equalization—United States.   2. College preparation
 programs—United States.   I. Tierney, William G.   II. Corwin, Zoë B.,
 1971–   III. Colyar, Julia E., 1969–   IV. Series.

 LC213.2.F76   2004
 373.18—dc22   2004041629

10 9 8 7 6 5 4 3 2 1

Contents

Acknowledgments

We sincerely appreciate the diligence of undergraduate research assistant, Rizza Gonzales, in compiling and verifying the references for this book. We also value the administrative support of Gina Lincicum, Monica Raad, and Diane Flores from our Center of Higher Education Policy Analysis at the University of Southern California. This book developed out of a larger research project administered by Oscar Porter and funded by the United States Department of Education [Award # R305T010143]. Denise Bell, Kristan Venegas, Susan Auerbach, and Paz Oliverez assisted in the development and articulation of this project; we thank them for their collaboration in the study.

It has been our pleasure to work with such esteemed chapter authors. Their insights have enlivened our understandings of college preparation programs and college going processes. Their work continues to inspire and engage us.

We also thank the many college preparation participants, program staff, and administrators for assisting our efforts. Our on-going partnership has been an invaluable aspect of this research.

Royalties from this book will be donated to the American Indian College Fund and SALEF (Salvadoran-American Leadership & Educational Fund) Education for Excellence Program.

ZOË B. CORWIN
JULIA E. COLYAR
WILLIAM G. TIERNEY

Introduction: Engaging Research and Practice—Extracurricular and Curricular Influences on College Access

Over the last generation, a myriad of experiments have attempted to bolster access to college. One of the more decentralized and significant attempts pertains to what we call "college preparation programs." Educational institutions, state and federal governments, and local communities have committed significant resources to the development of a wide array of outreach activities designed to identify and assist underrepresented students in their pathways to college. Programs such as Mathematics, Engineering, Science Achievement (MESA), Upward Bound, "I Have a Dream," Advancement Via Individual Determination (AVID), Puente, College Summit, and an extraordinary number of localized attempts have aimed to diversify the population of college goers. Although these efforts are well-intentioned, minority students remain underrepresented on college campuses. Opportunity, access, and attainment for minority students continue to fall below the levels afforded White and Asian American students (American Council on Education, 2002). Indeed, by the time children enter kindergarten, disparities in achievement among Whites, African Americans, and Latinos have already appeared. This "achievement gap" has been called *the* education issue of the new millennium in policy circles and popular media (James, Jurich, & Estes, 2002).

To be sure, college preparation programs cannot be blamed for the con-

1

tinuing disparities in educational achievement, nor should they be viewed as a cure-all for educational inequity. Structural inequity creates unequal opportunities, and the quality of one's schooling varies dramatically based on social class. Nevertheless, the remarkable diversity in college preparation programs raises a question that is the driving force in this book: with a finite amount of time and resources, which activities are most likely to improve educational achievement for underrepresented youth in the United States?

Our assumption is that college preparation programs cannot be all things to all people. All activities are not equal and some activities will be more effective than others. Unfortunately, there is very little evaluative data on what works in college preparation programs. As noted previously (Tierney & Hagedorn, 2002), most programs are underfunded and understaffed. Harried program directors seldom allot the necessary time or resources to conduct evaluations of their programs when they believe that direct services are paramount. While we understand the desire to focus direct services to populations that desperately need supplemental educational instruction, we also recognize that without effective evaluative mechanisms, programs run the risk of not providing the most effective services possible because staff do not have an understanding of what works.

Outreach programs have begun to come under increased scrutiny. Current programs are expected to meet higher levels of accountability from foundations and granting agencies. Yet there is still no consensus on what makes a program successful. Numerous programs have been created, revised, dissolved, and recreated, but programmatic success remains a mystery. According to many researchers, little empirical evidence has been collected about program effectiveness (Coles, 1993; Gándara, Larson et al., 1998; Perna & Swail, 1998).

In this book, we analyze and define the parameters of effective college outreach programs. This effort comes on the heels of a great deal of previous work in the area of college preparation. Many of the authors in this volume have significantly contributed to an understanding of college access for underrepresented students. Our work here, however, takes a different approach: rather than looking at college preparation writ large, we look specifically at various program components. In previous work, we developed and analyzed a taxonomy of college preparation efforts (Tierney & Hagedorn, 2002) and outlined the various components of different programs, such as academic preparation, mentoring, and counseling. Throughout this text, we examine how various components operate *within* the context of preparation programs, and the authors analyze how each contributes—or does not contribute—to program success. The goals of this work are not, then, simply to describe college preparation efforts, but to engage with the individual program elements—to provide a means by which discreet components can be studied, understood, evaluated, and improved.

DEFINITIONS: WHAT WE KNOW

College preparation programs are aimed at enhancing and supplementing a school's regular activities to assist primarily low-income, minority youth who might otherwise not be able to attend college. While individual programs vary in significant ways, there are several structural elements that are frequently employed across programs. Each chapter is based on a proposition that the authors have assessed. The propositions reflect curricular and extracurricular components that are integral to programs we have observed across the country over the past decade. We developed the propositions in argumentative fashion in order to stimulate the authors to take a stand and in an effort to foster meaningful dialogue about issues of access. Accordingly, the propositions for enabling students to get into a college or university are as follows:

1. It is helpful, but not critical, to emphasize the culture of the student.
2. Family engagement is critical.
3. Peer groups are helpful, but not critical.
4. Programs need to begin no later than the ninth grade and have structured activities throughout the year.
5. Having knowledgeable, available counselors at the core of the program is critical.
6. Access to a college preparation curriculum is the most critical variable.
7. Cocurricular activities are irrelevant.
8. Mentoring is helpful, but not critical.
9. There is a positive relationship between the cost of program delivery and achieving college readiness.

Clearly, the propositions are not exhaustive. We have not addressed the important questions of financial aid for college, differences in experience by gender, and retention in postsecondary environments. Many of the chapters do, however, address such questions within the context of the individual propositions. In addition, we do not discuss the underlying political context in which all of these questions are played out. There are structural and cultural constraints implicit in the educational system that impede access for minority and low-income students. The American educational system and urban contexts in particular are fraught with long-term problems that exist outside the purview of this book. Our assumption is that given these constraints, and given the knowledge that fundamental challenges exist for all schools, college preparation programs ought to be examined so that ways to promote success can be identified and enhanced.

In what follows, we discuss the assumptions that guide our research and the organization of this text.

FRAMING THE BOOK: UNDERLYING ASSUMPTIONS

The book's framework builds on two assumptions about the role of college preparation programs for historically underrepresented students: (1) students need appropriate *intellectual scaffolding* (skills and knowledge) to become college ready, and (2) college-going skills and knowledge are most effectively communicated by programs that build on a *cultural scaffolding* (that emphasize students' cultural backgrounds). While there is no universal formula for the expertise necessary for success in college, there is broad agreement that the following five competency areas are beneficial to stimulating college readiness: (1) academic preparation; (2) access to college planning information and navigational strategies; (3) development of self-efficacy and college-going aspirations; (4) strategies of socialization and acculturation; and (5) financial aid and financial planning skills.

The nine components of college preparation programs addressed in the following chapters influence the development of these essential skills in unique and complementary ways. As you will see, the chapter themes do not occur in isolation; they overlap, not only with each other, but with the development of the five skill areas as well.

Intellectual Scaffolding

ACADEMIC PREPARATION

As Laura Perna demonstrates in chapter 6, the most fundamental skill area and strongest predictor of success in college is academic preparation. Given that the development of academic skills varies tremendously between schools with regard to intensity, quality, and access to a rigorous academic curriculum (Hagedorn & Fogel, 2002; Oakes, 1985; Kozol, 1991; Mehan et al., 1996), there is an integral connection between participating in an academically rigorous curriculum and with all the other chapters, as they address strategies for surmounting shortcomings in academic preparedness.

ACCESS TO COLLEGE PLANNING INFORMATION AND NAVIGATIONAL STRATEGIES

Another factor in promoting college readiness is the ability to access knowledge about the college application process and college going in general. In order to better understand the mechanisms involved in college decision making, Hossler, Schmit, and Vesper (1999) advocate using an *information-processing model*: "a perspective (or lens) that makes gathering and processing information in a social setting an essential part of decision making rather than a prerequisite to it" (p. 151). When aiming to improve how students access and interpret institutional knowledge about college going, the chapters pertaining to social support networks are particularly valid. For example, low-socioeconomic status (SES) students, already considered at risk of not pursuing postsecondary education, are in particularly precarious positions with regard to access to information about college. Stanton-Salazar and Dornbusch (1995) note: "when lack of access to institutional funds of knowledge is combined with perceptions of discrimination, self-elimination is a likely result" (p. 118). If students in low-support environments do not receive adequate and appropriate guidance, their likelihood of dropping out or not pursuing a college education rises significantly. The chapters in part 1 of the text suggest the value of social support networks such as families, peers, school counselors, and mentors in disseminating information and aiding students to decipher information about college and navigate the college application process. Furthermore, by outlining the timing of key college-going hurdles in chapter 8, Marguerite Bonous-Hammarth and Walter Allen suggest a timeline for monitoring informational issues.

DEVELOPMENT OF SELF-EFFICACY AND COLLEGE-GOING ASPIRATIONS

Many authors have stressed the importance of developing college-going aspirations and building a sense of self-efficacy in bolstering academic advancement and college-going outcomes (Bandura, 1989; McDonough, 1997; Murray & Mosidi, 1993; Praport, 1993; Sutton & Fall, 1995). Related to the concept of building aspirations and self-efficacy are skills such as setting goals, persisting at a task, and maintaining college-going motivations and orientations (Hagedorn & Fogel, 2002). Aspiration development is discussed to various extents in many of the chapters, with special emphasis included in the chapters pertaining to social support networks.

STRATEGIES OF SOCIALIZATION AND ACCULTURATION

Positive adjustment to the intellectual rigors of college life in conjunction with a new social environment can be challenging for students and significantly affect chances of college completion. The challenges faced during the transition to college often affect low-income and minority students to a greater extent than their counterparts from higher SES backgrounds who, equipped with the cultural capital necessary to succeed in predominantly white institutions, do not have to make as many social adjustments to the new environment. Students of color and low SES have to balance time spent adapting and learning coping strategies for survival in college with academic achievement (Fleming, 1981; Gunnings, 1982). Consequently, college preparation programs and students' support systems can be proactive in preparing students for college persistence by enhancing academic preparation and reviewing social strategies for survival during the first college years.

FINANCIAL AID AND FINANCIAL PLANNING SKILLS

For many, one of the largest inhibitors to college going is the prospect of being able to afford a college education. Knowledge about the costs of college and the benefits of college graduation on lifetime earning power, and the expertise to manage college costs are complex skills to master. This topic is important enough to deserve book-length analysis such as that of Levine and Nidiffer (1996), St. John & Asker (2003), and Heller (2001). While we have not included a chapter on financing college, each chapter has significant repercussions for financial knowledge and management. Students' social support networks can help to decipher loan applications, financial aid packages, and the costs of living. Programs can provide instruction in applying for financial aid and understanding the costs and benefits of attending college. We hope that a discussion of how financial aid can be accessed, who can help, and the timing of the process is facilitated through the conceptual framework provided in each chapter.

Cultural Scaffolding

Rueda, Monzó, and Arzubiaga (2002) delineate the concept of *academic instrumental knowledge* as a particular subset of cultural capital and offer a framework for thinking about the attainment of the above-mentioned skills and school-specific knowledge while taking into consideration the sociocultural context in which knowledge is communicated. They frame the acquisition and use of knowledge, skills, and aspirations useful for academic success in a way that does not impinge on a student's cultural background. Rather, this approach employs cultural knowledge as an additional tool in facilitating the college-going process.

A reconceptualization of the role of culture in college preparation programs is evident throughout the book. In particular, in chapter 1, Octavio Villalpando and Daniel Solorzano establish the overarching orientation of the text. They point out that despite the increase in students of color involved in college preparation efforts, the numbers of these students enrolled in institutions of higher education is still disproportionately low. College preparation programs that emphasize students' cultures in conjunction with academic support, suggest the authors, have the potential of more positively influencing college enrollment rates than programs that ignore the role of culture. The colorblind approach that characterizes the majority of existing college preparation programs points to a need to redirect attention to the part that culture plays and has the potential to play in increasing the college attendance and persistence of students of color.

The chapters that follow draw upon a cultural integrity framework of college preparation programs that "call upon students' racial and ethnic backgrounds in a positive manner in the development of their pedagogies and learning activities" (Tierney & Jun, 2001, p. 211). Furthermore, a model based on cultural integrity assumes that a child's cultural background is a critical tool to be channeled for promoting success. Since culture has the capacity to influence how student learning is organized, how curriculum develops, and how teaching methods are implemented, an analysis of how culture pertains to various components of college preparation is integral to our understanding of how to improve such programs. Consequently, chapter 1 provides an orientation for the chapters and their discussion of social support networks and programmatic elements.

OUTLINE

This book is organized into two parts: Part 1: Social Support Networks and Part 2: Programmatic Elements.

Social Support Networks

The four chapters on social support networks segue from the beginning chapter on culture and build directly onto a cultural integrity perspective. Families, peers, mentors (including teachers and advisors), and guidance counselors comprise a critical web of support agents for students thinking about going to college. According to Stanton-Salazar (2001), "the very texture of an individual's daily existence (and ultimately his or her life chances) is fundamentally shaped by structured and accumulated opportunities for entering multiple institutional contexts and forging relationships with people who control resources and who generally *participate in power*" (p. 17). Furthermore, Stanton-Salazar asserts that an individual's social class, racial assignment, and gender influence how he or she interacts with educational institutions. Hence, relationships with individuals with institutional know-how or with people who can provide socioemotional support become integral in aiding students in negotiating the college-going process. In terms of accessing the above-mentioned academic instrumental knowledge, in their work with the parents of immigrant students, Rueda et al. (2003) found that having access to a mediator who had knowledge of the U.S. educational system, and who was open to answering questions about their children's progress, was a key element in increasing educational achievement for first-generation college-goers.

The four chapters pertaining to social support networks address the role of institutional mediators in college preparation programs while also emphasizing the distinct role that outside agents play. For example, after advocating an expanded definition of the role of families in college preparation in chapter 2, William Tierney and Susan Auerbach outline various ways that parents can support their children and college preparation programs can cultivate parental engagement. William Tierney and Julia Colyar, in chapter 3, take up the question of how programs can make best use of peer groups, suggesting ways that peers can serve as resources in building college-going culture within programs. Patricia Gándara and Maria Mejorado's discussion of mentors in chapter 5 discusses the role that formal and informal mentors play in providing extrafamilial socioemotional support and academic encouragement to students. Mentors also draw connections between career achievement and college going, a point frequently overlooked by program and school curricula. In chapter 4, Patricia McDonough explores how school and program guidance counselors serve as an important channel of communication about the college-going process. They can guide students on academic issues, help foster college-going aspirations, outline career goals, and provide socioemotional support.

Taken together, chapters 2 through 5 illustrate the web of support that children potentially have available to them. With the exception of teachers and guidance counselors, these support agents act externally to the school. Understood in conjunction with chapter 1, a notion of social support develops that acknowledges the unique and valuable perspective that extraschool agents can add to the college-going process. The chapters that follow look at the internal dynamics of college preparation programs.

Programmatic Elements

After an extensive review of college preparation programs in the United States, Tierney and Hagedorn (2002) found that most college preparation programs focus on academic, counseling, and social activities. In the latter chapters of this book, we discuss four key elements of programmatic design; academics, social activities, timing, and costs in an effort to provide a conceptual framework for how to tackle improving each component.

As suggested above, academic preparation is crucial to preparing students for college. In chapter 6, after delineating key arguments in favor of an academically rigorous curriculum, Laura Perna suggests how programs can capitalize on academic content. She advocates beginning preparation programs earlier, coordinating instruction between K–12 and postsecondary institutions, ensuring access to a rigorous academic curriculum and articulating academics through a culturally sensitive framework. James Hearn and Janet Holdsworth, in chapter 7, explore the role that social activities play in college preparation by discussing the types and implications of various social events. Ultimately, such activities can provide valuable links to the chapters related to social support. For example, how might a program include social events that foster family engagement and community building?

The final two chapters have significant implications for all of the preceding chapters. In chapter 8, Bonous-Hammarth and Allen review the importance of the timing of interventions. They explore what skills and knowledge can be developed over time and what critical hurdles in the college application process are attached to fixed deadlines. This chapter affects the implementation of recommendations from other chapters and provides insight into the broad picture of college preparation. In the final chapter, Watson Scott Swail tackles the challenges of determining the cost effectiveness of the various components of college preparation programs. He outlines the difficulties inherent in measuring the impact of programs and develops a framework for assessing the relationship between cost and program delivery.

Finally, in the conclusion, Robert Rueda summarizes the findings of the individual propositions and offers a synthesis of the larger questions of access. While he notes that none of the research areas provide definitive answers, he also suggests that policy can be guided by what researchers already know. In addition, Rueda provides a discussion of alternative frameworks that may enhance continued research efforts and underlines the interconnectedness of the propositions.

Far too often, we find ourselves in parallel universes. One world is the rarefied academic atmosphere where scholars try to develop with scientific and minute precision a particular finding related to access programs. The other world pertains to the classrooms and schools where these programs actually take place. Those who work in college preparation programs need large-scale answers to vexing problems: Should we spend more time on SAT preparation or on involving a youth's family in the program? Some might say that we have sought the proverbial cake and want to eat it as well: we have asked engaged intellectuals to develop nuanced texts that utilize their academic skills, and we intend for these texts to help shed light in the "real world" rather than remain simply as an academic treatise. It is our hope that this book serves as a guide to gauging what makes a college preparation program effective and engaging dialogue between researchers and practitioners.

Finally, we would like to stress that we do not intend to suggest that for a college preparation program to be successful, it need exhibit all nine components developed in the text. Some programs might offer a discrete activity that is of worth in relation to the other interactions that a student has during the course of his or her academic career. Another program might stress a competency area that is overlooked by students' extrascholastic support systems. Programs need to be aware of the contexts in which they operate and the unique requirements of their clients. Ultimately, we intend for this text to provide a roadmap of the kind of activities that appear to have the best chance of improving access to college for the students they serve.

Part 1

Social Support Networks

OCTAVIO VILLALPANDO
DANIEL G. SOLORZANO

Chapter One

The Role of Culture in College Preparation Programs: A Review of the Research Literature

The majority of precollege outreach programs that are designed to improve the college readiness of low-income students of color[1] are centered on academic enhancement activities. The main focus of these programs is to help students develop academic skills that will improve their likelihood of attending and succeeding in college. They operate under the assumption that students who participate in the programs are more likely to succeed in college than those who are not involved with the programs. But, while these programs probably do help students, as Gándara (2002a) observes, "it is virtually certain that they could meet with much greater success if the research were able to better identify which strategies are most effective for which types of students, under which conditions" (p. 100).

Indeed, despite decades of involvement by low-income youth of color in various types of college preparation programs, these students continue to be se-

We appreciate the feedback provided by William Tierney, Zoë Corwin, and the other authors who contributed to this volume. We also want to acknowledge the helpful research support provided at different stages in the development of this chapter by Philip Aletto, Steve Baumann, Peter Miller, Shad Sorenson, and Trina Valdez at the University of Utah.

verely underrepresented in higher education (Wilds, 2000). Their dispropor-tionate enrollment and success rates have led many to question the impact that precollege programs play in the preparation of these students for college (Tier-ney & Hagedorn, 2002).

In this chapter, we review the literature that focuses on the role of stu-dents' culture in college preparation programs. We synthesize the research that addresses the extent to which the transition of students of color to college is en-hanced when they participate in precollege outreach programs that include a focus on their culture.

We begin with a discussion of how cultural integrity and cultural capital frameworks often inform the concept of culture in the college preparation lit-erature. We argue that a cultural capital framework does not adequately capture the complex identities of students of color, which consequently helps explain why the present research in this area frequently reaches inconclusive or con-tradictory findings. We propose the consideration of a conceptual lens that builds upon the concept of cultural integrity to better understand the dynamic experiences of students of color who participate in college preparation pro-grams.

We then synthesize the research on the role of culture in college prepara-tion programs, highlighting the ways in which programs deliberately create initiatives and opportunities for students to integrate their respective cultural and racial identities as a way to make academics more effective. We conclude by discussing how to apply the conceptual lens proposed in this chapter to fu-ture studies of students of color and college preparation programs.

GUIDING QUESTION

Swail and Perna's (2002) exhaustive review of college preparation programs revealed that most programs include a strong emphasis on building academic preparation, but very little to no emphasis on integrating students' cultural identity, cultural needs, or cultural assets into the program. Why would pro-grams designed to enhance the college readiness of low-income youth of color not include an emphasis on their culture or cultural identity as a formal pro-grammatic focus? To some, while it might make sense intuitively that these programs should account for students' culture, there is little systematic investi-gation of the effects of incorporating culture in college preparation programs. A comprehensive research literature base does not yet exist to point programs toward the adoption of specific cultural components or related cultural strate-gies that can be helpful for students, although many scholars in this area have issued calls for the inclusion of culture and cultural components in precollege programs (see Tierney & Hagedorn, 2002). Thus, our understanding of the role of students' culture in college preparation programs has remained uninformed by the research literature.

As we embarked upon this review, our guiding assumption was that college preparation programs for low-income students of color were probably most successful when they included a focus on both the students' culture and on the development of academic skills. This assumption framed our attempt to synthesize the studies that examine the extent to which the goals of college preparation programs might be enhanced when they emphasize the culture of the student. We posed the following question as a guide for this review:

> To what extent is it essential for college preparation programs to emphasize the culture of the student in order to enable her or him to get into a college or university?

FRAMING CULTURE

Cultural Capital

Our review revealed that much of the literature that included a discussion of culture in college preparation programs borrowed Bourdieu's (1986) concept of cultural capital to frame the way in which programs view students' racial identities and cultural needs. Bourdieu (1986) considered cultural capital as a set of cultural knowledge, skills, and abilities that are possessed and often inherited by certain groups in society, and suggested that families from lower socioeconomic backgrounds do not have the privileged opportunities that families from higher socioeconomic backgrounds possess.

Even though Bourdieu explicitly conceptualized cultural capital as a class-based, not a race-based, analysis of culture, our review found that the literature frequently applies this framework to try to explain the complex relationships between the cultural needs of students of color and the role of college preparation programs. For example, in their review of the role of parent involvement in college preparation programs, Jun and Colyar (2002) address the importance of involving parents of color in college preparation programs as a way of transmitting cultural capital "from one generation to the next by parents who inform their children about the value, importance, and process of securing a college education" (pp. 203–204). The assumption is that a cultural capital framework helps to explain the experiences and needs of students of color who often come from working-class families and their interactions with educational institutions.

Cultural Integrity

Jun and Colyar (2002) also argue that accounting for family culture in college enrichment programs is essential to the success of students of color. They build upon the work of sociologists and cultural anthropologists, including Cummins (1997), Deyhle (1995), and Tierney and Jun (2001), to propose the adoption of a cultural integrity framework in college preparation programs that affirms students' cultural identity. A college preparation program designed within a cultural integrity framework reconceptualizes deficit notions of culture by viewing students' cultural identity as a set of positive traits in the learning process. This framework is premised upon the notion that the beliefs held by educators and teachers about students' identities and educators' roles in the structures in which the learning process takes place "are important in enabling or disabling the college intentions of low-income minority youth" (Tierney & Jun, 2001, p. 207).

We found that the literature sometimes links the concept of cultural capital to a cultural integrity framework. Cultural integrity emphasizes the importance of affirming students' cultural identities, while cultural capital is often used to reinforce the power and influence of culture in society. Both concepts are used together to persuade college preparation programs to reconceptualize deficit views of the identities of students of color.

The Concept of Culture for Students of Color

Culture influences how learning is organized, how the curriculum is developed, and how teaching methods are implemented. In our review, we found that the concept of culture for students of color took on many divergent meanings. Some research equated culture with race and ethnicity, while other work clearly viewed culture through a much broader lens of characteristics and forms of social histories and identities.

For the purposes of this review, our concept of culture draws from the work of scholars who have reconceptualized traditional sociological and anthropological deficit theories of culture (Tierney, 1993; West, 1993), language (Valencia, 1997), class (Giroux, 1983; Foley, 1997; McDonough, 1997), gender (Collins, 1986; Hurtado, 1989), and ethnicity/race (hooks, 1990; Solorzano, 1997) in order to provide more robust and valid explanatory frameworks for research in education and the social sciences. Building upon the framework of cultural integrity, we view the culture of students of color as a set of characteristics that are neither fixed nor static. We consider culture to be dynamic, cumulative, and an influence of the continuous process of identity formation. It is a process of behaviors and values that are learned, shared, and exhibited by a people. For students of color, their culture is frequently represented symbolically through language and can encompass identities around immigration status, gender, phenotype, sexuality, regionality, race, and ethnicity. The broader contemporary youth culture in society is very often also represented among students of color.

But perhaps the most important dimension of culture for students of color is that it is very often a guide for their thinking, feeling, and behaving— indeed, it is a means of survival. The cultures of students of color can nurture and empower them. Moll, Amanti, Neff, and Gonzalez, (1992) and Velez-Ibanez and Greenberg (1992) believe that, for Latinos, culture can form and draw from communal funds of knowledge, while Gordon (1995) views culture for African Americans as possessing a set of nurturing family characteristics.

Toward a Concept of Cultural Wealth

Despite Bourdieu's (1986) explicit intention to apply cultural capital to class-based analyses (see Dika & Singh, 2002), the college preparation literature borrows this framework to explain the experiences and needs of students of color. Based on our review, we propose an extension—or reconceptualization—of this framework when analyzing the relationship between students of color and college preparation programs. The conceptualization we propose here allows for a more robust interpretation of the role of culture for students of color in college preparation programs.

If we begin with the assumption that students of color, parents, and communities value educational achievement, and if we build on this assumption by using it as the basis for interventions like college preparation programs, then by adopting a cultural continuities approach (Weisner, Gallimore, & Jordan, 1988), we believe it is possible to improve the achievement of students of color. This approach examines the home and community for cultural activities that are compatible with school achievement. These culturally compatible activities are then adapted for program use. Indeed, like cultural integrity, viewing the student's home and community culture as a strength leads to intervention programs of mutual accommodation in which the schools, the student, and their families fashion their behavior toward a common goal of academic achievement. With this approach, we can ask whether there are forms of cultural capital that students of color bring to the college intervention table that cultural capital theory does not recognize or cannot see (e.g., parental value of education, awareness of parental sacrifices, hard work of the parents, etc.).

This approach allows us to identify and analyze how individuals and groups use different and often unrecognized forms of capital in response to educational subordination. Can these cultural and familial resources be considered a form of cultural resistance to educational subordination, a type of resistant cultural capital of those at society's educational margins (Solorzano & Villalpando, 1998)? In a sense, these questions represent a redefinition of cultural capital, since those who do not have the "traditional" forms might be displaying a different form of cultural capital than those society acknowledges and privileges. Indeed, if we frame the concept of cultural wealth within the context of higher education, we might be better able to see how individuals and groups use their marginal status as a source of empowerment.

However, we first have to reconceptualize cultural capital by focusing on those attitudinal, behavioral, and familial assets that students of color bring to their school experience. By increasing our focus on marginalized students who rely on different forms of cultural capital to complete a high school diploma and aspire to a college degree, we can begin to more fully explore how their success might be affected by (1) their dependence on other students and teachers of color for support and mentorship, (2) their response to a curriculum and teaching pedagogy that emphasizes their background, and (3) school "multicultural" policies and practices.

We propose the concept of *cultural wealth* to encompass, along with students' unique cultural capital, other accumulated assets and resources such as students' navigational capital, social capital, economic capital, experiential capital, educational capital, and aspirational capital (see Auerbach, 2002). Our notion of cultural wealth identifies individual indicators of capital that have rarely been acknowledged and used as assets in examining the cultural and social characteristics of populations of color.

Gender and Culture

While we recognize that culture intersects with many dimensions of the identities of students of color, clearly gender plays a very significant role in how students experience college preparation programs. Our review failed to identify published empirical work focusing on how gender and culture intersect in college preparation programs. However, it is imperative to point out that any omission of a discussion of major differences in the precollege experiences between women and men should not be interpreted to suggest that both genders share the same educational experience or outcomes. Despite the lack of empirical work, on the intersection of gender and culture in college preparation programs, wherever possible in this discussion, we attempt to raise questions related to possible areas where women might have a different experience than men in college preparation programs.

In the next two sections, we illustrate how a cultural wealth lens might allow for a more appropriate analysis of the role of culture for students of color in precollege programs. We begin by synthesizing the major published findings in this area and, in the latter section, apply a cultural wealth concept to reexamine components of programs that are cited as models of cultural enrichment and academic skills development.

CULTURE IN COLLEGE PREPARATION PROGRAMS

Our review of the research began by seeking studies of programs that exclusively emphasize culture and pay little attention to the development of academic skills. However, the published empirical literature we reviewed did not identify any such programs. Instead, we found that college preparation programs that emphasize culture almost always also included an emphasis on the development of academic skills or, at a minimum, an awareness about going to college. Most of these programs strove to improve students' chances for enrolling in college by emphasizing some dimension of students' culture and by attempting to improve their academic preparation (Lockwood & Secada, 1999; Swanson, 1993).

Indeed, in a national survey, Swail (2001b) found that college attendance was the primary goal of 92% of outreach programs, with 88% of the programs claiming that they strove to improve student academic skills and 66% listing culture as a main component of their programs. While clearly the most common purpose of college preparation programs is to increase the college attendance of program participants, Swail's (2001) study underscores the emphasis that college preparation programs claim to place on cultural enrichment goals. We found that the real difference was in the *degree* to which programs emphasized culture. Some programs appeared to be more overt and explicit than others in their emphasis on culture, but most seemed to share a similar programmatic interest in developing academic skills or an awareness about college.

With respect to how the programs conceptualize culture, the literature we reviewed suggests that some programs are more aware than others about the different ways in which culture exists and manifests itself, though most appear to premise their analysis within a cultural capital framework. For example, some programs are under the impression that their emphasis on students' culture only comes about as a result of a formal activity, such as taking trips to museums with ethnic displays, attending ethnic music concerts, or by offering classes or workshops on cultural topics or issues. Other programs are more clear and intentional about how they infuse culture. They are quite explicit about the need for and the process by which they involve students' parents and family, mentors, and peer groups. These programs appear to be aware that these activities serve to reinforce the students' cultural norms, beliefs, and values, even though it is accomplished in a less formal way than offering a course or workshop on a culturally specific topic. Thus, our review found that in some instances, the students' culture is infused into college preparation programs in a way that is not always apparent or necessarily deliberate. In other instances, programs are quite intentional about how to achieve some degree of academic success by striving for cultural integrity and viewing the students' culture as a form of wealth.

Our review did not identify any one particular culturally related activity that could be perceived as the best or most effective means of transmitting culture or achieving a modicum of cultural integrity. Students' parents and family, mentors, peer groups, and formal classes or workshops each appear to be important components of programs that allow students to maintain their own cultural integrity, ensuring that students' cultural backgrounds are viewed as critical ingredients for achieving success (Jun & Colyar, 2002). Other chapters in this book address the role of family, peers, and mentors in college preparation programs in detail, but below we offer a brief overview of how each of these components relates to the culture of students of color within these programs.

Family Involvement

Our review revealed that one of the most common ways that college preparation programs incorporate culture into their missions is by involving students' parents and/or their families. Swail and Perna (2002) discovered that more than two thirds of all programs offer a parental involvement component. For students of color, parent involvement in a college preparation program represents an important way of maintaining a connection with their culture. Jun and Tierney (1999) observed that while it was not possible to credit student academic achievement entirely to parental involvement, "it appears that many programs that make parents' involvement a priority also see student outcomes improve" (p. 57).

The literature suggests that a major reason for involving parents and family is to inform them about the various processes that they can undertake to help their children get prepared for and eventually admitted to college (Swail & Perna 2002; Gandara 2002a). According to Jun and Colyar (2002), this parental education component helps them acquire or develop the cultural capital necessary to help their children attend and succeed in college. Horn and Chen (1998) and Hossler, Schmit, and Vesper (1999) also found that students are more likely to enroll in postsecondary education when their parents have high expectations and are involved with them.

However, when viewed through a cultural wealth lens, involving families and parents of color in college outreach programs provides more than a vehicle by which information about or the value of college is transmitted or reinforced. As Gándara (1995) noted in her longitudinal study of educational mobility among Chicanos, the families and parents of students of color symbolize a powerful cultural representation that often enables students to shape their attitudes and aspirations around a sense of responsibility and commitment to their community. As Tierney and Auerbach elaborate in greater depth (chapter 2), programs that involve parents and, when appropriate, can provide services in their native language, do more than transmit cultural capital to the families. Parents can transmit various elements of cultural wealth to the students and to the program.

Peers

Peers of students of color are another means by which culture is integrated into college preparation programs. Even though the literature is inconclusive about the extent to which adolescent peers help or hinder student participants in college preparation programs, most programs that are aware of the importance of peers operate under the assumption that they can serve a useful function.

Most college preparation programs enable students from similar backgrounds to support each other's academic goals as they transition into new, alien environments (Gándara, 2002a; Perna, 2000a). Gándara (2001) also points out that most AVID (Advancement Via Individual Determination), Puente, SOAR (Summer Orientation and Academic Review), and Posse Programs have specific peer group components designed with the purpose of supporting student peers. In fact, one of the most overtly noticeable features of the highly successful AVID program is the supportive peer culture that develops among the participants, who not only meet for a class period each day but also eat lunch together daily (Swanson, 1993).

While peer groups exist naturally in college preparation programs, these programs seldom appear to organize peer groups in a purposeful manner to serve a specific function. In their review of the role of peer groups in college preparation programs, Tierney and Colyar (see chapter 3) cite a study by Mehan et al. (1996) that calls for a purposeful structuring of peer groups in a college preparation program as a way for students to affirm their own ethnic/racial backgrounds and academic identities. Tierney and Colyar urge programs to think about peer groups as a valuable component of learning by organizing them into purposeful and functional teams.

Mentoring

As Gándara and Mejorado illustrate (chapter 5), many college preparation programs utilize mentors as part of their strategy to benefit students. In several programs, mentors also provide students with access to individuals of the same racial or ethnic backgrounds who can exert a positive influence. Yet while such efforts are believed to be effective, they are very much dependent upon the talents and commitment of the mentors. For example, some programs enable student participants to spend a great deal of time over a matter of years with their assigned mentor. The outcomes experienced by students in these programs vary greatly depending upon the relationship with their mentor. According to Kahne and Bailey (1999), those who have been involved in programs with committed, long-term mentors have enjoyed college enrollment rates that are nearly double the rates of their peers who have not participated in such activities, while those who have been involved in programs with multiple mentors who lacked this same dedication demonstrated only minimal improvements on college enrollment rates.

Thus, while the role of mentors in a college preparation program can be quite powerful, it is a difficult kind of success to replicate consistently. Nevertheless, our review reveals that mentors for students of color are another way by which college preparation programs often infuse culture into their mission.

Cultural Instruction

The most formal way of bringing students' culture into college preparation programs is by offering workshops and/or courses on cultural histories and traditions. A cultural wealth lens recognizes this activity as a valuable way of acknowledging the social histories and identities of students of color. Our review found that college preparation programs that included some form of cultural instruction as a part of their program were usually very explicit about intentionally attempting to enhance the unique strengths possessed by students' culture. For example, the Frederick Douglass Academy in New York City focuses its college preparation efforts around the Black traditions of collective survival, racial uplift, and connectedness (Knight et al., 2000), while Puente teaches all of its courses using Latina/o resources and literature (Gándara, 2001).

Unfortunately, there are limited empirical published studies in this area, but the few available suggest that students of color exposed to cultural teaching strategies may demonstrate attitudinal improvements and a sense of cultural empowerment, although as Gándara (2001) noted, it is unclear whether their transition from high school to college is improved as a result of this specific strategy.

FOUR PROGRAMS PROMOTING CULTURAL ENRICHMENT AND
ACADEMIC SKILLS

In this section we review, through a cultural wealth lens, examples of four programs perceived to be exemplary in their attempt to achieve academic enhancement and culturally enriching outcomes for students of color.

Program 1: College Prep Academic Track

The literature we reviewed highlighted a program that claims as a key feature the removal of underachieving students from general education or vocational tracks and places them in rigorous college preparatory classes while providing them with extensive support services. Students meet every day with a program teacher and class where they participate in such activities as academic tutoring, writing development, note taking, test taking, study strategies, field trips, and motivational exercises (Fashola & Slavin, 1997; Gándara, 2001; Mehan et al., 1996). In addition, students are exposed to guest speakers who present information about preparing for college (Swanson, 1993).

The program claims to provide its students with "social scaffolding," which Mehan et al. (1996) defined as "the engineering of instructional tasks so that students develop their own competencies through their interactions with more capable peers or experts, and the building of a community of peers to support students' aspirations" (p. 78). Among the most notable findings from Mehan et al.'s (1996) evaluation of this program are: (1) improved college enrollment numbers; (2) particular effectiveness with African American and Latino students; (3) greatest effects on most at-risk students; and (4) the transmission of cultural capital. Even more than academic skill building, much of the program's impact is attributed to what is perceived as the transmission of cultural capital from teachers and mentors to the students. Services that help students improve test-taking skills and learn about the college application and decision process were believed to provide at-risk students with knowledge that they had previously not possessed.

The literature we reviewed on this program is guided by a cultural capital theoretical framework and frequently depicts student participants as deficient in a number of areas beyond academics. In fact, one of its main findings, the transmission of cultural capital, again assumes that the students did not possess any capital in their culture of origin and thus had to acquire it from the program. For example, an underlying assumption driven by this framework is that the students lack the motivation or desire to attend college because their families and communities have not valued education, as judged by the perceived disinterest among parents in becoming involved in their children's schooling. This myth continues to prevail, despite research by Gándara (1995), Stanton-Salazar (2001), Valencia, (1997), Valenzuela (1999), and others that clearly contradicts the misperception that families of color are not involved in or do not care about their children's education. It is one thing for the students to need information about college application procedures and college life, and quite another thing to conclude that they lack this information because their families have not valued their educational achievement enough to prepare them adequately for college. In contrast to a cultural capital framework, a cultural wealth lens allows for research that can reexamine "which strategies are most effective for which types of students, under which conditions" (Gándara, 2002a, p. 100).

Program 2: Promise of Financial Support for College

Our second example is of a program built on a promise to a class or group of elementary students that their college education will be paid for if they successfully make it through high school. The scholarships are provided by an individual or corporate donor. The program also includes support in the form of college scholarships, counseling, mentoring, and tutoring, all designed to attempt to help students graduate from high school and transition into college.

Yet, while this type of program component claims to provide both "academic and cultural services," Kahne and Bailey (1999) conclude that it is much more weighted toward the social and cultural realm, and cite the "social development goals" of the program as evidence. Again, a cultural wealth perspective would not identify social development as a primary goal of a college readiness program for students of color. The literature on this program, again premised upon a cultural capital perspective, presumes that the students of color who participate in the program possess cultural deficiencies that prohibit them from achieving academic progress. A cultural wealth lens would refocus attention on the deficiencies of the schooling processes that failed to provide adequate academic preparation for the students, shifting some of the major responsibilities for the students' academic needs from their families and toward the schools.

Program 3: Ethnic-Specific College Preparation and Mentoring Support

This program was designed to serve a particular racial/ethnic student group by providing a 2-year college preparatory English class, a dedicated guidance counselor, and a mentoring program (Gándara, 2001). The English course integrates literature into its core curriculum written by authors from the same racial/ethnic group as the student participants, and the mentors and counselors are usually also of the same race/ethnicity as the students, indications of the program's strong commitment to maintaining cultural integrity. Strong family and parental involvement form another important feature of this program. Families are regular participants in program activities that try to give both parents and students a sense of inclusion in the education process (Gándara, 2001).

Some of the most notable findings by Gándara, Mejorado et al. in their 1998 evaluation of this program are that: (1) there is an increase in knowledge of and value for the college application process; (2) increased rates of students reach their potential; and (3) parents play an essential role in the program. The program appears to have had a significant positive impact on students' attitudes, aspirations, and preparation for going to college. Perhaps largely as a result of these factors, program students enrolled in college at a higher rate than nonprogram students (84% compared to 75%). Similarly, the high level of family involvement in the students' education is attributed by the evaluators to the various meaningful ways by which parents are included in program activities, and to the counselors' and mentors' ability to communicate with the families in their own language.

The literature we reviewed on this program presents a strikingly different conceptualization of the program's goals and participants. Neither the students, counselors, nor mentors are depicted as culturally deficient, nor is the program itself described as an effort to remedy perceived deficits, other than academic. The literature indicates that the program readily acknowledges the importance of maintaining cultural integrity in its services and design by enlisting the participation of culturally conscious counselors and mentors and by providing services in parents' native languages when necessary. Though the literature we reviewed on this program does not explicitly name a cultural wealth perspective, clearly it seems to adopt this kind of lens by, among other things, attempting to account for the importance of the participants' lived experiences as a basis for learning. It describes the goals of the program as deliberate efforts to recognize the value of students' cultures of origin while simultaneously enriching their academic preparation.

Program 4: Summer Bridge Program

This type of program is most often available to students of color from low-income households who have expressed interest in attending college but lack the resources for doing so (Gándara, 2001; Myers & Schirm, 1999). The program is structured around 4- to 6-week summer workshops that are hosted by a college campus and provide students with an academically intensive precollege experience. The program is often coupled with supplemental academic courses and tutoring, cultural events, and career/college/financial aid counseling. While it does provide some culturally oriented services, it is most often recognized predominantly as an academic preparation effort (Myers & Schirm, 1999).

Myers and Schirm (1999) observed that this program appears to have its greatest impact on students who are most in financial need and does not appear to have very much of an impact on improving academic performance. While this program did not demonstrate a significant impact on college enrollment rates for all students, it did seem to benefit students who were from low-income households, whose parents had not gone to college, and who had previously been the poorest performers in school.

Even though this is one of the longest-supported programs in the United States, organizational models and functions seem to be vastly different between the regions in which the programs exist. For example, at some campuses, the 6-week summer bridge component incorporates formal culture-based courses (such as Chicana/o History or the African American Experience) alongside an introductory algebra course or an English composition class. At other campuses, the emphasis is strictly academic, with almost no focus on students' cultural identities. Thus, it is difficult to assess or generalize the success of this program in integrating cultural enrichment activities with academic achievement. What is clear is that a cultural capital approach that adopts a cultural deficit-based premise to designing its services or evaluating its effectiveness will likely fail to address many of the students' more relevant needs.

CONCLUSION

Our review reveals suggestive evidence that college preparation programs that have a focus on cultural enrichment *and* on the development of academic skills provide students with much-needed resources to enable them to attend college. The scant empirical work on the subject requires that we qualify our review of the evidence as merely suggestive rather than conclusive, though we concur strongly with the observations of important scholars in this area who agree that the most effective programs are those that include both academic and cultural components (see Gándara, 2001; Hagedorn & Tierney, 2002; Jun & Tierney, 1999; Kezar, 2000b; Oesterreich, 2000b; Perna, 2000).

Programs that only emphasize cultural enrichment strategies, while probably quite helpful, may offer only part of the solution. On the other hand, programs that utilize only academic services leave many of the most crucial life issues unaddressed for students of color (Kahne & Bailey, 1999). It is important to underscore that the real difference we found between college preparation programs was in the degree to which they emphasize culture deliberately to their advantage. Some programs appear to be very conscious of the benefits accrued from integrating a cultural enrichment emphasis with their academics, while others seem to be less aware or interested in placing much of an authentic focus on the students' culture.

In sum, the most significant findings resulting from our literature review are as follows.

College preparation programs framed by a focus on cultural wealth and academic skills development can have a substantial impact on college enrollment rates of underrepresented students. Even though these programs do not have a consistent effect on high school grades, students who have participated in them have demonstrated enrollment rates that are nearly twice as high as those of their peers who are not involved in such programs (Gándara, 2002a; Horn & Chen, 1998). Programs that can effectively incorporate both of these approaches can have an important influence on students' rates of college enrollment (Gandara, 2001).

Programs must be tailored to meet students' needs. While many programs may include some aspects of students' culture within their strategies, it is important that they continue to respond to individual needs to allow students to maintain and capitalize on their own cultural wealth. Hagedorn and Tierney (2002) note that "students approach school with multiple identities and if programs are to be successful they need to honor these identities in culturally specific ways so that learning fits" (p. 6). In other words, the implementation of generic cultural components may not be the best way to serve the heterogeneous student composition (even among the same race or ethnicity) of each precollege program. Programs should be developed based on the identified needs of specific students (Gándara & Maxwell-Jolly, 1999; Swail & Perna, 2002) and, since different students have different needs, different programs will need to be created to serve them (Jun & Tierney, 1999). Indeed, no one program can be considered a panacea for all students because there are so many divergent needs to be met and because of the large heterogeneous cultural composition of many college preparation programs (Swail, 2001b). Particularly important when considering students' needs is an understanding of how gender and culture intersect. While the empirical body of work around this important intersection is virtually silent, it is imperative that future studies take into account how women and men experience college preparation programs in order to ensure that programs meet their needs more adequately.

College preparation programs that provide a diverse array of components are most effective. The factors influencing college enrollment behavior between White students and students of color are different. While academic preparation tends to have the biggest impact on White students, more than any other factor, African American and Latino/a students have demonstrated a greater need for the acquisition of the knowledge and skills necessary to navigate the college application process (Perna, 2000a). Thus, it is impossible for a college preparation program to identify one or two factors that will have a profound universal impact on college enrollment rates for all students, since students are each affected by different factors based on their racial, ethnic, socioeconomic, and/or educational backgrounds.

FUTURE RESEARCH

Unfortunately, the single most important finding in our review was that not much empirical research has been published on the role of culture in college preparation programs. Most of the work we located was exhortative, and many of the evaluations and studies lacked methodological rigor in their design. As noted by Swail (2001b) and Tierney (2002), the evaluation of college preparation programs has proven to be a difficult task due to the lack of an overall schema consistently used in evaluating programs and because the evaluations are frequently carried out by untrained personnel.

There is an immediate need for research in this area that utilizes theoretical/conceptual lenses that do not presume that students of color are culturally deficient. We have proposed one such framework that views students' culture as having multiple assets, or as a form of wealth. Future research should consider how best to design college preparation programs that account for the role of the poor schooling that students of color are often exposed to.

Finally, to more directly answer the question that guided this review: *To what extent is it essential for college preparation programs to emphasize the culture of the student in order to enable her or him to get into a college or university?* Well, it depends. Even though the contradictory and elusive nature of the empirical research does not presently allow us to state that it is indeed *essential* to emphasize the culture of the student, we believe that more appropriate theoretical lenses that guide future research on the topic will provide more definitive evidence about the importance of students' culture in college preparation programs. At this point, our review leads us to conclude that the research only provides suggestive, though quite important, evidence of the value of emphasizing students' culture in order to enable them to attend college.

NOTE

1. For the purposes of this chapter, we define students of color as persons who identify as African American, Native American, Asian American, and Chicana(o)/Latina(o).

WILLIAM G. TIERNEY
SUSAN AUERBACH

Chapter Two

Toward Developing an Untapped Resource: The Role of Families in College Preparation

Throughout the 20th century, the family's role in enabling low-income children to gain an education was of great concern. By century's end, most parents of color/low SES aspired to college for their children, yet their students remained underrepresented in four-year institutions (Gándara, 1998; Solorzano, 1992a, 1992b). How critical is family engagement to college preparation for underrepresented students? Specifically, what types of family knowledge, beliefs, and practices are most effective in promoting college eligibility and access? What are the implications for policy and practice in academic outreach programs that aim to increase college access?

This chapter reviews the sociological literature on family engagement in education and college preparation to consider these questions. We argue that family engagement is critical to college preparation for underrepresented students and that parents want to be more helpful in this process, yet academic outreach programs rarely reach out in substantive ways to parents. Family engagement may be less essential to college access than rigorous college prepara-

Portions of this chapter appeared in Tierney, W. G. (2002). Parents and families in pre-college preparation: The lack of connection between research and practice. *Educational Policy, 16*(4), 588–606.

tory curricula and college counseling. However, we believe it is among the most important three or four components of successful programs. Indeed, enlisting parents as allies and integrating family education and support into all program elements strengthens their overall impact on students.

Family engagement is important for college preparation programs to consider because family members are potential allies—or obstacles—for every step in college access, from aspirations and academic preparation to taking entrance exams, applying, and enrolling (Levin & Belfield, 2002). The foundation for high educational achievement and aspiration is often in place long before programs encounter students; parents of all social groups are key players in creating that foundation. As we will show, parents' moral, emotional, and logistical support for college has motivated many students of color/low SES to pursue their goals, while older siblings and other family members have provided more specific information and guidance. Given that college entails sacrifices, opportunity costs, and unfamiliar life choices for low-SES families, it may provoke parent resistance that can waylay students' plans. If parents without college experience could learn about steps in the pathway to college as part of a supportive community of families and educators, they could offer more useful monitoring and guidance to their students in cooperation with program staff. It is especially urgent to enlist parent support in urban schools that do not provide sufficient academic support and college counseling for aspiring students of color.

This chapter begins with a brief historical sketch of how family engagement has been conceptualized by educators and researchers. Then it considers definitions of the family and family engagement, as well as theoretical frameworks that have guided recent research. Next, we review the evidence on how parent engagement affects academic achievement generally and college preparation in particular, with a focus on families of color/low SES. Finally, we examine the small body of literature on parents in academic outreach programs and offer recommendations for programs based on the literature.

THE EVOLVING ROLE OF FAMILIES IN SCHOOLING

The interpretation of the family's role in schooling has changed dramatically over the last century, conditioned by changes within and beyond schools. Parents moved from the position of outsiders, whose influence on education was seen as negative or negligible, to supposed partners in the world of schools (Swap, 1993).

In the early 20th century, educators and researchers assumed that the family actually caused harm to a child's educational welfare. Immigrant and Native American parents who held onto their traditional languages and customs were seen as impeding the assimilation of their sons and daughters into the mainstream (Cutler, 2000; Szasz, 1977). At its most extreme, this belief led to the creation of government-sponsored boarding schools that removed Native American children from their families for years without raising their educational levels to those of other children (Tierney, 1992; Wright & Tierney, 1991). A somewhat milder response was assimilationist parent education and social service programs in city schools. The assimilationist view persisted in the 1960s and 1970s in the prominent cultural deficit model, attributing the low achievement of poor and minority children to alleged inadequate parenting skills and low expectations. This initiated a push for parent education in compensatory education programs that continues today.

The idea of families as educators and of family-school partnerships gained currency in the 1980s and 1990s as a way to advance student achievement. During this time, there was a proliferation of partnership policies, programs, and research, from national Goals 2000 legislation and Title I funding guidelines to family literacy programs and the establishment of major research centers. College planning information campaigns, such as the federal *Think College Early* and California's *College: Making It Happen*, targeted parents of color/low SES as a key audience. Yet the ideal of two-way family-school partnerships was rarely realized, especially in high schools, minority communities, and college access programs (Delgado-Gaitan, 1994; Dodd & Konzal, 1999; Fine, 1991; Swap, 1993; Tierney, 2002a).

Broadly stated, researchers and policy analysts have moved from a stance that assumed parents were harmful to a child's welfare, to a position that assumed they were not important, and now to a perspective that assumes that parents, siblings, and extended families play a central role. A significant discrepancy exists, however, between what researchers say should be done and what is actually done, especially at the secondary level. Although researchers and many educators believe that families need to be more involved in the educational process, finite resources provide limitations and force trade-offs in schools and college preparation programs. We still do not know enough about how diverse families interact with schools and precisely what type and degree of parent engagement is most efficacious for certain students under particular conditions (Catsambis, 1998; Jordan, Orozco, & Averett, 2002). But we do know that family support in various forms facilitates student achievement and access to educational opportunities.

REDEFINING THE FAMILY AND FAMILY ENGAGEMENT

Until recently, the definition of "family" has been a static concept that has neither been questioned nor problematized. Researchers based their definitions on the 20th-century ideal of a nuclear family with a mother, father, and two to three children. Although such a definition was inappropriate for numerous groups, it is increasingly problematic in the 21st century. As William Julius Wilson (1996) has noted, patterns of family formation, especially in urban areas, and particularly with low-income families, have changed dramatically over the last generation. If we insist that mothers and fathers become involved in schools when a wider array of supportive individuals might be equally helpful, then we misplace our emphasis. The definition of family now needs to be more robust for virtually every group and culture.

Although most literature on family engagement in education focuses on parents, a growing number of studies suggest that minority students receive college encouragement and assistance from other members of extended families, especially older siblings who serve as cultural brokers for fellow first-generation students (Cooper et al., 1995; Gándara, 1995; Villanueva, 1996). In this review, we use the terms "family engagement" and "parent engagement" interchangeably to suggest a more flexible, protean definition of family that reflects changing social currents. We also use the term "parent" to denote either parent or guardian.

Just as we need a broader conception of the family and of family engagement, researchers have increasingly called for a more inclusive, flexible definition of parent involvement (Auerbach, 2001; Delgado-Gaitan, 1991; Fine, 1993; Mehan, Villanueva, Hubbard, & Linz, 1996; Valdés, 1996). Parent involvement is a floating term that is poorly defined in empirical studies and policy talk (Baker & Soden, 1998; Catsambis, 1998; Jordan et al., 2002). The traditional practices of White, middle-class parents are often treated as the standard for what counts as involvement (Lareau, 1989; Valdés, 1996). Most research of the past 15 years is based on the six types of parent involvement that Epstein's (1995) typology claims schools should promote, including the basic obligations of parenting, communicating with the school, volunteering at school, promoting learning at home, participating in decision making, and collaborating with the community. This framework is limited by its school-centered emphasis and its omission of key educational concerns for many parents of color, such as child advocacy and protection from racism and low expectations.

Parents of color/low SES are less likely to participate in school activities due to practical and structural barriers, from language and child care issues to a legacy of discrimination and distrust (Fordham, 1996; Lareau & Horvat, 1999; Moles, 1993). These parents often support their children's schooling with "invisible strategies" behind the scenes that are not recognized by the school, such as verbal encouragement and financial sacrifice (Clark, 1983; Mehan et al., 1996; Villanueva & Hubbard, 1994). Moreover, college-bound students of color often rely on help, information, and mentoring from older siblings and other family members (Gándara, 1995; McDonough, 1998). Thus, we need a broader concept of family involvement that reflects nontraditional strategies and participants. Meaningful family involvement in college preparation goes beyond attendance at an end-of-year celebration sponsored by a college access program. In this chapter, we use the term family engagement to suggest a wide range of formal and informal activities at home and at school that family members undertake over time as central actors in the education of their children.

THEORETICAL FRAMEWORKS FOR PARENT INVOLVEMENT RESEARCH

Parent involvement research has been notably undertheorized (Baker & Soden, 1998; Jordan et al., 2002). Most recent researchers cite Epstein's (1990, 1995) partnership model of "overlapping spheres of influence," in which families, schools, and communities share the responsibility for children's learning and development. Hoover-Dempsey and Sandler's (1997) model of parent role construction and sociological theory on cultural and social capital may be more relevant to the role of minority parents in college preparation.

Rather than prescribing types of involvement, Hoover-Dempsey and Sandler's (1997) model inquires into what motivates parent involvement. How do the identities and perspectives of parents and family members shape their view of their role, and what do schools expect of parents? Hoover-Dempsey and Sandler theorize that involvement depends on parents' role constructions, or "beliefs about the actions they should undertake for and with their children" (p. 11). In their model, strong parent role construction (a strong conviction that they should be involved) is the key predictor of involvement, followed by a strong sense of self-efficacy (the parents' perceived capacity to affect child outcomes). Somewhat less influential are what Hoover-Dempsey and Sandler call children's and schools' "invitations or demands" for involvement, which decrease significantly in the secondary school years. Though this model downplays the impact of class, race, and culture on parent roles, it is helpful for analyzing individual parent approaches.

Other frameworks that are increasingly utilized in this area are cultural and social capital (Bourdieu, 1977; chapter 1, this volume). These frameworks enable one to consider how parents might be more or less equipped to prepare their children for academic success. Cultural capital, a set of high-status linguistic and cultural competencies that children inherit from their families, is "the knowledge that social elites value yet schools do not teach" (McDonough, 1997, p. 9). Bourdieu (1973) writes, "academic success is directly dependent on cultural capital and the inclination to invest in the academic market" (p. 504). High-SES parents invest "time, effort, and money" in their children's education as part of a calculation to optimize advantage. Those without high-status cultural capital are unaware either that investments need to be made or how to make them appropriately.

DiMaggio and others observe that cultural capital not only structures inequality by equipping the upper class with the knowledge necessary to ask questions regarding educational outcomes, but also by enabling upper-class children access to the avenues to college, such as college preparation courses, SAT tutoring, and campus visits (DiMaggio, 1982; DiMaggio & Mohr, 1985). In addition, as Lamont and Lareau (1988) point out, what matters for students is how family cultural capital is activated and received at school. Marginalized families are subject to "moments of social exclusion," such as non–college preparatory track placement, in institutions that privilege high-status cultural capital (Auerbach, 2001; Lareau & Horvat, 1999; Yonezawa, 1997).

Important studies by Lareau, McDonough, and Gándara apply cultural capital theory to parents' role in education. Lareau (1989) documents contrasts in high- versus low-SES White parents' educational competence, occupational status, and social networks that allow higher-SES parents to obtain a "home advantage" by intervening in their children's schooling. McDonough (1997) illustrates similar class-based patterns in college choice: high-SES White parents "transmit cultural capital by informing offspring about the value and process for securing a college education, and its potential for conversion in the occupational attainment contest" (p. 9) while working-class students "who lack college choice cultural capital are dependent upon the sponsorship of the guidance counselor" rather than their families (p. 100). Gándara's (1995) study of highly successful Chicanos shows how their low-income immigrant families' mix of high aspirations, a strong work ethic, and "middle-class cultural capital," such as modeling reading and discussing current events, gave students the motivation and persistence to overcome barriers. Some college preparation programs aim to enhance the cultural capital of students from low-SES families (Mehan et al., 1996), but this may be difficult due to the long-term, cumulative nature of cultural capital development (Gándara & Bial, 1999).

Bourdieuan cultural capital theory may be limited in its application to lower-SES families of color, due in part to its implied deficit model of families who lack high-status forms of capital (chapter 1). Rueda and colleagues (2003) observe that the cultural capital of Latino immigrant parents is socially transmitted, negotiated, and embedded, with mediators helping to nurture the particular subset of academic instrumental knowledge that makes a difference in children's schooling. Smith (2002) identifies what he calls African American cultural capital, rooted in a history of oppression, which privileges caring and community ties over academic reputation and prestige in college choice. The cultural capital of families of color can be reframed in terms of a broader notion of cultural wealth (chapter 1), cultural integrity (Tierney, 1999), funds of knowledge (Moll et al., 1992), and moral, emotional, or navigational forms of capital (Auerbach, 2001), all of which college access programs could build upon as assets. Rather than negate or assimilate local identities, programs can work to affirm such identities while at the same time working to support a sense of active engagement and self-efficacy for parents and family members.

Like cultural capital, social capital is unequally distributed in society and affords advantage to families in pursuit of social mobility. Coleman (1988) defines social capital as productive relationships that lead to advantageous behaviors or outcomes within a social system. One's stores of knowledge, debts, and obligations derive from and are exchanged within one's social network. For example, high-SES White and Asian parents and lower-SES Black and Latino parents in Yonezawa (1997) had different approaches to and leverage with their children's high school class placement, based on their "information-rich" or "information-poor" social networks and the school's response to this capital. Increasingly, policymakers and researchers urge schools and outreach programs to focus on nurturing family social capital (Auerbach, 2002; Plank & Jordan, 2001; Shirley, 1997), which is more amenable to short-term change than cultural capital. For example, expanding parents' college-relevant social networks is listed as a key strategy for creating a "college-going culture" in homes and schools in the goals of UCLA Outreach (Oakes, Rogers, Lipton, & Morrell, 2002).

With these theories in mind, how might we understand trends in the literature on family engagement and the conditions that enable or constrain parents' active participation?

FAMILY ENGAGEMENT AND K–12 ACHIEVEMENT

In a review of the literature on family involvement over the last generation, Jun and Colyar noted, "A majority of the research indicated that students performed better and had higher levels of motivation when they were raised in homes characterized by supportive and demanding parents who were involved in schools and who encouraged and expected academic success" (2002, p. 195). Parent involvement at home and at school has been associated with higher rates of student achievement, attendance, homework completion, graduation, and college enrollment (e.g., Choy, 2002; Henderson & Berla, 1997; Scott-Jones, 1995). Aspects of parent influence most strongly correlated with achievement include parents' aspirations and expectations for their children, monitoring of behavior and school work, communication with school staff, and a warm but firm "authoritative" rather than strict "authoritarian" parenting style. These practices may not have the same viability or effectiveness in minority and immigrant families (Fordham, 1996; Okagaki & Frensch, 1998;

Valdés, 1996) due to structural and cultural differences. For example, high school students of color are more likely to be triply disadvantaged by lower track placement, by parents' lack of knowledge about and participation in the placement process, and by schools' greater responsiveness to the requests and demands of higher-SES White parents (chapter 6, this volume; Yonezawa, 1997).The modest literature on parents of color suggests that their role is foundational for K–12 student success but that their support takes unique forms due to their social and cultural location and schools' response to that location. Clark's (1983) classic study found that low-income African American parents of successful high school seniors used deliberate home pedagogy, close monitoring, and community resources over the years to "sponsor" their children's "competence in student roles." He asserted, "It is the family members' beliefs, activities, and overall cultural style, not the family units' composition or social status that produces the requisite mental structures for effective and desirable behavior" (p. 2). A more recent retrospective study of family influences on Black male college students reported similar parent practices, as well as strong discipline, open communication, affirmation of a positive Black male identity, and "judicious advocacy" with the schools (Hrabowski, Maton, & Greif, 1998). Among working-class Latino immigrant families, Delgado-Gaitan's (1992) study of home socialization for literacy found that the parents of the better primary-grade readers not only read with their children and helped them with homework but sought help and information from the school and communicated regularly with teachers. She suggests that the key to empowerment for marginalized parents is knowledge of the school system and community organizing to further collective concerns in a two-way accommodation with schools (Delgado-Gaitan 1991, 1994). In Gándara's (1995) retrospective study of 50 Chicano professionals with advanced degrees, immigrant parents created a "culture of possibility" through high expectations, stories of past family accomplishment, and the modeling of literacy and hard work.

Patterns of family engagement in education are fundamentally shaped by social class and race, and mediated by cultural and individual psychosocial factors (Auerbach, 2001). For example, parents of higher SES are more likely to have higher aspirations and expectations for their children's educational attainment (Sewell & Shah, 1968; Solorzano, 1992a, 1992b), more helpful information networks (Lareau, 1989; Yonezawa, 1997; Useem, 1992), and greater influence on schools (Lareau, 1989; Wells & Serna, 1996). Parents of lower SES are more likely to engage in more nontraditional, behind-the-scenes forms of support for education (Azmitia, Cooper, Garcia, & Dunbar, 1996; Mehan et al., 1996; Pérez, 1999; Villanueva & Hubbard, 1994); to hold beliefs that may be in conflict with school norms (Lareau, 1989; Lawrence-Lightfoot, 1978; Pérez, 1999; Valdés, 1996); and to delegate educational responsibilities to the school (Bauch, 1993; Lareau, 1989). Across lines of class and race, parent engagement is generally seen as women's work and, as such, is subject to additional tensions and power differentials in schools (Lawrence-Lightfoot, 1978). These findings confirm explanations of parent involvement as variously rooted in status variables, such as class-linked cultural and social capital, and process variables, such as Hoover-Dempsey and Sandler's (1997) role constructions.

Epstein (1990) insists that process variables, such as actual parent practices and the influence of parent involvement programs, trump status variables like race and class in patterns of parent involvement but concedes that status variables may take precedence in settings such as high schools, where parent engagement is typically not promoted. When teachers, administrators, and related school personnel believe that parents should be involved, then school involvement programs are stronger (Epstein & Dauber, 1991). As Cooper (1999) observes, school-based programs that enable families to be involved in systematic, culturally specific cooperative learning situations are more likely to succeed than those that are unidirectional and monocultural (Delgado-Gaitan, 1991, 1994). Extensive ethnographic research with a grassroots Latino parent organization that set its own agenda pointed out that cooperative linkages between families and schools increased student learning. Caplan, Choy, and Whitmore (1992), in a study of Indochinese refugee families, concluded that family engagement "must go beyond annual teacher-parent meetings and must include, among other things, the identification of cultural elements that promote achievement" (p. 42). Levin and Belfield (2002) have gone so far as to suggest that families ought to be viewed as contractual partners in education insofar as they are essential for the manner in which students approach education.

One of the most salient contrasts in parent engagement that may have relevance for college relates to parents' propensity to intervene in or proactively manage their children's education. Higher-SES White parents of average or low-achieving students appear to be the most likely to intervene to request assistance and special services or consideration (Baker & Stevenson, 1986; Lareau, 1989; Yonezawa, 1997). This is one of their strategies for managing their students' careers for maximum advantage. Immigrant and minority parents are less likely to intervene at school for a variety of reasons, including general low rates of participation at the school and differing belief systems (Fordham, 1996; Gándara, 1995). For example, in Delgado-Gaitan and Segura's (1989) case study of 10 Chicana mothers of high school students, all provided moral and emotional support and most offered homework support, but only a few intervened on behalf of their children at school. Despite these trends, as we will see, there may be more cause for parents of color to intervene and take on proactive roles when schools serve minority students poorly and perpetuate social inequalities.

The propensity to manage and intervene may be closely related to parents' sense of self-efficacy. If a parent thinks that his or her actions will lead to realizable goals of student success, then the parent is likely to be more committed and try to achieve those goals (Bandura, 1989). A sense of efficacy is particularly important with members of minority or low-SES groups. For example, Okagaki and Frensch's (1998) survey found that European American parents of fourth and fifth graders were more confident of their ability to help their children with school than Asian American or Latino parents, perhaps due to parent education and immigration effects. Again, those who have cultural capital relevant to American schooling assume they will reach their goals, whereas those who do not may not even have traditional educational goals or know how to pursue them. Parent efficacy typically declines as children mature and parents have less control over them (Eccles & Harold, 1993). Shumow and Lomax (2002), who found that parental efficacy was positively associated with parent monitoring of adolescents and parent-child communication, suggest that boosting efficacy be a goal of parent programs.

The assumptions that parents and family members hold about learning and intelligence also play a part in how parents perceive efficacy and see their role. As Hoover-Dempsey and Sandler (1997) point out in their article about parent involvement, "Parents' beliefs in the importance of developing conformity, obedience, and good behavior in children have been related to poorer school outcomes, while beliefs in the importance of developing personal responsibility and self-respect have been associated with better school performance" (p. 37). A parent or guardian who assumes that his or her role is to be actively involved in specific active learning tasks rather than merely rote and passive learning activities is more likely to raise the educational level of the child. Likewise, parents who believe that effort will produce educational gain are more likely to be involved in their child's education than those who believe in intelligence as a preordained gift (Hoover-Dempsey & Sandler, 1997).

While the effects of timing of parent intervention and student development are explored in greater depth by Bonous-Hammarth and Allen in chapter 8, it is clear that parent intervention and efficacy may be critical for college preparation during secondary school, especially for families of color who are more likely to be disadvantaged by discriminatory tracking structures and substandard schools (Oakes, 1985; Solorzano & Solorzano, 1995). Parent influence on student placement and access, rather than on achievement per se, becomes salient for some students at this time. For example, an analysis of National Education Longitudinal Study (NELS) data found that parent involvement had a greater impact on credits and course-taking patterns than on test scores of 8th through 12th grade students (Catsambis, 1998). College-educated parents are more likely to intervene to ensure higher 8th-grade math placement, to encourage their students to take algebra in middle school, and to help students choose high school courses that qualify them for college (Choy, 2002; Useem, 1992). Such intervention is predicated on the possession of college-relevant cultural and social capital, which is associated with social class. According to a study of six Maryland high schools (Sanders, Epstein, & Connors-Tadros, 1999):

> Most families know very little about high school course offerings, the consequences of special school programs for student advancement or remediation, and requirements for promotion, graduation or post-secondary education and are, therefore, less equipped to be effectively involved in their teens' learning. (p. 14)

As Yonezawa and Oakes (1999) suggest, schools need to include parents in the course placement process.

The obscuring of information about student placement is part of the general disincentive for family engagement at large, bureaucratic secondary schools. For example, one survey at five diverse California high schools found that 39% of teachers felt parents could not help students at this level; 62% thought teachers could not affect parents' home practices; and 63% initiated little or no contact with parents (Dornbusch & Ritter, 1988). Parent engagement generally declines during these years, constrained by both disinterested schools and teenage students' disinclination for communication and involvement (Dodd & Konzal, 1999; Eccles & Harold, 1993; Epstein, 1990). In Hoover-Dempsey and Sandler's (1997) terms, this amounts to a loss of both school and child "invitations" for involvement. The implications of this breakdown in family-school and parent-child communications are grave, given parents' heightened anxiety about their children's future prospects at this juncture and given the often-dire lack of access to college guidance in many high schools addressed by McDonough (chapter 4). Since parent outreach programs at the high school level have been shown to prompt greater engagement and get parents and students talking more about school (Sanders et al., 1999; Simon, 2001), college preparation programs would seem to have a unique opening to address this gap.

What do the findings reported here suggest about the structural conditions for family engagement? Parents and family members who reside in communities that have structural supports for their engagement—and who utilize these supports—are more likely to be involved than those who do not (Clark, 1983; Furstenberg, Cook, Eccles, Elder, & Sameroff, 1999; Hrabowski et al., 1998). When the school affords opportunities for parents and family members whose language may be different from the school's to become involved, participation is more likely (Delgado-Gaitan, 1994; Tierney, 2002a). If the contexts in which the child lives support a sense that he or she can learn and achieve educational goals, then achieving those goals is more likely (Clark, 1983; Gándara, 1995). When parents and guardians believe that their participation in education is welcomed and important, they are more likely to participate (Hoover-Dempsey & Sandler, 1997; Sanders et al., 1999). However, similar parent engagement efforts may not lead to the same benefits for all students, due in part to family social status, cultural and social capital, and the perceived exchange value of that capital at the school (Auerbach, 2001; Lareau & Horvat, 1999; Yonezawa, 1997). These structural constraints become particularly salient as students from lower-SES families pursue college goals.

Clearly, the role of the family in children's education has done an about-face from the assertions of the early 20th century. Rather than isolate the child from the family, researchers now argue that family engagement is crucial to the educational success of the child. Indeed, the belief that families should be involved in their child's learning has reached near paradigmatic status. The assertion that children learn irrespective of the family has been soundly rejected, along with the assumption that only a narrow range of family support strategies are helpful. Clark (1983) suggests that "a wide variety of specific parental practices may serve well in equipping school children with the comprehensive writing, reading, verbal, and social skills and personal qualities needed for learning" (p. 215). The same could be said of parent strategies to promote college preparation, although we still need more research on diverse families' role during the secondary school years and at crucial transition points (Jordan et al., 2002; Useem, 1992). As the next section shows, most of the information on the role of families in the high school–college transition comes from large-scale quantitative studies that offer little insight into the process of promoting college access.

FAMILY ASPIRATIONS, PARENTAL ENCOURAGEMENT, AND COLLEGE PLANNING

The evidence is mixed on the centrality of parents' role in college planning. A survey of high school students' college knowledge in five states found that parents and teachers were the main sources of help, with counselors rarely used (Antonio, 2002). Horn and Chen (1998) found that parental involvement increased the odds of moderate-to-high-risk students enrolling in some form of postsecondary education. Hossler, Schmit and Vesper (1999) contend that students rely on family information only until 10th grade, after which they shift to "external sources," such as teachers, counselors, and peers. The high-achieving Latinos in Gándara (1995) were mentored in their student careers by teachers (50%), older siblings (20%), and community members (15%); they had a "resigned understanding" of the limits to the educational help they could expect from their parents, given parents' low educational levels (cf. Auerbach, 2001; Cooper et al., 1995). Nevertheless, Gándara and Bial (1999) state in their survey of college preparation programs:

> The experience, knowledge, resources, and expectations of parents play a significant role in the kinds of choices that students make. Students with equal ability make very different decisions about their postsecondary education based on the guidance—or lack of it—that they receive from home. (p. 30)

The three main predictors discussed in the sociological literature on college enrollment are parent education, parents' educational aspirations for their children, and parental encouragement for college—all closely linked to class. Having college-educated parents confers advantage on students not only through its association with higher family income, student aspiration, and rates of enrollment directly after high school but through its association with practices like college encouragement, SAT preparation, and college visits (Choy, 2002). Studies have noted strong correlations between high parent educational aspirations and high student achievement, aspirations, and college enrollment (Catsambis, 1998; Conklin & Dailey, 1981; Hossler et al., 1999; McDonough, chapter 4; Paulsen, 1990; Sewell & Shah, 1968). Hossler et al. (1999, p. 24) call parents the "single most important predictor" of students' educational aspirations—more important than parent education level or student GPA. Cooper and colleagues showed how families of low-income minority students were able to inspire and help children set and maintain college aspirations (Cooper et al., 1994; Cooper, 2000). The fact remains, however, that there is a wider gap for families of color than for White families between college aspirations and actual attainment (Solorzano, 1992a, 1992b). This is an indication that broader structural constraints are at work and that aspirations are necessary but not sufficient for college preparation and enrollment.

Parental encouragement for college is generally defined in the literature as the frequency with which parents and students discuss school matters and postsecondary plans. Paulsen (1990) considers parental encouragement a "powerful intervening variable" that may have more impact on student aspirations than the "immutable" factors of family SES or student ability. In a longitudinal study of 5,000 White and Black students in Indiana, Hossler et al. (1999) report that 64% of students with "strong encouragement" from their parents enrolled in four-year colleges after high school, while only 39% of those with mere "encouragement" did so (p. 102). Similarly, Plank and Jordan (1997, 2001) found that "early and sustained discussions" with parents prior to senior year advantaged students, but did so indirectly through promoting actions like SAT taking and college applications (cf. Choy, 2002). Their careful analysis of NELS data shows how certain types of information, guidance, and action—measures of family social capital—weaken predicted SES effects on college enrollment. These large-scale studies are limited by reliance on subjects' self-reports and by lack of information about the quality, as opposed to the frequency, of parental encouragement.

Hossler et al.'s (1999) model of parents' role in college enrollment posits that "parent influence" sends signals of their expectations from an early age; that general "parent encouragement" of college is important throughout high school; and that tangible "parent support" or action for college, such as saving money or visiting colleges, is most important late in high school. These three phases correspond roughly to Hossler and Gallager's (1987) three-stage pre-disposition-search-choice model of college choice. Some aspects of this model are problematic for working-class families, who often begin preparing for college late and lack the resources for college visits and savings accounts (Auerbach, 2001; Post, 1990).

Not surprisingly, parents' college knowledge—a proxy for high-status cultural capital—figures prominently in how they become involved in college preparation. High-SES White parents who have been to college are more likely to know about the steps in college planning and "how, when and why they should interact with the school about their daughters' college choice processes" (McDonough, 1997, p. 152). By contrast, working-class families without college experience may not even be aware that such a process exists (Auerbach, 2001). About two thirds of Latino parents in a national survey by the Tomas Rivera Policy Institute lacked basic information about college, especially first-generation immigrants with limited education, English fluency, and incomes; a key recommendation of the study was making college information widely available in Spanish (Tornatsky, Cutler, & Lee, 2002). McClafferty and colleagues (2001) found that mere translation at parent college planning workshops was insufficient; Latino immigrant parents needed information geared to culturally specific concerns in the areas of college life and safety, the financial benefits of college, and immigrant status.

Parents' knowledge and perception of costs and financial aid play a crucial role in the college prospects of low-SES students, especially in a period of rising tuition and restricted grant-based aid (Levine & Nidiffer, 1996; Olson & Rosenfeld, 1984; Post, 1990). Most parents consistently overestimate the cost of all types of college (Antonio, 2002; Choy, 2002; McDonough, 1998). This can severely limit options for students from low-SES families, given their greater "loan aversion" and vulnerability to the opportunity costs of college (Olson & Rosenfeld, 1984). Studies indicate a "consumer gap" in college financial awareness for parents who need the information most, with better-educated parents most likely to seek out and understand their options and limited-English parents particularly lacking information (Horn & Nuñez, 2000; McClafferty et al., 2001; Olson & Rosenfeld, 1984; Pérez, 1999).

If college preparation programs are to significantly broaden access for underrepresented students, they need to make privileged information about college and financial aid much more easily accessible to families in linguistically and culturally appropriate forms (Auerbach, 2002; McClafferty et al.,

2001; Tornatsky et al., 2002). As the next section demonstrates, few college preparation programs are prepared for this challenge.

FAMILIES AND COLLEGE PREPARATION PROGRAMS

Despite the evidence on the foundational role of families in students' academic success and college pursuit, ongoing family engagement activities are still the exception in college preparation programs. In the College Board (1999) review of strategies for increasing the achievement of underrepresented minority undergraduates, *Priming the Pump*, parent involvement was not even listed as a strategy in the 20 programs that were studied. Gándara and Bial's (1999) national survey found parent components in 18 of 33 programs, though the extent of these components varied widely. In the California Postsecondary Education Commission's (1996) review of the major characteristics of college preparation programs in California, only one third of the programs listed parent engagement as part of a program strategy to fulfill their mission. In a longitudinal review of college preparation programs, Tierney and Jun (1999) reported that only 4 of the 12 programs, and Tierney and Colyar (2001) reported that only 3 of an additional 11 programs, had any component related to parents or families.

The National Survey of Outreach Programs, by contrast, found that about 70% of the 1,100 programs surveyed identified involving parents as an important goal and offered some kind of parent programming, with 58% claiming their activities helped parents learn about college (Swail & Perna, 2002). However, the example of half of all respondents requiring parents to sign a contract as part of student enrollment begs the question of what counts as parent involvement in these programs. Moreover, program staff's frustration with outreach to low-income parents suggests that activities may not be reaching their intended audience—perhaps in part because program staff do not typically have training or experience in working with families.

When these and other programs point out that they work with families, they mean parents only, and their interaction with parents or family members is generally minimal. For example, in one program that stated they involved parents, Jun and Tierney (1999) observed that only generic activities, such as parent nights, occurred once a year. Other programs may limit their parent engagement efforts to orientations, fund-raising, and a few voluntary meetings or social events. Such approaches to parent engagement are less likely to benefit students than ongoing, in-depth family education and support activities.

Most efforts to involve families do not take account of students' culture beyond offering language translation or celebrating ethnic foods. Based on the research reviewed here and notions of cultural integrity, one expects that most college preparation programs geared to cultural and linguistic minorities will feature parent programs that are culturally specific, or built from the ground up incorporating the assumptions of the participants (Cheng Gorman & Balter, 1997). Schools will develop strategies that call upon local languages and definitions of self and identity in order to enable parent/family interaction to occur with teachers, counselors, and administrators. However, this is generally not the case. Puente and the University of Southern California's Neighborhood Academic Initiative are notable exceptions for the high value that they place on family engagement in college preparation, as in requiring parent interviews as part of the initial student selection process and offering ongoing bilingual workshops and services for families. Such programs demonstrate how including family members in students' efforts to get to college becomes a critical way of affirming students' cultures (cf. chapter 1).

It is difficult to assess the effects of existing family components in college preparation programs, as they differ widely in how they conceive and implement these activities and as programs generally suffer from a lack of systematic evaluation (Tierney, 2002b). Among the few relevant evaluations is a longitudinal study of Puente by Gándara, Mejorado, et al. (1998), which found that students in the program not only had higher rates of college enrollment than their matched peers but also reported more parent engagement. Puente students availed themselves of help and advice from significant persons—especially parents—at a higher level than similar non-Puente students. They commented that parents were the primary individuals who influenced their work habits at school, their postsecondary aspirations, and their future goals (Gándara, 2002b).

Regardless of their particular sponsorship, structure, and approach, programs with an emphasis on parents appear to be vital to the college knowledge of their participants. In a survey of 45 parent programs with college components and college preparation programs with parent components in California, McDonough, Pérez, et al. (2000) found that the programs were the main source of information about college for the parents of color/low SES that they served. The most effective program elements in the view of program staff and participants were building trust in personal relationships with parents, bridging the information gap, and helping to empower parents as advocates; common problems included low parent attendance and inadequate staffing. Smith (2002) reports that single African American mothers with limited college experience used college outreach programs extensively to enhance their knowledge of "insider practices" and extend their social network. Another study found that parents were eager for a wide range of college information in their own language, preferably presented by college graduates of similar background on an ongoing rather than one-time basis (McClafferty et al., 2001). These studies suggest the need for greater collaboration between parent involvement and college preparation programs to share expertise and programming ideas. They also point to the lack of research on programs themselves—a gap the Pathways to College Network plans to address with the publication of research-based models for family engagement (Salchak, 2002).

As in K–12 education, the banking or transmission model of information transfer is inadequate for parent education. Parents without college experience need personal contact with individuals who can help them make sense of complex college information and show its relevance to people like themselves (McDonough, 1998; McClafferty et al., 2001). In one pilot program, parents rated the most helpful activity as hearing stories and personal testimony about college going from guest speakers of color, including college students, high school alumni, teachers, and fellow parents (Auerbach, 2002).

It is telling that students describe staff and students in outreach programs as being "like family" in the sense of encouraging, nurturing, and protecting them (Cooper et al., 1995; Serna & Collatos, 2001). Staff members become surrogate parents, and fellow students become honorary siblings and cousins in an expanded extended family. There is great potential here for programs to welcome students' own parents and siblings into this greater family to coordinate support efforts and maximize their benefits for students.

Given this potential, one might wonder why more programs do not feature regular family-centered activities. Research clearly supports family engagement in the education of their children. Policy suggestions from the federal government as well as state governments and foundations have offered recommendations about how to involve families in college preparation. Why, then, are not more programs mindful of the need to incorporate families?

The problem lies not with the findings or policies, but with the implementation of those policies. As Tierney (2002b) has pointed out, college preparation programs suffer from underfunding, short staffing, and a lack of evaluative mechanisms that enable practitioners to prioritize activities. Because families are secondary constituencies, activities geared toward them almost never rise to the top of any list; if the activities occur at all, they are seen as extraneous. In Swail and Perna's (2002) national survey, 27% of respondents reported that working with parents was problematic or needed more funding. Without an explicit mission that acknowledges the importance of family engagement and sufficient resources, practitioners will be hard pressed to incorporate the findings into their programs.

Clearly, the development of effective models for all aspects of college preparation programs, including family engagement, hinges on more systematic, reflective evaluations of diverse approaches (Tierney, 2002a, 2002b). It is likewise clear that programs can and should be doing more to invite parents into the college planning conversation through more sustained, culturally specific parent activities.

CONCLUSION AND RECOMMENDATIONS

We have seen that various forms of family engagement are associated with K–12 student achievement and access to educational opportunity. Higher-SES parents tend to take a hands-on, interventionist role focused on managing their students' careers, including their entry into a "good" college. Parents of color/low SES are constrained from many forms of proactive, instrumental engagement in their children's college preparation due to limited college knowledge and resources, as well as structural and practical barriers. They tend to offer crucial moral, emotional, and logistical support behind the scenes, giving students the motivation and determination to succeed. Many parents without college experience who aspire to college for their children desperately want more information and contacts so they can better help their children. This is an invaluable opening to which college preparation programs must respond.

There are both moral and practical reasons why these programs should invest in developing the untapped resource of parents as informed, supportive guides along the pathway to college (Levine & Nidiffer, 1996; McClafferty et al., 2001). First, engaging with families is a way of affirming students' cultures and building a more holistic college-going culture that pervades students' lives. Second, since college-educated parents deploy their considerable cultural and social capital to advantage their children in college markets, families without college experience need targeted information and support to help level the playing field. While programs already do this through staff mentoring of students, staff members are often overworked and unable to provide the ongoing monitoring and encouragement that many students need; parents are in a good position to supplement these efforts, given adequate information. Third, programs can help cultivate parents as helpful allies in the college preparation process rather than as passive bystanders or potential obstacles. As McClafferty and colleagues (2001) note, if we are serious about increasing college access, programs must "tap every potential resource in the advancement of student achievement" (p. 28). Finally, investment in parents as resources for college going can have educational ripple effects throughout marginalized communities. If college preparation programs began partnerships with parent engagement programs at elementary and middle schools, they could cultivate a base of students who came to high school with more college knowledge and better academic preparation. With family outreach at the high school, younger siblings, other family members, and even parents themselves may be inspired to continue their own education (Auerbach, 2001).

With finite resources, college preparation programs should plan at least a minimal family component for activities on a regular basis, beginning in late elementary or middle school (cf. chapter 8). Family awareness and action to promote college preparation go hand-in-hand. Programming should extend beyond family education for college awareness to guidance that helps parents take appropriate action for college access as their children's advocates and supporters. The research reviewed above suggests potential for beneficial family education and support activities in the following areas: (1) personalized information focusing on steps in the pathway to college and how parents can help, beginning in elementary school; (2) expansion of family social networks related to college options to include more educators, college students/alumni, and families like themselves; (3) reinforcement of parents' sense of self-efficacy, perhaps through workshops on adolescent development or advocacy training by community organizers; and (4) gathering with other families for support and fellowship in instrumental steps on the pathway to college, such as helping students choose classes, meeting with college counselors and representatives, visiting colleges, and filling out financial aid applications. Such activities could be accomplished relatively simply and inexpensively through monthly parent workshops or support groups led by program staff or other facilitators who share the families' cultural and linguistic background. Ideally, this would take place as part of school-university-community partnerships so as not to strain program resources.

Our point is surely not to prescribe the nature of parent and family engagement in all college preparation programs. Indeed, if we work from the notion of cultural integrity, then different programs will develop culturally specific pedagogy that meets the needs of local populations. For example, programs that work primarily with African American parents who have high school diplomas or community college experience will have different emphases than those that work with Latino immigrant families with less formal education and familiarity with American institutions (cf. McClafferty et al., 2001). However, we know a great deal more today than we did a decade ago. One clear finding is that families—broadly defined—can be of significant help in enabling children to graduate from high school and go on to college.

The challenge, then, is fourfold. Policymakers need to incorporate family engagement into a systemic and prioritized support system about what works for college access, as the Pathways to College Network has begun to do. Funders need to ensure that funding goes toward activities that are central rather than peripheral, and that evaluative criteria are in place for all components. Researchers need to move beyond metastatements about the importance of family engagement and offer more fine-grained analyses of specific activities that are successful and implementable with the families of low-SES students of color. We especially need more studies on the role of siblings in college preparation and of college-related encouragement and instrumental strategies used by African American, Asian American, and Native American parents. Finally, program staff need to develop an ongoing reflective evaluative framework that enables them to prioritize those activities that are key, and then utilize that framework to ensure that program activities achieve maximum effectiveness. Enlisting and developing the support of parents and other family members as allies will ultimately further this mission.

WILLIAM G. TIERNEY
JULIA E. COLYAR

Chapter Three

The Role of Peer Groups in
College Preparation Programs

INTRODUCTION

The significance of peer groups in the social and academic development of adolescents has long been discussed by parents, psychologists, school personnel, and public officials (Piaget, 1932; Hinde, 1987). In some respects, the importance of peers is deceptively simple. Except in cases such as home schooling, education is a social activity. Youth learn in groups. If education is a social undertaking, then the role of peers in learning is of critical concern.

A review of the literature reveals that few topics about the social processes of education have been as often studied as peer groups, and few topics have provided such varied interpretations. Peers are examined in studies of dropouts and identity formation. They are discussed at length in psychological and sociological literatures. They are viewed in terms of school and nonschool settings. Race and gender have been considered, as have the differences between urban and rural peer groups.

The 1966 Coleman Report, for example, supported the notion of racial balance in schools; poor Black children, Coleman noted, performed better in

We appreciate the comments of Zoë Corwin and Anthony Lising Antonio.

integrated, middle-class schools. These findings led to the busing of inner-city children to suburban schools, a practice that met strong resistance from many communities but underscored the importance of peer groups. Additional studies have focused on the social context of peer groups (Bandura, 1977; Hartup, 1992) as positive and negative factors in students' progress through school (Romo & Falbo, 1996; Azmitia & Cooper, 2001) and the ways in which youths learn from one another. Peer connections are thought to provide an important source of social support for children, particularly in periods of emotional distress. They have also been studied as sources of evaluation and reaction, as providing directive influence on children's behaviors and developmental processes (Chen, Chen, & Kaspar, 2001). Peers have been thought of as a subcultural group that provides agency for youth to resist the dominant culture on the one hand (O'Connor, 1997; MacLeod, 1995) and as a way for youth to navigate multiple and conflicting worlds on the other (Azmitia & Cooper, 2001).

The topic is important for college preparation programs because virtually all programs focus on cohorts or discrete groups of students. College preparation programs, by definition, are collective undertakings. The programs do not, in general, offer self-paced learning activities for an individual; instead, social, cultural, and academic college preparation programs occur in groups. As with other chapters, our central question here is the following: with finite resources and finite time, how much effort should be put toward enhancing peer relationships? Unlike a learning activity, a time frame, or a mentoring program, there is little choice for college preparation programs with regard to peers. That is, a program may concentrate on math skills or not; the program may begin in junior high or late in the senior year; a program may decide to have mentors or to ignore them. Regardless of the format, time frame, and inclusion of mentors, however, the tasks that take place will include one's peers.

Accordingly, unlike many of the other chapters, our purpose is not so much to decide whether to include peers in the learning process, but to consider how to make the best use of them. We begin by considering how peers have been defined and theorized, then turn to findings about the influence of peer groups in educational settings, and conclude with recommendations about how to utilize peer groups to increase college access. Although one might work from several different perspectives (e.g., psychology, anthropology), we base our discussion primarily in sociology and utilize the notions that Villalpando and Solorzano developed in chapter 1.

DEFINING PEERS

As Bradford Brown (1989) and others (Scheidlinger, 1984) note, the term "peer group" has been used inconsistently to identify close friends, classmates, groups of students, or the entire population of age mates. Peers have been defined as those with whom one interacts (Hallinan, 1979), shares specific activities (Crockett, Losoff, & Petersen, 1984), or attends the same school. Kemper (1968) uses the terminology "reference group" to describe the process by which individuals choose behaviors and actions; the reference group provides a set of explicit or implicit norms and values. In most cases, peer groups are defined by particular characteristics of the individual student members, and more specific distinctions follow from the number of students in a group. For example, one of the major topics of peer research has been overall popularity or rejection; peer groups are often classified as average, popular, scholarly, or athletic (Rubin, Burkowski, & Parker, 1998).

Peer groups are also discussed as closed, self-contained systems. Astin's (1993, p. 400) work uses such a definition, calling peers a "collection of individuals with whom the individual identifies and affiliates and from whom the individual seeks acceptance or approval." These two qualities—identification and the desire for acceptance—are necessary conditions for peer group status. Further, affiliation and acceptance are exclusively interrelated—each generates the other.

Other researchers provide more specific definitions based on the number of individuals involved. These definitions rely on the assumption of self-contained, self-regulated groups. In many ways, such definitions are more reductive than characteristic groups; they deal exclusively with group size. For example, in his study of informal peer groups in their natural settings, Dunphy (1963) notes that "cliques" are smaller than "crowds"—cliques with an average group size of 6.3 members, crowds with approximately 20. Cliques develop within crowds, usually not across crowds, and clique membership is a "prerequisite" to crowd membership. Dunphy argues that clique membership is the basic alliance that makes all others possible. Expanding contacts and establishing new ones occurs only within the stability of the clique, again emphasizing the closed nature of the groups. Coleman (1980) also argues for the closed nature of cliques. They form based on school or recreational activities, and they are not readily open to outsiders. Because of their size, Dunphy notes that cliques tend to be more intimate and coherent; they often provide an alternative center of security when family security is unavailable. At times, cliques can even be scornful of nonmembers. Such cliques are usually unisexual during early adolescence, but increasingly heterosexual as individuals age. Departing from Dunphy's model, Brown (1989) adds that crowds are reputation-based groups; these group affiliations denote the "primary attitudes or activities with which one are associated by peers" (p. 190). Crowds may be labeled to reflect these characteristics: brains, jocks, druggies, cheerleaders, and so on. While norms for cliques are generated by the members, norms for the crowd are imposed from outside, usually reflecting the stereotypes associated with the group.

Coleman (1980) adds to the definition of crowds and cliques by noting that cliques are generally composed of members of the same socioeconomic class and grade level in school. They tend to be preoccupied with internal activities such as conversation, and crowds tend to be concerned with external social activities such as parties, dances, or other cocurricular activities. Further, Coleman indicates that the significance of the crowd is that it "provides a means of transition from unisexual to heterosexual social relationships by facilitating interclique activities"—cliques come together under the umbrella of the crowd, allowing individuals to interact with others in a "protected setting" (p. 418).

A final set of definitions has to do with peer pressure and peer conformity. According to Santor, Messervey, & Kusumakar (2000), the central feature of peer pressure is the tendency for individuals to think and act in specific ways because they have been urged or pressured to do so. Brown, Clasen, and Eicher (1986) mark the differences between pressure and conformity this way: peer pressure represents an attitude, and conformity represents a behavioral disposition. Pressure is defined as a subjective experience, whereas conformity assesses the degree to which individuals adopt a set of actions sanctioned by their peers.

How one defines a peer group obviously has implications for how one thinks about and studies peers. For example, using Kemper's (1968) notion of reference groups, if the peer group is conceptualized as one that provides explicit guidance, then large populations such as an entire campus or a dorm can serve as the model for the norms, values, and beliefs of the group. From this definition, interaction is not necessary and nearly impossible with all individuals in the peer group; norms exist external to individual students and interactions. However, if peer groups are more specifically defined as friendship groups where, by definition, interpersonal interaction and affiliation are mandatory, then an entirely different theoretical and practical standpoint is assumed. Peer groups that peers create and maintain may be viewed in one light, and peer groups that adults create for peers may be studied in another. Shared and consensual sets of norms are much more cocreated through interpersonal interaction in a friendship group; they are much more preexistent in a reference group. Although no definition is paradigmatic, we highlight here the import of definitions; these terms are also discussed below. We now turn to a discussion of theories that have been used in analyzing peers.

THEORIZING ABOUT PEERS

The variety of definitions applied to peer groups and peer influence is nearly matched by the theoretical lenses that articulate such definitions. In what follows, we offer five sociological lenses with which to view peers. As with any theoretical framework that is not paradigmatic, each lens is an ideal type that covers a great deal of conceptual territory.

Role Theory

Briefly introduced above, one theoretical cornerstone of peer group research is the reference group; this framework theorizes about the roles that individuals assume. Though Hyman is usually credited with the first reference group study in 1942, the framework is best known from Newcomb's (1943) study of female students at Bennington College in the late 1930s. The study was concerned with the role of peer groups in students' changing political views that came about with their orientation and integration into the college. Throughout the 1960s and into the 1970s, researchers continued to use the theory as they looked at the ways in which peer groups shape the attitudes and behaviors of individuals (Milem, 1998).

Like the definitions of peer groups, cliques, and crowds, reference groups provide an uncomplicated theoretical lens through which to view interactions. Reference groups provide explicit guidance by providing clearly articulated roles, norms, and values, or a set of guidelines from which to negotiate. The role an individual adopts is related to the dynamics and values of the group, which exist with or without individual membership. Reference groups, then, play a role not only in how members act within the group, but also with regard to an individual's socialization; while the reference group can provide the "perfect" example of behaviors, it is ultimately the individual that performs those roles. Kemper offers some clarification on this point: "a reference group is a group, collectivity, or person which the actor takes into account in some manner in the course of selecting a behavior from among a set of alternatives, or in making a judgment about a problematic issue" (1968, p. 32).

As the name implies, individual decision making occurs in reference to a peer group, without consideration of external or nongroup characteristics. Kemper (1968) describes this framework as both popular and "devoid of any real theory" (p. 31). The problem, he notes, is that "we have a concept and some cognate concepts such as role set, role model, reference set, reference group and the like" (p. 32)—but none of these help explain how reference groups are chosen. Reference groups cannot serve as predictors of a role that an individual will assume, Kemper maintains, but simply as "worn-out" postdictors.

Role theory proponents argue that individuals imitate the behavior of one or more peers whom they respect (Hallinan & Williams, 1990). Rather than negotiating a decision based on the parameters established by the group, the individual directly imitates another in the peer group. Critics argue that this theory does not provide information about how a peer group is selected. Hallinan and Williams (1990) explain: "the theories do not identify which individuals are vulnerable to influence or who possess the power to influence and they do not specify the conditions under which influence occurs" (p. 122). As a result, role theory lacks explanatory power and predictability.

Social Comparison Theory

A second interpretive framework that is related to role theory is social comparison theory. Festinger (1954) hypothesized that individuals evaluate their opinions, behaviors, and talents by comparing themselves to others—particularly with those they believe are similar to themselves. Similarities can be considered in a global sense (a female student) or by more specific criteria (a female student majoring in English). Friendship groups (or membership groups) are often pointed to as examples of social comparison arenas. Unlike reference groups, friendship groups develop shared values through interaction; group norms do not exist independent of individual membership and, in some cases, comparison. The goals of comparison are self-improvement or self-enhancement; self-improvement is provided by looking to individuals with superior skills in order to learn these skills or become more motivated, and self-enhancement comes from comparisons focused on an individual considered to be less skilled. Comparison with those who are less fortunate or less skilled may cause an individual to reevaluate their own behaviors or situations (Antonio, 1995).

Developmental Theories

In some respects, a developmental framework is more psychological than sociological insofar as it returns the focus to the individual student and articulates the ways in which cognitive, emotional, and intellectual development informs peer group processes and influences. It is nearly impossible to consider the influence of the peer group without also marking the characteristics of adolescence. When children enter school, they spend less time with parents and more time with friends and peers. Increasingly, their spheres of social meaning expand to include agents other than parents and siblings. With new contacts in the world, children and adolescents develop new cognitive skills, communication skills, concepts of friendship, and acts of friendship (Epstein & Karweit, 1983). Over time, children develop more accurate perceptions of self and other, awareness of errors in judgment, and increased problem-solving skills (Erikson, 1968).

Perhaps more important, children develop the tools to consider simultaneous points of view as well as individual details within a collection of ideas (Epstein & Karweit, 1983). In addition, the ability to think from multiple perspectives assists adolescents in developing "realistic expectations of their friends, of themselves as friends, and of friendship as a social relationship" (p. 44). While there is a great deal of argument about the causes of these developmental changes—are they neurological or based on experience?—researchers agree on the fact that adolescence is a time of changing social relationships.

Fictive Kinship

A fourth framework is based on the work of John Ogbu (1978, 1991; Fordham & Ogbu, 1986) and oppositional identities. Rather than the more psychological explanations of developmental theories, fictive kinship utilizes cultural-ecological approaches to understanding peer groups. This framework, writes Fordham (1988), "refers to a kinship-like connection between and among persons in a society, not related by blood or marriage, who have maintained essential reciprocal social or economic relationships" (p. 56). The peer group is one example of a fictive kinship. Insofar as peer groups often function by way of racial identity, fictive kinship is a cultural marker of collective identity, which is constituted by, but more than, skin color. That is, fictive kinship is not merely that people of one race are involved in a common group, but that a particular mind-set or worldview is also involved in that grouping.

This theory is quite different from the previous theories for several reasons. First, the theory emanated from scholars trying to understand how racial and ethnic minorities functioned in educational arenas as opposed to theories that in large part ignored or overlooked race as a defining characteristic. Second, each theory that we have mentioned up to this point also has been researched by scholars who had varying interpretations of peer groups. Some have assumed that peer groups are important and others have not, even though they may have utilized role theory, development theory, or social comparison theory. Fictive kinships, however, in large part deny agency to individuals. The assumption is that the collective identity of what Ogbu (1984) termed involuntary or castelike minorities is so great that those racial minorities must adopt certain behaviors within the educational peer group. Proponents of fictive kinship argue that schooling for African Americans causes a chronic sort of schizophrenia such that the student has to choose: either be black and poorly educated, or be raceless and earn an education. Needless to say, fictive kinship has garnered its share of critics and, like the other theories, remains controversial and still debated.

Social Network Theory

The goals of social network theory are to articulate more accurately the "various and simultaneous ways class, gender, race, and ethnic forces affect the daily lives of low-status adolescents, particularly in the development of adolescent relationships and social support systems" (Stanton-Salazar, 2001, p. 5). As Stanton-Salazar points out, social networks have been defined as "social webs" or "support systems" that connect people to one another and to the larger society. While they can be pipelines through which valuable resources or information are transmitted, they can also be instruments that keep resources from certain populations. Networks are fluid entities, constantly assembled and reassembled through social interactions and institutional settings (Cochran, Larner, Riley, Gunnarsson, & Charles, 1990). A peer group is one such network.

Individual network orientations are defined as a constellation of skills, dispositions, and beliefs that assist in adaptation to particular environments. Unlike reference groups, which often focus on interpersonal influences as the basis for peer influence, network orientation is concerned with all aspects of the environment: peers, social groups, neighborhood, recreational centers, churches, gangs, and more. J. Clyde Mitchell (1969) defined a social network as a "specific set of linkages among a defined set of persons" (p. 2). As opposed to fictive kinships, which provide a relatively stable understanding of what counts as a peer group, social networks are quite broad and not easily defined. If all aspects of the environment fit within the possible definition of a peer group, the predictive ability of the theory is virtually absent. The strength of such an approach is that it is especially helpful with regard to protean communities where members enter and leave. While stable membership communities might have existed a generation ago, groups in the United States today do not exhibit such stability.

No theory is paradigmatic, and a fair amount of conceptual confusion exists. Interestingly, however, there is an increasing sense that regardless of the theoretical stance one assumes, peer group affiliation is an important component of educational success. A great number of studies have looked at the various ways in which peers interact and influence one another in high school and college settings. In general, these studies approach the topic from a combination of theoretical approaches. That is, they begin with the assumption that peer groups are closed, self-regulated systems that provide guidance through a set of group norms or values. If one works from the perspective of fictive kinships, however, then the ability of a youth to negotiate a successful outcome is problematic. If one accepts the notion of social networks, then how these networks get created is essential for success. We turn now to a discussion of the research on peers in educational settings to highlight how these various theories get played out.

RESEARCHING PEERS

Background on Peer Influence

For many years, one stream of research about peer influence in adolescence was decidedly negative. Peers or adolescent peer pressure were credited for various forms of misconduct, including alcohol and drug abuse, illegal or dangerous activities, and apathy toward school (Coleman, 1961; Kandel, 1973; Pearl, Bryan, & Herzog, 1990; Snyder, Dishion, & Patterson, 1986; Brown et al., 1986). The term itself—peer pressure—came to suggest force, coercion, or constraints, always with negative associations. In particular, researchers in the late 1960s and early 1970s often discussed the harmful impacts of adolescent peer groups. Peer groups were seen as "sub cultures," a part of society found in "halls and classrooms of the school, the teen-age canteens, the corner drugstore, the automobile" (Coleman, 1961, p. 4). High school students were thought to be more interested in popularity than intellectual development, growing up to be rock stars rather than nuclear scientists. To gain admission to the leading crowd, students needed "money, fancy clothes, good houses, new cars, etc.—the best," and being active in school meant cheerleading or athletics, rarely the honor roll or school leadership (Coleman, 1961, p. 38). Braham (1965) went so far as to suggest that the peer group subculture was an "educationally negating force that legislates against widespread intellectual activities during the intellectually important period of secondary education" (p. 248). The impact of such a force was not restricted to adolescents, however. Braham was concerned that "over the long run this would . . . be restrictive of personal, cultural and species evolution" (p. 248).

Coleman's concerns in his 1961 landmark study are still worth noting, in large part because they had such a significant influence. In a postindustrial age, children spend more time in schools, and take longer to acquire job skills, than ever before. Adolescence itself is a life period marked by extensive changes in the individual and the social environment, a time when youth must reorganize their concepts of self and the world (Pombeni, Kirchler, & Palmonari, 1990). Even before the age of the Internet, Coleman cited the rapid communication systems and spread of ideas as a means by which cultures form and thrive; in the 21st century, the capacity to communicate is far beyond anything Coleman could have predicted. New cultures and groups, including adolescent cultures and groups, can and do form and, as Coleman suggested, these subcultures have "languages all their own, with special symbols, and most importantly, with value systems that differ from adults'" (p. 3). The underlying assumption of these studies was that peers made a difference in identity formation by way of modeling particular behaviors to one another, and that for the most part the impact of peers was negative.

A different stream of research concluded that peer groups were insignificant in identity formation. Cohen (1977, 1983), for example, conducted a series of studies that concluded that the magnitude of peer influence on college aspirations was relatively meager. Kandel and Lesser (1969, 1970a) had multiple articles in which they compared the effects of parents and peers on the educational plans of students and found that "parental aspirations and participation in a college preparatory program each have a strong and independent effect that is much larger than that of peers" (1970b, p. 270). Haller and Butterworth (1960) also offered tentative support for the assertion that peers did not influence one another's levels of educational aspiration.

Yet an additional line of research had the opposite finding: peers not only made a difference, but they had a positive impact. Beginning with Piaget (1932) and Sullivan (1953), many researchers have argued that peers play an important role in identity formation and college-going aspirations. Rather than assume that the role is negative, more recent research has tried to conceive of ways that peer groups might be structured to enable positive outcomes. Youniss and Smollar (1985) have pointed out that peer groups enable youth to develop a mature sense of self; in effect, adolescents need to break away from the parental bond and peer groups enable the young to develop an independent identity. Michael Ungar (2000) has noted the term peer pressure may more accurately be considered an adult construct than a true reflection of adolescent realities. Eckert (2000) has looked at the way peer groups foment or retard identity formation through the use of linguistic constructions.

Other researchers have found the peer group to be essential for cognitive and emotional development (Newman & Newman, 1976; Furman & Gavin, 1989) or as a source of support for difficult tasks. Pombeni and colleagues (1990) suggest that "the nature of the group individuals join is of minor importance, whereas the relationship established with peers is crucial" (p. 351). Epstein and Karweit (1983) and Steinberg, Brown, Cider, Kaczmarek, and Lazzaro (1988) point out that peers influence achievement behavior. Authors have found that students whose friends have college aspirations are likely to go to college, while those who befriend students with no college-going aspirations are less likely to attend a postsecondary institution (D'Amico, 1975; Rumberger, 1991).

Studies have investigated distinct populations as well, such as college students (Feldman & Newcomb, 1969; Astin, 1993). Unlike the literature on peer groups and high school youth, studies on college students have offered nearly unconditional praise for peer group influences. Peer groups afford opportunities for socialization into the postsecondary setting; they provide encouragement for pursuing graduate studies, and they act as academic and personal support networks. "Peer pressure" gives way to "collaborative learning," and student groups are highlighted for their positive influences on academic outcomes.

Race has been looked at from a variety of perspectives. Fordham (1988), Fordham and Ogbu (1986), and Matute-Bianchi (1986) have concluded that peer groups do not foster an environment for educational advancement among African American and Latino youth because academic success is equated with "acting White" with their peers. O'Connor (1997) has disagreed with this assertion, and has suggested that students of color have much greater agency in the process; they do not necessarily think of academic success in a particular way. Steinberg, Dornbusch, and Brown (1992) have found that White and Asian youth benefit from peer support for achievement, whereas Hispanic and African American youth do not. The studies of Azmitia and Cooper (2001), Gándara (1995), Cooper and Cooper (1992), and Stanton-Salazar (2001) have argued that peer group formations play a crucial role for minority youth if rightly conceptualized and orchestrated.

Although the literature appears robust, there are also areas that are understudied. There is little comparative work, for example, about the differences in outcomes between groups that come together by themselves as opposed to groups that adults form for adolescents. Researchers have not looked at the effects of putting students in magnet schools or particular after-school programs; these parental and/or academic decisions, however, invisibly shape peer groups. Little work has been done on the academic success of peer groups that are explicitly based on gender, race, sexual orientation, and the like in comparison to heterogeneous groupings. Adolescents also frequently inhabit multiple peer groups simultaneously, and not much research has investigated how individuals make sense of groups that frequently require different identities.

Nevertheless, findings in the general literature support a variety of conclusions. Peers make a difference. Peers do not make a difference. Peer groups are harmful cliques to be avoided, destroyed, or overcome. Peer groups are helpful subcultures for identity development and need to be fostered. We turn now to a more in-depth discussion of the educational contexts of peer groups.

Junior High School and High School

When adolescents begin high school, they enter a context that frames social situations, networks, daily activities, and systems of support. A ready supply of bystanders is available to confirm or withhold status or to influence the decisions students make about school, family, or social activities. In some ways, then, the school context is set up as a high-stakes arena; the structures students must learn to negotiate are already in place, independent of student characteristics, family values, or cultural norms. How students respond to this environment is a complex mixture of their cognitive abilities, the school climate, and the peers with whom they spend their time (Van Acker & Wehby, 2000; Berndt, Hawkins, & Jiao, 1999).

A school is a dual context. Although parents and teachers may look on the school as an educational arena, youth look on it as a social locale as well. Students come to learn; adolescents come to meet and be with their friends. Just as adults carry multiple identities with them to the workplace, adolescents come to school with multiple agendas and identities. Osterman (2000) has studied how peer groups meet these various needs. On the one hand, peer groups parallel tracking mechanisms: low-track students are in one group and college-bound students in another. On the other hand, when adolescents get tracked in this manner, it also helps determine a student's sense of belonging and community. Thus, a catch-22 exists for the low-tracked student whereby a sense of belonging to the school is diminished because of his or her place in a particular peer group. That sense of belonging, however, is ultimately what motivates and encourages students to higher achievement.

The notion that peers have a largely negative influence on learning can be found in much of the research on high school students, particularly in studies conducted prior to 1980. In fact, considerable support can be found for the role of peers in encouraging antisocial behaviors (Glynn, 1981; Kandel, 1973). Mounts and Steinberg (1995) studied more than 6,000 high school students attending schools in California and Wisconsin, and they found that peers had a "significant, direct effect" on drug use (p. 919). Other researchers have suggested that peer groups discourage academic effort: John Goodlad (1983) found high school students passive, and others (Bishop, 1989; Braham, 1965) have noted that poor student motivation is caused by peer pressure against studying hard.

The assertions about peer influence are not always supported by data, and studies correlating peer influence with positive educational outcomes are easily found. Even Mounts and Steinberg's (1995) study of peer influence and drug use revealed that adolescents with high-achieving friends tend to do better in school than those with lower-achieving friends. Essentially, students in their study became more similar over time. Brown and colleagues (1986) also found that students influence one another in more prosocial than negative ways; students in their study reported that peers pressured them to work hard and get good grades more often than they discouraged schoolwork. In Stader and Gagnepain's (2000) study, a structured peer mentoring program provided an opportunity to develop healthier and more positive student relationships and interactions.

Influence and discussion between friends has also been studied with respect to peer groups in high school. Berndt, Laychak, and Park (1990) posited that students would develop similar attitudes toward academic achievement after they discussed dilemmas related to achievement. In the study, 118 junior high students were divided into friendship pairs and asked to work toward decisions on different dilemmas. In each, they were asked to decide between actions that reflected either high levels of achievement motivation or low levels, and these decisions were compared to pretested results. They found that their hypothesis was consistent with the student behaviors: friends' decisions were more similar after their discussions, even if their discussions were very brief. These results also supported the hypothesis that similarities increased when the discussion involved close friends. Of particular interest in this study is the fact that student discussions focused on academic motivation issues. More often than not, student discussions led to changed attitudes in motivation.

McDill and Coleman (1965) took a different approach to studying peer groups and school motivation. They examined the "peer status" of students in leadership positions and their academic aspirations. While students with high peer status raised their aspirations and expectations for college and beyond, the aspirations of nonleaders (lower peer status) dropped. These findings occurred even when the father's educational background was not controlled. McDill and Coleman asserted that this points to a shift away from family education and socioeconomic level as the primary determinant in college aspirations; instead, the students' personal achievement and status among peers was seen as a more important influence on success. Rehberg and Schafer (1968) added to this discussion by asserting that athletic participation is another important variable in success, particularly in students without parental encouragement and/or lower levels of academic success.

While these studies support the notion that peers are influential with regard to academic outcomes, the process of such influence is not clarified by the findings. In general, researchers have not asked questions about gender differences, language abilities, cultural expectations, or socioeconomic positions. In most cases, peer influence is imagined as occurring in one dimension with only a few outcomes—peers influence or they do not, peers are positive influences or negative.

Some studies have added contextual elements that have problematized the findings. Irene Cota (1997) looked at students' second-language ability and the role of parents, siblings, and friends in developing English language skills that can lead to academic achievement. Eder, Evans, and Parker (1995) investigated how peer groups vary by gender and how masculinity in boys is often worked out in extracurricular activities such as sports. Calabrese and Noboa (1995) looked at Mexican American adolescents, and they pointed out that students often "weigh the benefit" of joining a gang or opting for the traditional value and social structures offered in the school setting (p. 226). Ide, Parkerson, Haertel, and Walberg (1981) looked at the correlation of peer group variables and a range of educational outcomes, including standardized test scores, course grades, educational aspirations, and occupational aspirations. In all students grades 9 through 12, Ide et al. found a correlation between peer influence and outcomes; in the majority of cases (105 out of 110), the correlations were positive. In particular, Ide et al. found stronger correlations with students grade 10 and above, and in urban settings. A more recent study on urban high schoolers supports their findings: Hebert and Reis (1999) looked at a group of high-achieving students in large, economically deprived urban environments and found that as students advanced through high school, "peer network[s] became stronger as they interacted with other high-achieving peers in various extracurricular activities" (p. 447). These high-achieving students also worked in peer groups to complete projects, and they participated in "an active network for each other," supplying help, peer counseling, and the support needed to over-come problems at home and school (p. 447). Bonous-Hammarth and Allen (chapter 8) review literature on the timing of peer influence on developmental stages of students.

Gándara, Gutierrez, and O'Hara (2001) conducted a study of White and Latino peer groups in rural and urban schools and discovered a number of dif-ferences based on locale. Similarly, Goodenow and Grady (1993) argued that many urban adolescents have a poor sense of school belonging, which can lead to low academic motivation and persistence. Further, while urban adolescents were no less academically motivated than their middle-class suburban counter-parts, they "expressed far lower levels of social and personal connection to oth-ers in the school, a lower belief that others in the school were *for* them, and less confidence that their friends valued school success than did suburban students" (p. 67). The importance of school belonging was particularly important for Hispanic and female students (see also Urberg, Degirmencioglu, Tolson, & Halliday-Sher, 1995). Rosenthal, Moore, and Taylor (1983) also noted the complexities of ethnicity in school settings, and suggested that student adjust-ment and belonging is related to different groups' desires for assimilation and the nature of institutional support.

As we have mentioned, other researchers have looked at the comparative roles of parents and peers in adolescent aspirations. In 1969, Kandel and Lesser began a study aimed at examining the simultaneous influence of parents and peers in the educational process in an effort to bring together the work that had until then been carried out individually. Perhaps not surprisingly, previous work suggested mixed findings: McDill and Coleman (1965) and Herriot (1963) concluded that peers are more influential than parents; Simpson (1962) found that for both middle- and lower-class boys, "parental influence was more strongly related to aspirations than peer influences" (p. 521); for Brown, Mounts, Lamborn, and Steinberg (1993), parental influences are mediated through the peer group indirectly—that is, parents influence the behaviors by which teenagers become associated with particular groups.

By looking at over 1,000 interrelated triads of lower-class and rural stu-dents—two students, paired with one of their mothers, for a total of over 3,000 subjects—Kandel and Lesser (1969) hoped to untie the complexities of family and peer influence. They found that while both parents and peers are influential in how students report educational aspirations, parent influence is greater, par-ticularly when the parent and peer do not hold similar views or expectations. Kandel and Lesser report that 49% of adolescents "plan to continue beyond high school when their mothers have college plans for them and their best-school-friends intend to stop at the high school level" (pp. 216–217). In addi-tion, Kandel and Lesser reported that parental influence remains stronger than peer throughout adolescence.

In 1981, Kandel returned to the question of parental influence with Mark Davies and again studied triads of adolescents, best friends, and parents. Supporting the earlier study, Davies and Kandel (1981) reported that parental influences were "much stronger than the influence of best friends" (p. 370). They also found that peer effects, though overall weaker than parental, were stronger for girls than for boys. Another important finding was that parental aspirations were based on socioeconomic status—not on the student's school performance. It is important to note that Davies and Kandel did not assert a direct relationship between socioeconomic status and student aspiration; the effect was considered mediated through the parent, and possibly through the peer. It is difficult, however, to attribute outcomes to peer influence in light of this finding. Davies and Kandel suggest that a student's choice of friendships may reflect homophily on the basis of social class background as well as potential parental control of a student's choice of friends (p. 374).

Picou and Carter (1976) also looked at the role of significant others in educational aspirations. Their study of high school seniors in Louisiana added a layer of complexity to the question of whether peer groups made a difference when compared with parental influence: they noted a difference in types of influence, "modeling" and "definer" modes. Peer influence was considered to operate via modeling, while parents, teachers, and others did so through the definer role (McDill & Coleman, 1965; Kandel & Lesser, 1969; Sewell, Haller, & Ohlendorf, 1970a). Though these distinctions had been asserted in past research, Picou and Carter argued that they had never been tested. Further, Picou and Carter were interested in whether peers acted as both models and definers, or if they were confined to the model role. Through surveys and group interviews of 1,200 white male students, they found that peer influence came exclusively through modeling. They also found differences in the strength of influence based on community origins. While urban students were more influenced by parents than peers, rural students were more influenced by peer modeling.

The diminished strength of peer influence in adolescent aspirations was also tested by Jere Cohen (1983). Previous studies of peer influence, Cohen noted, used peer similarities as an indicator of peer influence without controlling for similarities that might have existed prior to the friendship (e.g., Haller & Butterworth, 1960; Duncan, Haller, & Portes, 1968). When similarities are controlled, the effect of peer influence on college plans decreases dramatically. In his study, Cohen looked for homophily and controlled the project through respondents' early reports of college aspirations. Peer effects on college aspirations were not eliminated in his study, but they were greatly reduced: the effect was noted as one of the "weakest areas" of peer influence (p. 773). While peer influence was significant in other areas, it was not central to college aspiration.

In contrast to Cohen, the point that one's peer group influences college plans is supported by the work of Alexander and Campbell (1964) and Hallinan and Williams (1990). Both studies support the assertion that when an individual is a member of a college-going group, then the individual is more likely to attend college as well. Questions of homophily are also problematic in Krauss's (1964) study of working-class youth. Krauss looked at high school seniors in the San Francisco Bay area, and he noted that working-class students whose friends were planning to go to college were more likely to go to college themselves. Those without friends planning to go to college were less likely to make college plans—only 10%, compared to more than 80% among students with college-going friends (p. 874). Krauss also asserted that students who are active in extracurricular activities are more likely to aspire to college; in particular, cocurricular activities are important for encouraging working-class students. With these findings, however, Krauss also noted the primary influence of family conditions. Student aspirations were related to peer influence, but also to family educational history, father's occupation, and downward mobility in the family.

Spady (1970) pursued the question of college aspirations one step farther with a longitudinal study aimed at understanding how adolescent goals are transformed into achievement in college. He surveyed 300 senior high school boys who planned to do postsecondary work, and then checked on their status four years later. Though 71% of the high school students indicated college attendance as a goal, only 49% had completed more than one year of college after four years. Spady determined that the most important factors in predicting college success were academic talent, high school GPA, participation in extracurricular activities, and actual peer prestige. He points to peer status as one of the most important findings of his study; in particular, "The feeling of being recognized," Spady asserts, "stimulates a desire for further status and recognition after high school" (p. 700).

Spady's study, like many others, was limited in that it focused only on male students. Studies that have included both male and female students have noted differences in the experience of peer influence. Brown (1982), for example, argued that peer pressure is more dominant in high school life for girls than for boys. Not only were pressures for girls more intense, they were also more closely related to specific behaviors (p. 131). It is important to sound a note of caution about these results, however. Brown's study called for retrospective accounts of peer pressure. That is, Brown asked college students to reflect back on the pressures they experienced in secondary schools. Their responses might have been influenced by their new situations.

Perhaps the most controversial area of study with respect to peer influence is ability grouping or tracking. Ability grouping is "the practice of organizing classrooms . . . to combine children who are similar in ability" (Kulik &

Kulik, 1982, p. 415). In their meta-analysis of 51 different studies, Kulik and Kulik found that ability-grouped students performed better on examinations than their counterparts in ungrouped classes, had better attitudes about the subject matter, and had better generalized attitudes toward school. These effects were stronger for high-ability students; lower-ability groups had a near-zero effect. Other research shows that students tend to choose friends from within their own track, which means that noncollege and college-track students have little time to interact (Oakes, 1982, 1985; Karweit, 1983).

MacLeod (1995) and Vigil (1999) looked at students who had dropped out and how peer affiliations enabled them to have some sense of identity. Both studies looked at gangs and how they form, their role in identity creation for the members, and how streets and schools interact. Again, both authors call upon various theoretical frameworks to analyze gang behavior and peer pressure.

College

The specific literature on peer influence in college (rather than college aspirations) is more extensive and varied than that of high school. In an effort to focus this discussion, we review only the literature on college student peer groups during the first year of college. Walter Wallace (1964) studied socialization patterns and the effects of peer influence on freshmen attitudes toward school and their futures. Through peer group interpersonal communications, Wallace asserted, freshmen are socialized to the new environment and turn from a strong to a lower emphasis on grades; this lower emphasis was the prevailing notion among their peer hosts. Instead of grades, peers—particularly nonfreshmen—were concerned with problems of the life cycle, including life goals, parents, religion, sex, politics, and friendship (p. 317). Wallace also looked at aspirations for graduate study (1965), and he noted that freshmen were more inclined to accept advice from seniors or upperclassmen rather than their same-class peers. He found that freshmen were socialized by "old-timers" to change their aspirations to include postgraduate studies.

Bruce Sacerdote (2001) took up the different ways in which freshmen influence one another in a study of Dartmouth College roommates. In some areas such as choice of major, roommates did not exert influence upon one another, but in others peer effects were clearly important. Decisions about academic effort, membership in a social organization, and membership in a fraternity or sorority were related to the influence of randomly selected roommates.

Some of the most celebrated research on peer groups in college is Uri Treisman's (1992) work with minority students in calculus classes. In 1974, Treisman was teaching calculus at the University of California, and he noticed that the failure rate of Black students was dramatically higher than that of Whites—nearly 60% compared to the 15% rate of White students. In addition,

Treisman noticed that black students tended to study and struggle alone while Asian American students worked in groups to confirm difficulties and solve problems. In response to the disparity in achievement, Treisman developed a community model for teaching and learning. Students participated in a "workshop" associated with their calculus course, which offered a challenging and supportive environment in which to work. The emphasis on working with peers helped change the ways Black and Latino students approached the subject as well as their education more generally.

Other researchers have been concerned with peer influences on college attrition. Anderson (1981) looked at student persistence with respect to the types of colleges students are enrolled in (two- or four-year schools). She asserted that students in two-year schools had lower odds of persistence than their peers in four-year schools, particularly in the transition between the second and third year. The difference, she suggested, is in the influence of college type on the peer group. Peers in a community college are more likely to "encourage the student to consider leaving an academic track for vocational schooling or employment," or to become more involved in a job that distracts from their academic goals (p. 13).

Terenzini et al. (1994) also examined the roles of high school peers in the transition to college. They noted:

> High school friends were instrumental in how successfully . . . new students made the transition to college. When a student knew high school friends who were also new students (or friends or siblings already enrolled) at the same institution, these precollege friends functioned during the early weeks or months of college as a bridge from one academic and interpersonal environment to the next. (p. 64)

On the other hand, high school friends who did not go on to the same school or any college served to "complicate and hinder" the transition. They tended to hold students in the networks, patterns of behavior, and interests established in high school.

College Preparation Programs

Finally, the research specific to college preparation programs is relatively slight. Mehan and his colleagues (1996) undertook a study of one such program and argued that the structure of the peer group in a college preparation program was a form of "untracking" where students learned that they were able to celebrate their own cultural identities while at the same time affirming academic identities. They argued that the bonding that took place within the peer group enabled the students to envision attending college while at the same time affirming their own ethnic and racial backgrounds.

Although peer groups obviously exist in virtually all college preparation programs, the only other current research project that we have found pertaining specifically to peer groups is Puente. In the work of Gándara (2002b), peer group behavior is noted as a route to in-group bonding that contributes to academic success. Although peer groups are not of central concern to the studies that pertain to Puente, they are mentioned as a successful variable rather than one that is neutral or negative.

CONCLUSION

Research on the influence of peer groups does not provide a clear-cut answer about their influence on the college-going patterns of low-income urban minority youth. Although, for the most part, the research has moved away from portrayals of peer groups as breeding grounds for failure, we would be remiss if we stated the opposite: that the research on peer groups finds that they are conclusively an essential ingredient for improving college going. Indeed, much of the research on peer groups and college preparation programs is so sketchy that one can conclude little about their influence.

At the same time, as we noted at the outset, peer groups almost by definition are part of any college preparation program. One cannot decide whether to have peer groups; they already exist, and they will form spontaneously insofar as college preparation programs are not hermetically sealed educational exercises. Students are part of peer groups before they enter a college preparation program, and they will be part of peer groups once they are finished. With the realization that peer groups exist and/or they will form whether one wants them to or not, what might one suggest based on the wealth of literature that has been touched on here? We conclude by offering five suggestions.

Consider the type of peer groups "produced" by college preparation programs. If peer groups are not a monolithic entity where new members must simply conform to preexisting norms, then as Allen and Bonous-Hammarth suggest in chapter 8, one needs to consider how peer groups change over time. The assumption here is that peer groups are malleable and will change. Such a perspective suggests that attention needs to be paid to the characteristics of these groups and how the processes of interaction might be made more effective in affecting students' educational aspirations or self-confidence.

Think of peer groups as a resource to be developed. The likelihood is that a greater positive impact will occur if one thinks of peer groups as a valuable component of learning that can provide a positive sense of self-efficacy. Such a suggestion is in keeping with the argument made by Villalpando and Solorzano (chapter 1) at the outset. Peer groups occur for multiple reasons, and their purpose often has to do with a sense of belonging and a desire for community. The needs and problems of inner-city youth are all too often portrayed using a deficit model—that the youth themselves are somehow inadequate or that they are the problem. Instead, acknowledge the reality of peer groups and work toward enhancing their potential.

Develop a sense of teamwork within the peer group. Although the impact of peer groups may be debatable, research also points out that individuals who work in isolation frequently do not do as well as those who work in groups. Peer groups in college preparation programs have the potential of enabling students to learn from one another. Such a group process not only has the ability to increase student learning, but students also learn a valuable study skill for when they enter college.

Acknowledge the sociocultural aspects of peer groups. Even though the research does not offer a singular voice on the impact of peer groups, for over a generation there has been the recognition that there are differential effects for different groups. That is, those who are likely to attend college are more likely to participate in a peer group in which others are likely to attend college. Social categories such as "jocks" or "Goths" are also often the basis for a peer group to exist.

Our point here is not so much to suggest that those in a college preparation program treat any particular group in a specific manner. Rather, one needs to acknowledge that such groups exist and then consider how to involve them in positive learning experiences. In our research we have seen, for example, a college preparation program that was populated by above-average youths and had a preponderance of girls. The program, however, was not looked on as "cool." In subsequent years the program sought out members of the football team to participate in the program, and its tasks—such as writing college essays—suddenly became "cool," thereby undermining the kind of problems discussed by proponents of fictive kinships.

Undertake additional research on peer groups. The learning potential of peer groups waits to be exploited, but to do so one needs empirically based studies about how to construct such groups. Researchers need to move away from assertions about the relative worth or harm of a group and acknowledge them as a social fact. Insofar as peer groups exist and researchers and practitioners recognize that adolescence is a time when individuals work out who they are and who they are going to be, research on peer groups ought to take on increased importance. The potential for a greater understanding of peer groups by way of qualitative and quantitative methods is vast, and the lack of such research will only retard the field's ability to enable greater access to college for low-income youth.

PATRICIA M. MCDONOUGH

Chapter Four

Counseling Matters: Knowledge, Assistance, and Organizational Commitment in College Preparation

INTRODUCTION

A fundamental principle of organizational effectiveness is that if a task is important, it has to be written into the mission statement and organizational structure through the job descriptions of appropriate staff members, including organizational leaders (Scott, 1998). Moreover, an accountability system for ensuring completion of key organizational missions must exist. Across the spectrum of public systems of K–12 education, the college enrollment of graduates is not built into any school accountability system. Few staff members have college preparatory responsibilities as their main job, nor is there a regularly identifiable K–12 staff member who is held accountable for graduates' college enrollment.

Counselors are the logical choice to be the K–12 staff member responsible for college access preparation and assistance and are often assumed to be handing this role, yet they are inappropriately trained and structurally constrained from being able to fulfill this role in public high schools. Nonetheless, counseling has long been identified as both a direct and indirect asset to students' college aspiration development, preparation, choice, and enrollment

(Adelman, 1999; Boyer, 1987; Plank & Jordan, 2001; McDonough, 1997; Oakes, 1995; Orfield & Paul, 1993; Romo & Falbo, 1996).

This chapter looks at the history, role, effectiveness, and needs for college counseling in high schools and in college preparation programs. The first caveat is that an extensive literature on the impact of counselors on students' college preparations does not exist. Given what literature exists, this chapter is heavily focused on school counseling because the literature is more developed. It draws on an extensive survey of counseling and college access research to set the framework for reconceptualizing school counseling to incorporate college advising and support.

The chapter begins with a context-setting history of public high school counseling, contrasts that with the evolution of private school counseling, describes the roles of school counselors today, presents information on how high schools structure students' college planning and ultimately their opportunities, reports on the empirical evidence of the impact of counselors and counseling, and concludes with suggestions for effective college counseling. But first, I present some definitions of counselors and counseling.

Counselors are "certified/licensed educators" and "advocates who work cooperatively with other individuals and organizations to promote the academic, career, and personal/social development" of students, and counseling is a relationship that helps students "resolve or cope constructively with their problems and developmental concerns" (American School Counselor Association, 1999, p. 1). Counselors are legally mandated to have a psychological, developmental, and problem-solving knowledge and skill base. The major functions of school counseling are scheduling, testing, and discipline (DeLany, 1991; Lombana, 1985; McDonough, 1997; McDonough, Ventresca, & Outcalt, 2000; Monson & Brown, 1985; Wilson & Rossman, 1993), with secondary functions of dropout, drug, pregnancy, and suicide prevention, as well as sexuality and personal crisis counseling. Generally, a very small subset of selected counselors provide college counseling in addition to their primary responsibilities. Counseling is a formal relationship between a student and trained, certified educator and is different from mentoring, which Gándara and Mejorado (chapter 5) define as a voluntary relationship of guidance and encouragement that may take the form of a caring role model or informal advisor.

HISTORICAL PERSPECTIVES ON SCHOOL COUNSELING

From the beginning, the role of school counseling in public schools has been contested. Conflict sprang from multiple sources as well as the pressures on a new profession. The tensions included the evolving role of psychological development and testing, the proper functions of counselors, understandings of the college counseling task, and whether the counselor should be a facilitator or gatekeeper, as well as training and identity issues.

School counseling began as vocational guidance in the early 20th century and was initially viewed as a curricular subject focused on dispensing information pertaining to jobs and educational planning (Aubrey, 1982; Beale, 1986). The word "counseling" was rarely used and, beginning in the 1930s, guidance began to take on elements of psychology and the normal developmental concerns of individuals (Aubrey, 1982; Coy, 1991). Eventually, psychology became foundational to guidance along with counselor roles in testing and individual pupil assessment as the subfield of psychometrics developed.

Beginning in the 1960s, three forces converged to set the stage for school counseling in public high schools as we understand it today. First, the school counseling profession evolved to the point that personal, therapeutic counseling was a major emphasis (Armor, 1971). Although some scholars expressed concern that psychotherapeutic models were often in conflict with educational objectives (Aubrey, 1969), developmental approaches so dominated the profession's conception of its mission that one leading researcher cautioned school counselors about their role and suggested that they had conflated the purpose of counseling with the location where the function was performed, notably schools (Arbuckle, 1976).

Second, college counseling was a small, growing, and hotly contested part of counselors' work. Debates raged within the counseling practitioner journals about whether college counseling was the most or the least important counseling function (Muro, 1965; Tibby, 1965). Arguments against college counseling were that it was not actual guidance but, at worst, was the unseemly work of subtle persuasion or salesmanship, such as writing letters of recommendation for college applicants (Tibby, 1965), and at best was little more than simply proffering information. This articulation of the college advising function as information dispensing dominated the counseling literature into the 1990s (Cole, 1991) and a significant segment of the college advising support industry, which I discuss later, is premised on this fundamental assumption.

Also, many counselors opposed to the incorporation of college counseling viewed college advising as esoteric (Cole, 1991) and in conflict with counselors' identities as mental health agents (Carroll, 1985). These same counselors bristled at the elitism inherent in providing disproportionate institutional resources for college advising to small numbers of college-bound students (Avis, 1982; National Association of College Admissions Counselors [NACAC], 1986).

The third force influencing the development of modern school counseling was a growing body of sociological research identifying and criticizing counselors' gatekeeping functions, which significantly influenced public discourse and policy debates (Rosenbaum, Miller, & Krei, 1996). Cicourel and

Kitsuse (1963) described and critiqued counselors' exercise of professional responsibility for determining which students were college material based on
their personal assessments of students' character, maturity, and appearance. In
the 1970s, Rosenbaum joined this research tradition and critiqued counselors'
practices in thwarting working-class students' access to college preparatory
curricular tracks and other means of discouraging students' college aspirations.

Other historical tensions affecting the development of counselors' complex, oftentimes conflicting, and always unmanageable roles have included the
following:

- Counselor efforts to remain separate from, yet influencing and affecting, teachers and administrators (Arbuckle, 1976)
- Major mechanical and technological advancements in guidance (Kroll,
  1973; Tiedeman, 1968; Vriend, 1971) complicated by counselors'
  sometimes resistance to technology (Avis, 1982; Carroll, 1985)
- Alternating economic cycles of boom and bust that triggered expansion and contractions in school counseling positions (Hull, 1979)
- Counselors' inability to demonstrate their effectiveness in terms of student learning or development, which led to vulnerability in times
  of budget cuts (Aubrey, 1982; Avis, 1982; Carroll, 1985; Cole, 1991;
  Kehas, 1975; Miller & Boller, 1975)
- Escalating demands on principals, leading to counselors assuming administrative duties (e.g., scheduling) which blurred counselor and ad-
  ministrator roles and further confused counseling missions (Cole,
  1991; Day & Sparacio, 1980; Monson & Brown, 1985)

A final historical perspective comes from an overview of training and
identity issues. Over the last several decades, many counseling programs mi-
grated from education departments, into psychology departments resulting in
increased family and clinical practice training, a more desirable and higher-
status role (Aubrey, 1982; Carroll, 1985), and a shift in identity to mental
health agents whose primary goal is helping adolescents through the challenges and pitfalls of adolescence (Aubrey, 1982; Carroll, 1985; Huey, 1987).
This identity and training also offered an occupationally viable alternative
when school counseling positions have been eliminated (Carroll, 1985). This
role conception—resolving students' social-emotional problems—has consistently put counselors at odds with principals, who seldom perceived it as a central role for counselors and who instead perceived counseling as primarily academic advising (Chapman & De Masi, 1984). Finally, training in counseling
(Hossler, Schmit & Vesper, 1999; McDonough, 2002; NACAC, 1991) has historically not included preparation in the area of college counseling.

In an interesting contrast to the public school counseling profession's
evolution, in college preparatory or prep schools, counseling as a profession

began in the 1950s when the number of college applicants in the United States grew and heads of prep schools could no longer call admissions offices and place their students in a small number of elite colleges. In stark contrast to public schools, counseling positions in prep schools developed exclusively for the purpose of college counseling, and the psychological counseling components so prevalent in public schools was and is outsourced to private therapists who have minimal connection to the school (Powell, 1996). Furthermore, another big public school counseling function—scheduling—is not a function in prep schools because of their generally small size and their singular mission; therefore, all courses are college preparatory.

HIGH SCHOOL COUNSELING RATIOS, AVAILABILITY, AND ROLES

Both the American Counselor Association (ACA) and the American School Counselor Association (ASCA) recommend a maximum counselor-to-student ratio of 1:250. Yet the national average is 1:513 (ACA, 1999). In a study of the largest U.S. cities (which have the highest concentrations of students of color), the average high school counselor-to-student ratio was 1:740 (Fitzsimmons, 1991), which is three times larger than the recommended ratio. Yet some states, notably California and Minnesota, averaged over 1,000 students per counselor (ACA, 1999).

ASCA recommends that school counselors spend at least 70% of their time in direct services to students, but a recent national study found that, at best, public school counselors spend 50% of their time in direct service work. Furthermore, across multiple surveys, counselors report a lack of time and attention for college counseling. In the most recent national study of secondary school counselors (which oversampled college counselors), Miller (1998) found that public school counselors spent an average of 20 hours per week in direct contact with students, carried an average caseload of approximately 330 students, and their perceptions of their most important jobs were college counseling, personal counseling, academic counseling, scheduling, and testing. Although this study was unable to parse out exactly how much time counselors devoted to each task, with five crucial tasks competing for 20 hours per week to work with 330 students, these structural conditions effectively leave precious little time for individual college counseling. An earlier study that was even more nationally representative found that counselors reported valuing assisting students in making plans for college equally alongside helping students with personal growth and development. Yet they reported that 25% of their actual time was spent in personal counseling, and only 13% of their time was spent in college guidance (Moles, 1991).

The National Association of College Admissions Counselors (NACAC, 1986), the professional association with the highest stake in college counseling, found that the great disparities in college counseling resources and activities are a direct result of the social class of the communities in which these high schools are located. Specifically, they found that school counselors in upper-income neighborhoods spent more time on college counseling. However, it is important to note that those who are especially hard hit in terms of unmet or inadequate counseling are communities, schools, and students of color (McDonough, 1999; Paul, 2002).

African American and Latino students are significantly more likely to have their college plans influenced by their high school counselors (Lee & Ekstrom, 1987; Plank & Jordan, 2001), and yet these are the students who are least likely to have counselors, the most likely to have underprepared counselors, and the most likely to have counselors pulled away from college counseling to work on other counseling tasks (Paul, 2002). Furthermore, students of color often express reluctance to use counselors because they are perceived to be uninformed and hostile (Gándara & Bial, 2001), have well-documented reputations for placing students in non–college-recommending classes (Atkinson, Jennings, & Liongson, 1990), and historically have thwarted students' and their parents' educational aspirations (Lareau & Horvat, 1999; Pérez, 1999).

COLLEGE ACCESS INFLUENCES

How do students get to college? The research evidence on college access suggests that students enroll in college through a complex, longitudinal, interactive process involving individual aspiration and achievement, organizational structuring of opportunity in high school, and institutional admissions. Four key components of the high school have a tremendous impact on college attendance: (1) a college preparatory curriculum; (2) a college culture that establishes high academic standards and includes formal and informal communication networks that promote and support college expectations; (3) a school staff that collectively is committed to students' college goals; and (4) resources devoted to counseling and advising college-bound students (Alexander & Eckland, 1977; Bryk, Lee, & Holland, 1993; Coleman, 1987; Coleman, Hoffer, & Kilgore, 1982; Cookson & Persell, 1985; Falsey & Heyns, 1984; Hotchkiss & Vetter, 1987; McDonough, 1994, 1997, 1998; Powell, 1996).

Besides the role of academic preparation and familial support, both examined elsewhere in this volume (see chapters 2 and 6), one common thread running through the research evidence on the school's role in structuring students' aspirations and actual college preparatory opportunities is that guidance and counseling staff can help to establish a school's college culture. But that culture needs to be held and acted upon by knowledgeable staff who affect students in daily interactions apart from specific college preparatory programs (Hotchkiss & Vetter, 1987; McDonough, 1994, 1997; McDonough & McClafferty, 2000). For example, students' educational expectations play a major role in college enrollment (Cabrera & La Nasa, 2000c; Hearn, 1987) and oftentimes are the single strongest predictor of four-year college attendance (Thomas, 1980). Longstanding college goals can be resources: intending to go to college increases the likelihood of going by 21% when that intention develops prior to 10th grade, compared to plans formulated in senior year (Alexander & Cook, 1979). Additional recent research establishes that early college expectations, especially if developed by the eighth grade, stimulate planning for college as well as providing motivation for students to maintain grades and engage in necessary extracurricular activities (Cabrera & La Nasa, 2000c; chapter 7, this volume; Hossler, Schmit, & Vesper, 1999; McDonough, 1997).

HOW SCHOOLS STRUCTURE COLLEGE OPPORTUNITIES

Since having college plans by the eighth grade is an essential precondition to planning for a college-track curriculum and extracurricular activities in high school, maintaining good academic performance, and ensuring college enroll-ment (Cabrera & La Nasa, 2000c; chapters 6 and 8, this volume), the expecta-tions that teachers and counselors have of students even early in their academic courses are integral to the development and maintenance of college aspirations. Too often, students are labeled early in their educational careers as college bound or non–college bound, and those labels tend to have a profound impact on the choices students make, the options they see for themselves, and their ideas about what are realistic aspirations (Oakes, 1985). But college plans do not simply happen. They must be fostered and encouraged through a school's culture (McDonough, 1998) and the counselor is key to this development (McClafferty & McDonough, 2000).

A student's plans for college are affected by the normative expectations that exist among the students, parents, and personnel of a high school, as well as by anticipated consequences, and what alternatives will be considered or ig-nored. Not surprisingly, the latter variables are highly susceptible to influence from the school's counselors. The end result is that the students who are ex-pected to go to college, by and large, do so (McDonough, 1997). Those for whom the expectations do not exist are never given the chance to make it to college because they are denied the support, information, and resources neces-sary to get there. Clearly, schools, through counselors and other leadership, must set high expectations for all students, and must set the enabling school conditions so that students' college choices are not limited in ways that are be-yond their control.

If all students are to receive the guidance and preparation that will allow them to make well-informed decisions about how to effectively prepare for and choose a college, we must change not only the structure of counseling, but also the cultures of our schools. Research indicates that students desperately need basic information about college options, particularly for more selective colleges (McDonough, 1999). Moreover, students need to receive it early enough in their educational careers (by eighth grade) for them to enroll in appropriate classes. Middle and high schools have important and irreplaceable roles to play in guiding each student's decision making about whether or not a four-year college is an option.

Besides assisting with the development of college plans, high schools, through their counselors, influence students' college options and decisions by how they structure the flow and content of information, make explicit expectations that highlight or downplay specific options, limit the search for alternatives, and impose a specific schedule (McDonough, 1997). The critically important question in evaluating the high school's role in the transition to college is: What impact do high school counseling operations have on enabling or constraining students in securing adequate college preparation and the necessary information on college choice?

High schools have different structural arrangements for counseling in general, and college advising in particular (McDonough, 1997). Guidance counselors have a direct impact on students and, more important, they create and implement the school's normative expectations for students' college destinations and how to prepare for them. They create a worldview for students and their parents that delimits the full universe of 3,000 possible college choices into a smaller range (1–8) of cognitively manageable considerations. Schools and counselors construct this worldview in response to their perceptions of the parents' and community's expectations for appropriate college destinations, combined with the counselor's own knowledge and experience base.

Also, most public high schools' minimal guidance services are developed in reference to the identified needs of the normative student in that school. Sometimes because of desegregation and other reasons, high schools have racially and socioeconomically disparate student populations with widely varying needs and family resources that they can use to supplement school assistance. Any definition of normative in a heterogeneous population runs the risk of privileging those students who fit the norm and disenfranchising those students whose needs are silenced by the operation of a single, dominant norm (Gibson, 1986). For example, we often find in large urban school districts with students of color bused in from other neighborhoods that schools within schools develop. In these situations, White and more economically advantaged students end up in college prep tracks while students of color and poor students end up disproportionately in general or vocational tracks (Horvat, 1996).

Daily, the frequency and nature of students' and counselors' college preparatory interactions are shaped by a school's policies, resources, and organizational structures. This guidance process impacts students through subtle and unobtrusive controls. This process assumes that students are familiar with the communication channels for the transmission of college information, know the specialized college choice vocabularies, and are aware of the necessary preparations, prerequisites, tests, financial information, deadlines, and appropriate timetables (McDonough, 1997). Information about a school's policies, resources, and organizational structures offers insight into why student outcomes happen, for example, whether and how high school students are encouraged and assisted to go to college. Fundamentally, these organizational arrangements and policies are the artifacts of a school's decisions about what is important, and how and why school resources are allocated as they are.

COUNSELOR IMPACT ON COLLEGE ACCESS

Counselors and counseling matter in college access. We have adequate amounts of literature that empirically document the specific impacts that counselors have related to students' college aspiration development, college preparation, and college choice processes. However, we still have a long way to go to fully understand counselors' impacts and roles in college access.

In a pivotal study that employed exhaustive reviews of existing empirical evidence and new analyses on a nationally representative database, Cabrera and La Nasa (2000c) found many important influences on students' college aspirations and enrollment, including early college plans, taking the appropriate college preparatory curriculum in high school, and information about colleges and their costs. As is often the case in college access research, counselors are not among the major influences. Yet this lack of finding should not be overinterpreted. First, the data from Cabrera and LaNasa's study came from the National Center for Educational Statistics, the federal agency that routinely collects in-depth data on every aspect of our educational system. However, that data behemoth historically has not collected any data on school counselors except a simple head count in full-time equivalents. Clearly, counseling functions and their operations are not considered a data priority. Moreover, most of the national studies draw from this database or analogous databases because of the desirability of large-scale, nationally representative data. These facts mean that we are captives of our data collection capacities, or lack thereof, and are ill prepared to fully understand counselors' impacts. Nonetheless, the next section examines the literature on counselor impacts directly on students and indirectly on students through their parents.

Students

Counselors have an important positive influence on students' motivations and expectations, especially through the provision of information regarding college preparations (Fallon, 1997). Also, counselors, through group guidance activities, can introduce students to postsecondary educational opportunities, high school course preparation, admission testing, financial aid, and college decision making. Fallon (1997) identifies that middle school counselors can have a positive influence if they help students understand college, the advantages of a college degree, and the importance of a strong academic record. However, a study of students in one (not necessarily nationally representative) Midwestern state found that counselors have a negative influence on the early development of college aspirations (Hossler et al., 1999). Although we do not have the empirical evidence to mediate the differences between these two studies, still there are conclusions we can draw and speculations we can suggest.

The first conclusion is that the act of counselors distributing information seems to have a positive impact on helping students understand what they need to do to prepare for a possible college future and that early academic preparation is crucial to college success. Moreover, we know that counselors have been found to have a positive impact on parents in their efforts to foster early college aspiration development in their children. Why, though, would counselors have a negative impact, specifically on aspiration development? We know that early aspiration development is now thought to take place at least by eighth grade (Cabrera & La Nasa, 2000c) and we know that counselors are even less available in middle and junior high schools than they are in high schools. Finally, if counselors are unavailable and overworked, we would not expect their influence to be positive. However, neither would we expect it to be negative and so future research would need to tease out and confirm the actual differences between these findings.

In the area of academic preparation, one study found that students state that they usually saw their counselors only for scheduling classes (Hutchinson & Reagan, 1989). Nonetheless, counselors, as early as junior high school, develop curriculum assignments and group counseling activities to encourage students to gather college information, both of which impact students positively (Hossler et al., 1998). Also, counselors have been found to provide positive support to students as they progress through a college preparatory curriculum (Hossler et al., 1998; Rowe, 1989).

In contrast to this research, many other studies have found that counselor support is differentially available to students based on social class and race (Gándara, 2002a; Gándara & Bial, 2001) as well as gender and rural statuses (Lee & Ekstrom, 1987). Other studies have found that a general lack of counseling or wholly inadequate counseling has been found to be a major barrier to college preparation (McDonough, 1997; Oakes, 1985; Romo & Falbo, 1996). Plank and Jordan (2001) found that college counseling, which is often absent for low-SES high school students, explains much of the college underenrollment of low-income students.

In a study of first-generation college students, Matthay (1989) found that students who were dependent (no family resources to draw upon) on their high school counselor's help were less satisfied with their counselor than those students whose siblings had already attended college and could provide other college knowledge and assistance. Many minority students resist using counselors' services because they are perceived to be ill-informed about the situations and needs of students of color and because counselors have a reputation for advising low-income students and students of color to take general education or vocational classes (Atkinson, Jennings, & Liongson, 1990; Gándara, 2002a; Oakes, 1985; Rosenbaum, 1976).

Again, we have seemingly contradictory findings. Yet what also seems to be the major insight to be drawn vis-à-vis counselors' abilities to impact academic preparation for college access is that counselors' roles in scheduling students could be a major vehicle for increased college access for nontraditional college-bound students (e.g., first-generation, low-income students of color) if counselors understand the consequences of their roles and choose not to be gatekeepers. In fact, Rosenbaum, Miller, and Krei (1996) have conducted research that found that some counselors do not want to give students "bad news" about their college prospects, are avoiding any responsibility in this domain, and feel that parents and principals accord them no authority for this unwanted task.

Counselors become more influential over the high school years, especially by the junior year of high school, when students are engaging in their choice phase (Hossler et al., 1999). Specifically, counselors provide students with valuable assistance in the development of the set of target colleges to which students will consider applying. Rowe (1989) found that students perceived school counselors to be influential as college advisors, but only discussed their educational plans with counselors twice in their senior year. This finding suggests a possible mismatch between students' perceptions of the utility of counselor services versus their actual utilization of (or ability to access) counselor services.

One Midwestern state study found that 90% of students felt that their school counselor was a knowledgeable and approachable source for information about colleges and universities. In fact, this was the number one item for which students felt they would seek out a counselor's help (Hutchinson & Reagan, 1989). Given other empirical evidence about counselor knowledge and availability, this finding seems hopeful, yet hard to believe. One possible explanation is that this state is more racially and ethnically homogeneous and less urban than many other states and this demographic difference may influence the study's discrepant findings. However, Hutchinson and Reagan also found that students felt that they were not getting the *assistance* they needed from counselors. Presumably, these findings mean that information is, in and of itself, a necessary but insufficient condition for meaningful college assistance.

Counselors themselves reported that their biggest difficulty in advising students on college choices are "logistical," making sure that students secure accurate information in time, staying up-to-date with ever-changing college admissions information, and advising students and parents on financial aid issues (Chapman & De Masi, 1984). This same study found that counselors reported that they spend 20% of their time in college advising, and that this percentage was an appropriate allocation of time.

Boyer (1987) found that most high school students and their families do not have access to adequate information in making their college choices. In another study related to college information needs, Hutchinson and Bottorff (1986) found that 79% of the students surveyed identified college information as an important need, yet only 59% of these students felt that counselors were able to provide college information.

Orfield and Paul (1993) found that students and parents were uninformed of the necessary college access information, including an understanding of the influence of high school track, college admissions requirements, and the system of college costs and financial aid. These authors then criticized high school counseling as being inadequate to the task of improving the transition from high school to college. Hossler and Vesper (1993) found that if counselors provided guidance, not just information, it had a critical influence on students' college pursuits. Fallon (1997) found that counselors were influential in students' college choice processes and in helping students develop a college "mind-set."

A number of policy reports have addressed counselors' roles vis-à-vis college access. The Institute for Higher Education Policy (1997) recommended increasing the availability of college awareness, information, and college counseling, while the Center for Higher Education Policy Analysis (2002) identified counseling services as one of the two strongest predictors of improving access to college. Finally, in the largest review to date of special college preparation programs for underrepresented students, a federal commission found that one of the most common program elements is counseling (Gándara & Bial, 2001).

King (1996) found that low-SES students were more likely to attend a four-year college if they frequently met with a supportive counselor. Lapan et al. (1997) found that students who were enrolled in high schools with fully implemented guidance programs reported receiving more career and college information. Similarly, Rosenbaum, Miller and Krei (1996) found that if counselors have the ability to provide students with high levels of information and guidance, the counselors have a significant positive impact on students' enrollment in a four-year college.

Finally, in a very tightly designed national study using careful statistical controls, Plank and Jordan (2001) found that counselors who provide high levels of guidance and assistance increase a student's likelihood of reaching a four-year college. Moreover, Plank and Jordan concluded that efforts to improve high school counseling and equalizing students' access to these services would be likely to have significant impact on improving college access for underserved populations.

Parents

In the early stages of college aspiration development and persistence of educational plans, internal (self, family) sources of support and information are important. Thus, one way that counselors impact student plans and progress is indirectly through their parents (Hossler et al., 1999). Although much has been known for a long time about the fact that parents tend to be the most powerful influence on their students' educational aspirations in general and college plans in particular, it was only beginning in the mid-1980s that parents were identified as a service population for counselors as a means of serving students in the college-going process (Boyer, 1987; Chapman & De Masi, 1984; NACAC, 1986). Boyer identified parents' need for basic college information, while Chapman and De Masi pinpointed major parental needs regarding financial aid, and the NACAC study showed that, even though most high schools had college fairs and college information sessions, nonetheless over 400 high schools across the United States did not even have these simplest of parental college informational and engagement activities.

Beginning in the early 1990s, one of the leading researchers of college choice and preparation, Don Hossler, and a colleague published a study that demonstrated the strong influence that parents have in shaping students' college aspirations and in helping them to maintain their plans for college. Bouse and Hossler (1991) called for counselors to work with parents in order to help students develop college aspirations and plans. Fallon (1997) also called for counselors to work with parents in shaping students', particularly first-generation college-bound students', college aspirations and plans.

In a major empirical study of how students developed, maintained, and actualized their college aspirations, McDonough (1997) looked at the roles that parents and counselors played. She specifically documented that parents participated in their children's college-choice processes through encouragement, involvement, and as knowledge providers and interpreters and that counselors' major work with parents was to provide them with informational materials and meetings. Another major finding was that middle- and upper-middle-class parents often were dissatisfied with inadequate school counseling services and sought extraschool supplemental services. The two major extraschool services parents most often sought were information resources (i.e., guidebooks/rankings magazines) and private counselors.

Hossler et al. (1999) in a longitudinal study also found that counselors can and do have an impact on parents, who are the number one influence on their children's college aspiration development and persistence. Hossler et al. strongly suggested that counselors need to educate parents on the roles they play in their children's life and educational aspirations.

Finally, the Hossler et al. study, as had previous studies, identified the critical need parents have to understand college costs and the financial aid system and the impact counselors have in educating parents and assuaging their concerns. In the most recent study of counseling impacts, Plank and Jordan (2001) investigated the influences on students' postsecondary plan maintenance and implementation and found that communication among students, parents, and school personnel significantly increased an individual's chances of enrolling in college. However, Tierney and Auerbach (chapter 2) assert that few college preparation programs adequately and appropriately work with parents in efforts to increase college going.

Interestingly, not all parents need counselors' assistance in understanding their role in aspiration development or financial aid. These parents are upper-middle-income professionals who have more advanced needs and seem to be highly responsive to counselors' impact. The availability of high-quality counseling had a significant impact on parents' decisions to enroll their children in costly private college preparatory schools (Cookson & Persell, 1985; McDonough, 1997; Powell, 1996). What these schools offer is extensive insider information for parents on the college admissions process and expansion of parents' opportunity horizons by identifying a wider range of good colleges (Powell, 1996).

Private Schools and Private Counselors

This section examines two smaller but important comparative streams of college advising research on private schools and the private counseling industry. Cookson (1981) found that public schools had much less organizational effectiveness than prep schools in facilitating comparable students' enrollments at more selective colleges. Private schools enable their students' college aspirations better than public schools through small counselor-to-student ratios, more resources devoted to counseling and advising of college-bound students, and the nature and quality of their college counseling (Alexander & Eckland, 1977; Coleman et al., 1982; Cookson, 1981; Cookson & Persell, 1985; Falsey & Heyns, 1984; McDonough, 1997; Powell, 1996).

One significant area of the research base on private schools comes from prep schools. Private prep schools invest significant fiscal, human, and symbolic resources in their college counseling operations (Powell, 1996) and they define the state of the art of good college counseling. They are strategically attuned to the increasingly competitive college admissions process through highly professionalized counseling operations. Their college counseling operations are designed to reduce anxiety and provide technical assistance through (1) extensive practical information for students and families about how college admissions works, including timetables; (2) guiding students away from minor but damaging application mistakes and toward more effective means of self-presentation; (3) self-reflective exercises that help students become more aware of a wider range of good colleges and finding the best personal match; (4) using school documents to present their students in the most effective ways; and (5) maintaining close personal connections with college admissions officers (Cookson & Persell, 1985; Powell, 1996). Finally, the single most important tool used by schools in the college counseling process is the school letter (Powell, 1996). These letters go through extensive development by counselors and extensive review by teachers and heads of schools.

A related area of counseling research is the college advising support industry, which is made up of two major components: private college counselors and commodified college knowledge. If high school counselors are unavailable, what do individuals do to strategically meet college assistance needs? Because college admissions has become a complex, high-stakes venture in which information, particularly insider information, is difficult to come by, students and their parents look to private counselors for the following:

- A way to compensate for their dissatisfaction with the high school's counseling services
- Access to the specialized knowledge and contacts of a power broker
- Application profile enhancement in the form of test coaching and essay assistance
- Deep knowledge of the student and suggestions for college choices that are reputable and attainable
- An adult whose job it is to help the applicant get organized and stay on task and on time in the application process
- Alleviating anxiety and help with peer pressure
- Help with special circumstances (such as learning disabilities)

Private counselors spend more time with college-bound students than any type of high school counselor, public or private, and most are available both by phone and in-person during evenings or weekends (McDonough, 1994; McDonough, Korn, & Yamasaki, 1997).

For those who cannot afford private counselors, an industry has sprung up to satisfy at least the information needs of students and their families: magazine rankings of colleges, guidebooks, CD-ROMs, Internet, laser discs, and so on. These phenomena are strong indicators of both the need for college knowledge and that it has become a commodity, something that can be codified, packaged, and sold. The profit-making sector has stepped into a college counseling vacuum and filled in the gap.

Yet available evidence suggests that even the most inexpensive of these resources, college rankings magazines, have not filled a democratizing function because they are only used by the most economically and educationally advantaged students, and students need more than information to make their college choices. Ordinary college-bound students from ordinary public schools are not using the rankings magazines to satisfy their college knowledge needs (McDonough et al., 1997).

CONCLUSION

After such a jumble of contradictory study findings on the impact of counselors, what can be said? First, counselors can and do have impacts, positive and negative, on students both directly and indirectly. Second, some of counselors' negative impacts have to do with their inadequate availability for college counseling tasks, which speaks to a policy implication of needing more counselors, with more time committed to college counseling tasks. Third, counselors are needed to help all students, but the evidence documents the crucial needs of most students of color, poor students, rural students, women, and first-generation college-bound students.

So let's think about the potential positive impact of counselors as the developmental process that it is. In middle school, the evidence is somewhat consistent across studies. If counseling is available, three ways that counselors can have positive impacts are (1) structuring information-gathering activities that foster and support college aspirations and understandings of college and its importance; (2) assisting parents in understanding their role in fostering and supporting college aspirations, setting college expectations, and motivating students; and (3) scheduling students into college-track classes (Fallon, 1997; Hossler et al., 1999). In high school, counselors need to be consistently available to students throughout grades 9 through 12 to provide basic college information as well as financial aid and costs information. Second, empirical evidence indicates that the more available counselors are to students for guidance, and not merely information dispensing, the better prepared students are and the higher the likelihood that they will enroll in a four-year college (Hutchinson & Reagan, 1989; Hossler et al., 1999; McDonough, 1997, 1999; Plank & Jordan, 2001; Powell, 1996; Rowe, 1989).

Debates about college access often are predicated on commonly held values of merit and equality of opportunity. We are often divided about the meanings of these values, and they are "cultural arbitraries." In different historical moments we invented college entrance exams and discretionary admissions criteria to select the lucky applicants who would gain access, so we also invented counseling in public and private schools with very different goals. I say "invented" to remind us of our tendencies to view merit criteria as the end result of an inexorable march toward maximal educational efficiency and equity and thus the highest and only reasonable altar on which to make admissions decisions. There are many ways to structure counseling and our structures are both a moving target and a cultural arbitrary. Moreover, our focus on merit is a misrecognition of power—not every student has equal access to the conditions that can provide evidence of their merit, and counseling differences are a key part of this.

Equality of opportunity in college access is often framed as the right of individuals to compete equally at any given point in their educational careers. However, we tend to discuss college access as if it were like the spin of the roulette wheel, where every moment is perfectly independent of the previous one and thus the conditions of competition to win are equal. These conditions are not equal and an important caveat implicit in perfect competition is the principle of ceteris paribus, or "all else equal." When it comes to K–12 systems and college counseling and preparation, all else is anything but equal.

We live, not in the world of roulette, but in a social world that comes with a history, structure, regularities, and constraints. Moreover, it is a world created for particular social purposes by particular social groups that is constantly being transformed by individuals who are either trying to maintain or improve their social status. Advantaged college applicants and their parents constantly stack the deck in their own favor by improvising counseling supports. In contrast, underrepresented minorities who are primarily first-generation college bound are making their college access decisions in the post–affirmative action era constrained by lack of individual, parental, and school college knowledge and experience; lack of trained professionals to advise them; and often in a climate of presumed lack of merit, racial hostility, and unwelcomeness. These students struggle to get basic information and meet published eligibility requirements in schools without adequate honors and advanced placement classes; they are unaware of the improvised practices of their high-SES competitors and could not afford to engage in these practices even if they knew about them.

Are knowledgeable and available counselors an essential component of an effective college preparation program? This chapter responds to that query with "Yes! Absolutely!" I have provided evidence to support that claim by offering comparative perspectives on college counseling from public and private sources and by comparing the negative and positive impacts that counselors have been shown to have on students' college aspiration, preparation, and choice processes. As GEAR-UP (Gaining Early Awareness and Readiness for Undergraduate Programs), AVID (Advancement Via Individual Determination), Puente, federal TRIO programs and other college preparatory and counseling initiatives have mushroomed, alongside the growing private counseling industry, students, parents, and entrepreneurs have acknowledged college counseling needs. Educators and policymakers need to do the same.

If we are to reconceptualize counseling, what are the professional norms of good school counseling that can be inferred from the empirical evidence on negative and positive impacts of college counseling? Certainly, three challenges for reconceptualized college counseling would be ensuring enough counseling help to meet students' needs, helping counselors build trust with poor and underrepresented minority students and their families, and providing for the professional development of counselors for the college advising task. Other specific recommendations for changes include:

- Increase counselor availability in middle schools and mandate counselors to work with students and parents to set college expectations, to establish college preparatory curricular choices, and improve the transition to high school.
- Lower counselor-to-student ratios to provide for long-term and deep engagement in college advising.
- Build counseling resources devoted to the ever-changing and obtuse college admissions, costs, and financial aid information needs of students.
- Improve counselor training in college counseling, including building basic college knowledge.
- Effective college counseling operations in junior and senior years should be designed to reduce anxiety; provide application profile enhancement in the form of test coaching, essay assistance, proofing, and effective means of self-presentation; help students realize the wide range of college options and find the best personal match; present students in the most effective ways; and maintain professional networks with college admissions officers.

None of these recommendations is sufficient on its own. Having better counselor-to-student ratios would mean nothing without improved knowledge and training, and better informed counselors would not be useful to underrepresented students who will not use counselors because they have proven to be untrustworthy.

When considering the myriad influences (families, school, peers, etc.) on students as they prepare for college, think of a mobile. For each individual student, every influence has a different weight, and the mobile hangs in a unique way. When the family is silent because of lack of relevant college knowledge, or passive because of competing responsibilities, then school and friends may be stronger influences than the family. If students come from families and communities where college knowledge is not available, then the role of the school and the need for trained, available, trustworthy counselors becomes paramount. As Plank and Jordan (2001) have shown, the effectiveness of schools and families in advising students for college is interconnected and interdependent. Thus, in order to have equitable college preparation, schools need to structurally provide high-quality counseling comprehensively attentive to college advising and preparation needs (Noddings, 1984), be attuned to what different student populations need and what family resources can be used to supplement school assistance (Beck, 1994; Mayeroff, 1971), and be aware of how students' different racial and socioeconomic statuses affect their ability to access the school's college choice resources (McDonough, 1994, 1997).

Also, counselor effectiveness is only possible by meeting counselors' preservice and in-service professional development needs. Strong college counseling and support systems that assist students (and parents) with their college preparation and complex admissions information needs will be possible only if counselors are provided appropriate training (Hossler et al., 1999). Moreover, counselors' training needs to make clear the differences between dispensing information and helping students interpret the meaning of admissions information in the context of their individual circumstances (McDonough, 1998).

One concern is: Are traditional counselors the right professionals for the college advising job? Certainly, as these professionals are now trained, counselors seem more focused on psychological counseling than on being organizers, strategists, and agents of transformation. Yet if schools are to reconceive their missions to make college preparation a serious priority, then traditional counselors need to lead the call for changed master schedules and changed school cultures (McDonough & McClafferty, 2001).

Plank and Jordan (2001) suggest that efforts at providing better guidance and information need not require huge fiscal commitments, but they will require serious human capital (developing a college knowledge infrastructure within high schools) and social capital (interconnected and interdependent schools and families). Such capital commitments are likely to generate profound results in making college more accessible for all students.

PATRICIA GÁNDARA
MARIA MEJORADO

Chapter Five

Putting Your Money Where Your Mouth Is: Mentoring as a Strategy to Increase Access to Higher Education

Mentoring has become increasingly popular as a strategy for improving social, behavioral, and academic outcomes for at-risk youth (Grossman and Johnson, 1999; "A Meeting of Minds," 1997; Governor's Mentoring Partnership, 2001). For example, then governor of California, Gray Davis, set a goal of finding mentors for 1 million young people with the objective of helping them to become "productive individuals." Mentoring has also received considerable attention at the national level as a potentially potent weapon in the war against adolescent malaise, underachievement, and truancy among the nation's youth. In 1997, the Clinton administration, under the leadership of General Colin Powell, kicked off a major mentoring effort under the auspices of America's Promise: The Alliance for Youth. At one point in 1997, 2,000 corporations were enlisted in helping to fund and provide other resources for the effort. The goal was to increase volunteerism, with an emphasis on helping youth, largely through mentoring. In an interview on the *Today Show*, General Powell was asked whether there was any evidence that mentoring worked. His response was, "I don't know of any statistics, but I know it works" (January 21, 1999). Powell's blind faith in the universal effectiveness of mentoring is mirrored in the many testimonials to these programs and the almost total absence of hard data to back up these beliefs (Royse, 1998).

Although the Clinton administration's initiative received a good deal of national press, the challenge proved to be greater than anyone expected. Less than a year after the program was launched, Colin Powell was quoted as saying that coordinating such an effort was a "more difficult challenge than mobilizing an army in the Persian Gulf" ("A Meeting of Minds," 1997, p. 5). Two years hence, he had concluded that the project would need to be long term, taking perhaps 5 to 15 years to realize. However, he left the helm by the end of 1999. One study estimates that mentoring programs currently serve approximately 5 million youth nationwide (McLearn, Colasanto, Schoen, & Shapiro, 1999).

There are ostensibly a number of reasons for this intense interest in youth mentoring. Research on youth development has consistently found that a significant adult in the life of a young person is the critical feature of healthy and successful development (Garmezy, 1985; Rutter, 1987; Werner & Smith, 1982). Mentoring also makes a great deal of intuitive sense. There is little disagreement that good parenting is more apt than not to yield happy, healthy children. And a mentor is akin to a good parent—someone who provides appropriate and consistent guidance. Therefore, mentors *must be* a good idea. Most successful people can point to at least one person who aided, inspired, or guided them along their successful path. Levine and Nidiffer (1996), in their study of 24 first-generation college students, found that all had a mentor who had encouraged and guided them through the path to college. Finally, mentors appear to be a cost-effective strategy for addressing the needs of youth. Find a willing adult who is a good role model, match that adult with a young person who can benefit from the guidance provided by this individual, and arrange for the two to interact. This does not require expensive technology. Mentors are almost always volunteers, so there is no payment involved, and the primary activity is just "hanging out," which does not necessarily cost anything. It is little wonder that mentoring has gained widespread popularity. However, the reality is much more complex and costly. And the impact is far from certain. While *informal* mentoring relationships that arise out of a natural affinity between two individuals almost certainly play a pivotal role in many people's lives, *formal* mentoring relationships may be quite different. Formal, or arranged, mentoring relationships appear to vary much more in their impact. Programs that arrange mentoring relationships for youth considered to be at risk have proliferated, but they are often vague about their goals and unspecific in describing their strategies. As we discuss below, "mentoring" can mean many things.

Perhaps the most surprising aspect of the huge growth in popularity of mentoring programs is the extent to which they are advocated as a means of increasing academic achievement and college access given that there are so few data to support their effectiveness in these domains (Roberts & Cotton, 1994; Royse, 1998). This chapter reviews the issues associated with using mentoring as a strategy to increase academic achievement and access to college for underrepresented students, examines the data on the effectiveness of mentoring for this purpose, draws some conclusions about the conditions under which mentoring may be a viable and cost-effective strategy, and suggests where new research might be helpful for future policy and practice.

DEFINING MENTORING

The original definition of mentoring grew out of a corporate practice in which a seasoned professional provided guidance and encouragement for a junior-level employee. The use of mentors in the workplace proved effective in the career advancement of the novice while the mentor gained visibility and prestige within the organization (Kanter, 1977; Roche, 1979). Moreover, the organization benefited from a reduction in employee turnover and enhanced productivity of the protégé (Zey, 1984). Mentoring has also been used as an effective strategy to increase diversity among the ranks of administration in higher education. Female administrators, in particular, have been shown to benefit from having a senior manager "show them the ropes" and provide support and advocacy in the largely male enclave of higher administration (Johnsrud, 1990). Formal mentoring programs for undergraduate and graduate students have also demonstrated positive outcomes with respect to increased self-confidence (Busch, 1985) and likelihood of underrepresented students going on to graduate school (Martinez, 2000). In these cases, the mentoring relationship was normally between a faculty member and a student and involved ongoing advice, encouragement, and engagement in research and academic activities. All of these types of mentoring have several things in common. They involve adults both as mentors and protégés; they are completely voluntary on the part of both individuals involved in the partnership, and both are autonomous individuals, generally with the ability to remove themselves from a relationship that is not viewed as beneficial. All of these kinds of mentoring relationships also involve individuals with relatively high social status who are not particularly at risk.

Mentoring at-risk youth involves a substantially different and more complex set of relationships than exist in the corporate or higher education contexts. For example, the age differences and power differentials between teenagers and adult mentors are a significant aspect of the relationship. Youth are still dealing with important developmental milestones, while their adult mentors have long ago addressed these life changes. A common complaint of mentors is that the young person does not return telephone calls or is uncommunicative. This may be interpreted as irresponsible or, at the least, unresponsive behavior on the part of the young person. Teenagers, on the other hand, report that they are reluctant to call their mentor because they feel shy or awkward. Young people simply lack the skill to express themselves with strangers, or the confidence to initiate meetings. Even in face-to-face encounters, a gap of 20 or 30 years can be difficult to bridge in terms of understanding the life circumstances of the other member of the dyad.

Another significant difference between adult mentoring relationships and those that involve adolescents is the fact that teenagers also normally have parents and other family members who provide guidance, which may or may not coincide with that provided by a mentor. Where the guidance provided is consistent, it can be reinforcing of the parental role, but where it is at odds, it can create serious conflicts in the student's life (Morrow & Styles, 1995).

Although the role of the mentor may be relatively clear in a corporate or graduate school setting, this is often not the case in mentoring programs serving adolescents (Johnson, 1998). Mentors may sign on to provide advice and guidance about school or careers when the student is simply interested in having a friend who will provide unconditional support. Gándara and colleagues (1998) found that while mentors of high school students in the Puente program were most likely to report that they initially saw their role as "role model" or provider of specific guidance, students most often reported wanting the mentor to be a friend. It is not uncommon for the adolescent protégé and the mentor to have very different ideas about the role of the mentor, and far too often programs do not provide sufficient guidance to mentors about their roles (Grossman & Johnson, 1999; Johnson, 1998; Gándara et al., 1998). In sum, mentoring adolescents is very different from mentoring junior colleagues, or other adults, and it is important that both the mentor and the protégé are in agreement about what they are seeking in the relationship.

MENTORING FOR WHAT PURPOSE?

Most mentoring programs reported in the literature have focused on mentoring as a strategy to affect behavioral outcomes for young people who are at risk for engaging in negative behavior. The programs attempt to decrease truancy, dropping out, drug use, and fighting, for example. The greatest successes of mentoring programs appear to be in these areas (Sipe, 1999; Grossman & Garry, 1997; Foster, 2001). Some mentoring programs also focus on academic outcomes, such as grades and test scores, but usually in the context of a more comprehensive program that provides other support and resources in addition to the mentoring (Sipe, 1999). In these cases, it is difficult to know whether improved academic outcomes are the result of the mentoring program or of other interventions provided by the program. Programs that target academic achievement and in which mentoring is the sole intervention are a minority of such interventions, and tend to show a very modest impact on academic outcomes, or none at all (McPartland & Nettles, 1991; Sipe, 1999). In sum, whether a mentoring program is deemed to be effective depends greatly on what its goals are. When the goals are specified, the greatest success appears to be in behavioral outcomes. There is much less evidence to support the effectiveness of mentoring for increasing academic achievement. Where it is one strategy among others, few studies have attempted to address the independent effects of the mentoring component of the intervention.

TYPES OF MENTORING PROGRAMS

Mentoring programs can vary along a number of dimensions. They may include one-on-one mentoring, in which one student is matched with one mentor, or they may consist of different kinds and configurations of group mentoring strategies. The programs may consist of mentoring only, or they may embed the mentoring component in a much larger, more comprehensive program. Finally, they may target behavioral problems, academic issues, or simply getting students to go to college.

Most of the research on mentoring programs that shows significantly positive outcomes has studied one-to-one mentoring programs (Sipe, 1999) in which a student is matched with an individual mentor and the relationship is maintained over a lengthy (at least 12 months) period of time. Mejorado (2000) found that the longer the relationship lasted, the more it was perceived by the student to have an impact on his or her decision making. This, of course, should not be surprising, since the length of the relationship could be considered to be, at least in part, a proxy for the level of satisfaction that the individuals experienced. It could be inferred that a satisfactory relationship would be more likely to result in positive influence than an unsatisfactory one. There is, however, a startling lack of evidence in the published literature on the nature of these relationships or the amount of contact time that individual students have with mentors. Nonetheless, studies suggest that one-on-one mentoring relationships in which there is a long-term commitment on the part of both individuals yield the most positive student outcomes. The substantial commitment of time required for these relationships is often difficult for mentors, as well as students, to sustain. Mejorado (2000) found that only about one third of the mentoring relationships she studied were sustained for one year or more, even though the initial commitment was to have been for at least two.

Because the commitment of time is so great and the skills necessary for the job so considerable, it is often difficult to recruit sufficient numbers of mentors to meet program needs. For this reason, some programs turn to group mentoring, peer mentoring, and other alternatives to one-on-one mentoring relationships. In a study of college access programs, Gándara and Bial (2001) found that about one third included a mentoring component, and these could be categorized into four types: peer-based, school staff and faculty-based, community volunteers, or corporate/professional volunteers. The most common was faculty and staff acting as mentors for students. This was a function of the availability of school faculty and staff and the lack of resources to recruit from outside the schools. However, some observers have suggested that these school-based programs may have advantages over others in that supervision of the mentoring relationships is easier and therefore tends to be better. It is also easier for mentoring contacts to be made when all parties are on the campus. Of course, an obvious downside is that there are limited numbers of people on the campus who are willing and available to take on the responsibility of mentoring.

While it makes sense to maximize human resources to meet the needs of as many students as possible, there is little evidence that these alternative strategies, such as peer-based models or group mentoring, are as effective as one-on-one student-adult models (Sipe, 1999; Foster, 2001). Again, whether or not they are effective almost certainly is a function of the goals of the program. If program goals include reducing truancy by providing productive activities with a positive role model, the effectiveness of a group mentoring model may be different than if the goal of the program is to raise a student's school grades through tutoring and close monitoring of schoolwork. However, since there is no research on this topic, it remains an unanswered question. Table 5.1 provides a typology for considering key variables in youth mentoring.

Little is known about how each of these mentoring variables interacts with the others; however, the literature suggests that each, on its own, does play a role in how effective the relationship is for particular students. In the next section we discuss the theoretical frameworks that drive the kinds of activities in which mentoring programs engage.

TABLE 5.1.
Typology of Mentoring Variables

Key Feature	Variable Conditions
• Target outcomes	Academic enhancement, college going, personal development, behavioral change
• Status differential	Outside adult/student, school personnel/student, peers
• Intensity of relationship	Frequency of meetings, duration of meetings, formal versus informal meetings
• Role of mentor	Counselor, career or academic guide, information source, role model, friend
• Relationship type	One-on-one, group

MENTORING THEORY

Most mentoring programs, as well as the evaluations of them, are atheoretical in their approach. That is, they lack an articulated theory of action or set of beliefs about the causal link between program interventions and student outcomes. The literature on mentoring programs typically describes what they do, without providing any particular rationale for why they do it. The assumption is that something about the mentoring relationship results in improved outcomes for students, but the something is rarely defined. There is, however, an implicit theory of action behind many of these programs that is related to the activities in which they engage students. These implicit theoretical frameworks include: (1) development, (2) identity, (3) guidance, and (4) family support.

Development

The developmental framework is based on the assumption that adolescence (and overwhelmingly mentoring programs are targeted to teenagers) is a period fraught with stress and turmoil for many students (Csikzentmihalyi & Schmidt, 1998). Students in disadvantaged environments are particularly vulnerable to negative influences because of an intense need to be accepted by peers who often exhibit negative behaviors. Some programs also target students from single-parent homes because of a belief that they are especially vulnerable to negative peer pressure and lack of positive direction. The implicit theory behind these programs is that mentoring can directly affect the healthy development of a young person at risk for negative developmental outcomes by providing emotional support and unconditional acceptance during a difficult period in the young person's life, thereby obviating the sole reliance on peers for personal validation. There is, in fact, some support for this position in the literature on adolescent development. For example, some researchers (Grotevant & Cooper, 1985; Cooper & Cooper, 1992) argue that the data show that adolescents in supportive environments usually navigate this period of life successfully and emerge with a reasonably stable and satisfying sense of self. Stanton-Salazar (2001) avers that, even in low-income families, extended kinship networks can often provide a "buffering system" that holds environmental stressors, including adolescent distress and alienation, at bay (p. 56).

Those who do not weather these storms successfully, however, are disproportionately from lower income and marginalized groups where there may be fewer healthy alternative avenues for adolescent expression in their neighborhoods and communities (National Research Council, 1993; Stanton-Salazar, 2001). For example, Foley (1990), in a study of a south Texas high school, demonstrated how the same rebellious adolescent behavior was perceived as normal among White adolescents, but viewed by school personnel as expressions of deviance among Mexican American and other marginalized youth. It is in these circumstances in particular that mentors may be a viable re-source for at-risk adolescents. Theoretically, mentors can affirm the self-worth of such marginalized students while interpreting the cultural norms of the dominant society to them and helping them to establish a healthy identity in an otherwise hostile social context. Some programs report significant effects of mentoring on adolescents' positive self-concept (Rhodes, Grossman, & Resch, 2000).

It is also clear that ethnic minority students face different challenges in developing a personal and academic identity than other students (Steinberg, 1996; Steinberg et al., 1992; Steele, 1997; Phinney, 1990), and that these chal-lenges can lead to overidentification with marginalized peer groups. Whereas the values of peers and family may be relatively consistent for White or Asian youth, they are often diametrically opposed in the case of students of color (Steinberg, 1996). Thus, while peers may not represent a significant challenge to parental values for many White and middle-class students, this may be quite different for low-income and minority youth. The fear of failure, particularly when it is witnessed by mainstream individuals for whom it can be a confir-mation of their stereotyped views of persons of color, has also been shown to depress the achievement and aspirations of underrepresented students (Steele, 1997). The fear of appearing to betray the ethnic group in favor of "acting White" (Fordham & Ogbu, 1986) can also shape the educational futures of these young people. The complexity of these countervailing pressures on at-risk, low-income, and ethnic minority youth introduce real challenges for men-tors and raise very real questions about who can most effectively mentor them. But it also raises the possibility that additional adult resources—persons who are neither teachers nor parents and therefore are not evaluating or judging the young person—may provide a steadying force in a tumultuous sea of change. Many mentoring programs support the notion that an adult friend can provide a steadying influence on young people faced with many opportunities to lose their footing (Sipe, 1999).

Some literature on adolescent development has focused on the problem of insufficient support and direction for American young people in making im-portant life decisions. Hersch (1998), in an ethnographic study of adolescents in the eastern United States, argues that adult society has abdicated its respon-sibility to adolescents and allowed them to create a separate world in which adults have little influence. She finds that peers have enormous impact on young people's decisions, not because of peer pressure as it is often construed, but because adolescents live in a world with a separate set of norms, norms that often do not support the values that their parents hold. Similarly, Schneider and Stevenson (1999), based on a series of case studies of American youth, argue that, contrary to popular stereotype, American adolescents are not "slackers" with no ambition, but simply lack sufficient direction to transform their very ambitious plans into reality. Like Hersch, Schneider and Stevenson theorize that the problem with American adolescents is a lack of sustained, positive contact with adults who can provide support and direction for them. This literature makes the case for a potentially important role of mentors, in addition to much more engaged parents, in shepherding adolescents safely into adulthood and into productive adult roles. From this perspective, the impact of the mentor would be through providing support and supervision for a young person whose family may have abdicated this responsibility, or may simply not know how or not have the resources to provide it.

Identity

The identity framework approaches mentoring from the perspective that adolescence is intimately associated with the process of identity development (Erikson, 1968; Marcia, 1980). Erikson describes the primary task of adolescence as one of trying on different personas in a search for an integrated ego identity. The young person who one day is interested in school and going to college may shift focus the next day and be more concerned about getting an invitation to the prom than acing chemistry. To some extent this will depend on the affirmation he or she receives from peers. In early adolescence, teachers and parents may have less influence on these role choices than age peers (Hersch, 1998; Markus & Nurius, 1986), although the relative influence of parents and peers may change substantially over the course of adolescence (Gándara, O'Hara, & Gutiérrez, 2004).

An important assumption of the identity framework is that mentors, in the form of role models, can help students shape their identity. As young people experiment with different "possible selves" (Markus & Nurius, 1986), they draw from their own sociohistorical contexts and the significant others in their environment for prototypes of role possibilities. Usually this involves parents and other family members, peers, and to a lesser extent, school personnel and other members of their community (chapter 3, this volume; Phelan, Davidson, & Yu, 1998; Cooper et al., 1995; Brown & Theobald, 1998). For young people in the mainstream of society, many role models are available in their own surroundings, as well as in the media. However, for low-income and minority youth, models of high achievement and social and economic success may be very limited. Therefore, some mentoring programs view an important function of the mentor as being a role model—someone who represents a model of achievement (Gándara, 2002b). For these programs, the implicit theory of action is that mentors directly affect aspirations and achievement by causing the student to want to emulate the mentor. There is little empirical evidence for this belief, however.

The identity that adolescents negotiate during their high school years not only has major implications for their personal and social adaptation to adult society, but will also lay the foundation for future educational and occupational choices. Adolescents who are encouraged to see themselves as smart and academically competent are far more likely to have high post–high school aspirations than those who either do not see their identity as closely connected to school (for example, students who reject the culture of schooling through truancy or dropping out) or who are perceived as unsuccessful in school (Kao & Tienda, 1998). Unfortunately, because Black and Latino students are more likely to be stereotyped as underachievers than are White and Asian younsters (Kao & Tienda, 1998), they can come to see themselves in this light. From the perspective of the identity framework, an important role of mentoring programs is to provide support for the development of an identity that includes expanded "possible selves" and eschews a stereotype of low aspirations.

Guidance

The guidance framework assumes that students' decisions to attend college are influenced by providing essential information and specific guidance in navigating the process of college preparation. A study by Plank and Jordan (2001), based on the National Educational Longitudinal Study database, tested this proposition and concluded that indeed information about college and guidance directed toward college options did predict college going within two years after high school graduation. The operating assumption of programs that adopt a guidance model is that students lack certain kinds of information and personal networks (social capital) and class-based knowledge and habits (cultural capital) that promote successful academic outcomes and that these can be provided, at least in part, by a mentor. Social capital can be transmitted to the student via informational counseling and by introducing the student to networks of supportive individuals. Thus, the mentor may provide information about the process of preparing for college and may introduce the student to college-educated individuals or to contact persons at college campuses. Cultural capital can be partially provided by a mentor who introduces the protégé to experiences like going to cultural events, by initiating him or her into the language and customs of the college educated, or simply by visiting college campuses. The risk inherent in this model, as noted by Dika and Singh (2002), is that low-income and students of color can come to be seen as chronically deficient because they do not possess critical social and cultural capital. Stanton-Salazar (2001) and Lareau (1989) have endeavored to show, however, that access to important information and social networks is actively withheld from the lower classes by those who are intent on maintaining their privileged position in society.

Family Support

The family support framework is based on the notion that mentors can reinforce the role of the parents as important guides for their children and lend credibility to the role of parenting. Rhodes, Grossman, and Resch (2000) theorized that the impact of mentors in the Big Brothers/Big Sisters mentoring program might be due to indirect effects on students through strengthening relationships between students and their parents. Indeed, their path analyses suggested that, to a large extent, the effects of the program on both attitudes and performance in school were indirect and mediated by family relationships. The investigators concluded that an important function of the mentor is to bolster the parent-child relationship, which in turn increases the salience of parental advice and guidance for the child. Data were collected from self-report interviews, and effects were found only for students who had significant contact with mentors for at least one year. It is also important to note that virtually all of the nearly 1,000 11- to 13-year-old students in the national sample were from single-parent homes, and so it is not known to what extent similar findings could be expected for young people from two-parent families. Nonetheless, the study shows that family support can be an important potential mechanism for affecting the outcomes of at-risk youth.

WHO IS AN EFFECTIVE MENTOR?

Individuals who are selected to be mentors for minors must meet stringent criteria. In addition to possessing a number of personal attributes like patience, persistence, sensitivity to others' needs, and honesty, they must be free of criminal histories and other characteristics that would make them bad role models or place the young people at risk. They must have good interpersonal skills and be able to elicit trust from the students. If they are volunteers, they must have sufficient resources to support the relationship—a way to get back and forth to meet with the student, funds to pay for simple outings. For obvious reasons, most programs attempt to match same-sex dyads of students and mentors, especially in the case of female students. But particularly for young males without fathers in the home, many people believe that a male mentor can provide an important role model and source of guidance.

The question of who is an effective mentor becomes more complex when the objective of the program is to increase students' aspirations, preparation, and access to college. Must the mentor be a college graduate? Can a mentor who has not graduated from college be a credible role model or advocate for college going? Often individuals who work successfully with youth in minority communities are not themselves college graduates. And professionals with college degrees in these communities may be called upon so frequently that they have difficulty making the commitment to mentor a student as well. An alternative is to recruit mentors from outside of the students' community. The research suggests that a caring individual who sustains a relationship with a student over a long period of time (generally a year or more) can be an effective mentor regardless of the gender or ethnic match (Foster, 2001). However, it is not clear if this person can be as inspiring as someone from the same background as the student, who can call upon experiences similar to those of the student.

Some programs attempt to tap successful professionals as mentors because of the role models that they represent, especially when the program's goals include inspiring students to do well in school and go on to college. Lawyers, doctors, judges, teachers, and business executives may be prime targets for these mentoring roles. However, such individuals are usually very busy people, and the hours spent with a 14-year-old who is not yet very focused on either school or future goals might well be invested in fund-raising for the organization that could yield support for many more mentors or staff assistants. The 14-year-old might even prefer a mentor closer in age who could relate to his or her interests and adolescent issues. Gándara et al. (1998) examined this question in the context of the Puente program and concluded that busy professionals may not always be the best match for young adolescents who have not yet developed focused career or educational goals. In too many of these cases, the mentor who thought she or he would be helping a protégé make college and career decisions was frustrated by the realization that the student was not really interested in these topics at the beginning of high school. The literature suggests that the most effective mentors are those who are prepared to be a friend to the student, rather than a surrogate parent. However, when the goal of the program is to promote college going, the assumption is that the mentor will also provide monitoring and guidance related to schooling and college. These two roles may be in conflict.

Some programs have experimented with using college students as mentors for high school students, with the assumption that a college student is a good role model if the objective of the program is to increase college going. Coordinating mentoring activities with college students can be even more complex than coordinating these activities with busy professionals. College students, if they are available in the community in which the program operates, may have unreliable transportation and variable schedules that make it difficult to meet on a regular basis. Their class schedules change every semester, and often their work schedules must change to accommodate their classes. Both Puente (see Gándara et al., 1998) and AVID (Mehan et al., 1996), two large-scale college access programs in California, have experimented with the use of college students as tutors and mentors, with uneven results. Nonetheless, Mejorado (2000) found that high school students tended to show a preference for college-age mentors when asked what they thought was the ideal age of a mentor.

Because mentoring programs have not generally theorized about the mechanism by which they may have an impact on student outcomes, the personal characteristics of mentors have not been linked to these processes. Nor is it clear how the timing of mentoring interventions impacts interaction with students (see chapter 8). However, the gender and ethnicity of the adult mentors may be a factor in their potential impact. Whether the challenges of mentoring can be met as well by a mentor from the dominant culture as by one from the student's own ethnic community is an unresolved question in the literature. Studies generally find no statistically significant relationship between the demographic characteristics of mentors and student outcomes. However, studies also find weak relationships between mentoring and academic outcomes overall. Thus, the question may not be well tested in the context of these studies. Mejorado (2000) found that while a majority of Mexican-origin students in her sample of 114 students in a college access program responded in a survey that the ethnicity of their mentor did not matter, they also indicated that it was important for the mentor to be able to speak to, and become acquainted with, their parents who spoke only Spanish. This finding also points to the volatility of student responses to some forms of data collection.

IS MENTORING A COST-EFFECTIVE STRATEGY TO INCREASE COLLEGE GOING?

While mentoring programs are often simplistically seen as win-win arrangements in which students benefit from the attention of a caring adult and the adult is able to pass on accumulated wisdom to a young person, and all of this is accomplished cost free by volunteers, the reality is quite different. Mentoring programs that serve youth are labor intensive. To be successful, they require extensive recruiting, screening, matching, training, and monitoring.

Few studies have looked at the costs of mentoring programs, and few programs provide the kind of data about their costs that allow this question to be examined. However, Fountain and Arbreton (1999) pooled available data from several studies to answer the question of how much it costs to run a mentoring program. They found that the average program served about 291 students and employed one FTE (full-time equivalent person) for every 61 students. This person's job was primarily administrative. These programs utilized one volunteer FTE for every 25 students in the program. Seventy-five percent of the volunteer's time was spent on mentoring activities, and 25% on administration and support activities. This suggests that the average student in these programs was receiving a little less than five hours of mentoring contact per month. The average cost for a program was about $1,100 per student, excluding the cost of the time of the mentor. When the cost of the mentor's time was calculated, the annual cost per student for the mentoring program was approximately $2,300. Although the authors do not specify, the assumption is that these were 1998–1999 dollars. Additional donated resources, such as office space in schools or community centers, materials, and equipment are not calculated into these figures. Averages also obscure the variation in the numbers and there is a wide range in the size and costs of these programs, from less than $200 per student to more than $6,000. Moreover, the range in costs is no doubt related to the amount of time students spend in contact with the program, its size, and the numbers of additional elements that the program provides, none of which is specified in the study.

Rumberger and Brenner (2000) also studied a small mentoring program in California that focused on young adolescents and examined the per-student costs to run that program. First-year startup costs were almost double the annual costs thereafter, but on average it cost the program over $1,000 per student annually to recruit, screen, match, and monitor student-mentor relationships for 32 to 67 students over a three-year period from 1996 to 1999. The researchers questioned whether this was the most effective use of funds to achieve the modest outcomes reported for the program.

Grossman and Tierney (1998) reported that it took nearly a year to put a mentor in place in the Big Brothers/Big Sisters (BBBS) program, from initial recruitment to final matching with a student. Sipe (1996), in an overview of the BBBS mentoring program studies conducted by Public/Private Ventures, noted that the cost of just recruiting, screening, and matching each student-mentor dyad for the program was approximately $1,000 in mid-1990s dollars. This did not, however, include the cost to train and supervise the mentors and administer the program. Rumberger and Brenner (2000) also noted that many students in the program they studied were unable to be matched with a mentor until the second year of the program because of the limited numbers of volunteers and the labor-intensive nature of recruitment. Nonetheless, the per-student cost for the program was no less whether students had a mentor or not. And after the student and mentor have been matched, careful monitoring and support of the mentoring relationship are essential for an effective program (Sipe, 1999). Moreover, while an estimated cost of the volunteer's time was calculated by the Fountain and Arbreton (1999) study, this did not include an estimate of the opportunity costs of volunteering as a mentor. That is, what alternative kind of service might the same individual provide for the student, the family, the program, the school, or the community with this time? And might this alternative investment provide equal or greater impact on college-going outcomes?

HOW EFFECTIVE IS MENTORING AT INCREASING COLLEGE GOING?

We have suggested that most mentoring programs have focused on changing the behavior of young people at risk, and although there is evidence that recently established programs are focusing much more on academic outcomes (Foster, 2001), the bulk of the meager research on mentoring is on behavioral change. There are very few studies that examine the effect of mentoring on changing academic outcomes, including college going. Those that do seldom attempt anything like an experimental design, such that conclusions are generally based on postintervention surveys without any true comparison group, or anecdotal accounts of the effectiveness of the program (Sipe, 1999). A common attitude is "we know we are effective, so there isn't any need to evaluate." A further problem is that there are virtually no studies that look at the impact of mentoring on college-going behavior longitudinally. For example, we do not know the long-term outcomes of mentoring. However, a few studies have attempted to systematically examine the issue of effectiveness in either enhancing academic achievement or increasing college going. We look more closely at those.

Grossman and Tierney (1998) studied almost 1,000 students who were enrolled in Big Brothers/Big Sisters programs in eight different metropolitan areas. A community-based effort, BBBS has been in existence for almost 100 years. It focuses on the personal and social development of youth, largely between 11 and 14 years of age, who are growing up in single-parent, low-income households. Youth who participated in the study were randomly assigned to an experimental (participants) or control (nonparticipants) group. The study was conducted over an 18-month period in the mid-1990s during which the youth experienced a mentoring relationship with a young adult (usually between 20 and 29 years old) for approximately one year. (Because it took four to six months to match students with mentors, and about 40% of the mentoring relationships were terminated before the end of the study, the average time that students spent in such a relationship was less than the duration of the study.) The findings of the study were very encouraging with respect to behavioral and attitudinal change. Students who had been mentored were significantly less likely to initiate alcohol or drug use during the period of the study than were their nonmentored peers. They felt more competent about doing schoolwork and were less likely to skip school. They also reported better relationships with parents and peers. Self-reported grades, however, were affected only marginally, not at a level that was statistically significant. That is, the changes observed in students' grades may have been due to random error. Overall, the study demonstrated that mentoring can have a substantial impact on behavior and attitudes of youth and may have a very modest effect on academic achievement, at least during the period of time that they are being mentored. The researchers cautioned, however, that their findings do not suggest that any mentoring program can be effective. The BBBS program has very high standards and is relatively expensive to operate.

The BBBS program conducts an extensive, months-long screening of every potential mentor; matching procedures take into account the preferences of the youth, mentors, and parents; mentors are carefully trained on communication skills, limit setting, and developmental issues of young people; and the mentor relationships are closely supervised by a case manager who makes frequent contact with parents, mentors, and youth, and provides assistance and intervention as needed. Mentors and youth in the evaluation study met, on average, three to four times each month for about three and a half hours each time, totaling an average of 144 hours of direct contact.

Royse (1998) studied a mentoring program for African American adolescent males from low-income, mother-headed households in Kentucky. The program also targeted students who were not doing well in school. The 36 young men were 14 to 16 years of age at the time they were paired with a mentor, and all continued the mentoring relationship for at least six months, with a median length of relationship being 15 months. The objective of the program was to increase self-esteem, affect attitudes toward drugs, and enhance academic achievement. Students were randomly assigned to the experimental and control groups. The first postintervention assessment occurred, on average, when students had been in the program for 10 months. Several assessments were conducted thereafter, about a year apart. Royse found no statistically significant differences for any of the behavioral measures or for grade point average between the experimental and control groups at any assessment period. He explains the lack of differences as probably due to the fact that little was known about the quality of the mentoring relationships or the amount of time that students actually spent with their mentors. Royse underscored the problem of gaining access to good data on the nature of mentoring relationships. He hypothesized that strong relationships may have produced important outcomes, but because of both the small size of the sample and the variability in the mentoring experiences, it was not possible to detect differences between the groups. In sum, Royse questioned the degree to which the mentor relationships were adequately monitored by the program.

Johnson (1998) studied the Sponsor-a-Scholar (SAS) program, which targets high school students from low-income families in the Philadelphia area who are performing in a middle range of achievement (B's and C's). Students in the program, however, tend to come from stable homes in which approximately half have parents with more than a high school education. The objective of the program is to increase academic achievement and college going, and it lasts from ninth grade through the first year of college. The program provides a number of support services—college counseling, scholarships, tutoring, SAT preparation, and summer activities and jobs—in addition to mentoring. The evaluation design included 180 program participants who were each matched with two nonparticipants on gender, race, and school attended. There was also an attempt to match on academic achievement by pairing each participant with nonparticipants who had GPAs close to that of the participant (one higher and one lower). The program had very high rates of retention; approximately 85% of participants were still in the program by the first year of college.

Johnson found that the SAS program appeared to have a significant effect on college going—85% of SAS students enrolled in college after high school compared to only 64% of the comparison students. There was also a modest (2 percentage points), though statistically significant, difference in GPA in the 10th and 11th grades, although no difference was found by the 12th grade. By the second year of college, however, there was no statistically significant difference in college retention. Johnson concludes that the SAS mentoring model is effective in enhancing school performance and college attendance. She also found that some students—those with the least personal resources—tended to benefit most from the program. While the program did appear to have some impact on students (although whether this endured much beyond high school is questionable), it is not clear that the impact can be attributed to the mentoring component. The SAS program included many intervention components, and Johnson was not able to control for the effects of all of the other intervention strategies.

Rumberger and Brenner (2000) investigated a small mentoring program in southern California that focused on "average" academic performers in the fifth grade. The study did not specify what the criteria were for selection for the program. They compared students who were randomly assigned to mentors in the fifth grade with other students who were not, and tested academic and behavioral outcomes for both in the seventh grade. These researchers found that seventh-grade students who received mentoring over the three-year period marginally outperformed students who were not assigned to mentors with respect to GPA. Moreover, the researchers noted that there was a threshold for effects. Students who received less than 39 hours of mentoring did not show any grade improvement. Mentoring appeared to have an effect on students' awareness and access to helpful resources. Eighty-five percent of the mentored students could identify available resources to help with homework versus only 55% of the nonmentored group. The study is limited by the small size of the sample (32 to 67 students over the three years) and lack of detailed information about the nature of the mentoring relationship. We also know little about the characteristics of the students—income, parental education, family circumstances, or whether they were considered to be at risk for poor performance— and other studies have shown that effects may vary according to the different characteristics of the students. Rumberger and Brenner also noted that the program directors decided, on the basis of the evaluation, to incorporate more supports for students in addition to mentoring in an effort to strengthen the effects of the intervention. This echoes much of the literature on mentoring programs that target academic achievement. This study does suggest, however, that a small-scale mentoring intervention conducted over a lengthy period of time may have a small, but positive, effect on some students' achievement and related behaviors.

McPartland and Nettles (1991) conducted one of the most thoughtful studies of mentoring found in the literature. They evaluated the effectiveness of Project Raise, a program that provides mentors and student advocates for at-risk middle school students in the Baltimore area. The objectives of the program include increasing grades, on-time grade promotion, school attendance, and test scores. The intervention is designed to last for two years, during sixth and seventh grades. As other programs that target academic achievement, Project Raise included components beyond mentoring. Paid student advocates monitored grades and provided tutoring as well as occasional field trips to museums and sporting and recreational events.

McPartland and Nettles (1991) studied seven Project Raise sites, each with between 41 and 57 students, and compared the outcomes for these students over two years with students in the same schools who were not participants in the program. All schools were in very impoverished, high-risk neighborhoods. These researchers found that program participants showed a marginally significant increase in English grades (although no significant increase in either math or overall GPA), and increased their school attendance at a level significantly different from that of the comparison students. These modest outcomes, however, are moderated by possible selection bias, as some of the sites rejected the most at-risk students from their participant pool, biasing the sample in favor of better-performing students. Program effects also did not always correlate with programs that included a strong mentoring component. Only three of the seven sites actually showed statistically significant effects on grades and school attendance, and one of these did not have a mentoring program in place. On the other hand, one of the seven sites with a very strong mentoring program did not show any significant effects on student outcomes. The researchers, however, conclude, "although strong one-on-one mentoring is not an *essential* component of an effective program that uses outside adults to assist at-risk middle school students, the RAISE model is much more likely to show positive effects once one-on-one mentoring *has* been strongly implemented" (p. 581). Further, the researchers examined their data to determine for whom the program appeared to have the greatest impact. In this regard they concluded that "effectiveness is more likely for smaller groups of students who do not begin far below grade level. . . . effects are more likely for sponsors [program sites] who serve at-risk students with less severe initial educational disadvantages" (p. 581).

Mejorado (2000) investigated the impact of the mentoring component for students enrolled in the high school Puente program. Puente is a four-year program that provides multiple interventions for mostly Latino students. Students are assigned to a special Puente English class in the 9th grade and 10th grades, and are monitored by both a counselor and individual mentor, ideally throughout high school. In actuality, it is uncommon for the mentoring relationship to last the entire four years of high school, and, as with almost all other programs reported in the literature, finding sufficient mentors for all program participants is a chronic challenge, so students often have to wait a year to be placed with a mentor. Thus, students' contact with mentors varies greatly. Mejorado hypothesized that if the mentoring program was successful, then students with longer-term and stronger mentoring relationships would increase grades, aspirations, and college going more than students who did not have such strong relationships with their mentors. Comparing 44 students with strong mentoring relationships (lasting one year or more with high student satisfaction) with 36 students who had weaker relationships (less than a year with lower satisfaction), Mejorado (2000) found no difference in grades but did find a statistically significant correlation between the strength of relationship and perceived influence of mentors on post–high school plans. She also found that students in the middle range of achievement (neither very low achievers nor very high achievers) were most likely to report influence by mentors. Of course, as with other studies that have investigated the impact of mentoring in the context of program interventions with multiple components, it is difficult to disentangle the relative importance of the mentoring intervention compared to everything else. This study does lend support, however, to the finding in the literature that length of mentoring (and strength of relationship) are key variables in producing positive outcomes, and it reinforces the limited impact that mentoring appears to have on raising GPA.

CONCLUSION

To date, there are more questions than answers about the effectiveness of mentoring as a strategy for increasing academic achievement and college going. It is not clear if the reason that few studies are able to show a significant impact of mentoring on these outcome measures is because of the lack of specificity of the variables, inadequate data collection, poor study designs, or problems with the models themselves. Programs that attempt to affect student achievement and college going suffer from an additional problem—the mentoring component is usually only one of a multitude of interventions, and so it is frequently difficult to specify what its role has been in any observable student changes.

One area in which the literature has been almost silent is the role of mentors in the identity development of underrepresented students. A large literature in sociology has demonstrated powerfully that students of color and other at-risk youth often do not see themselves as high academic achievers or college goers. For many of them, this is not a "possible self" they can envision (see Markus & Nurius, 1986). Moreover, even admitting to a desire to be so can carry costly social consequences among peers. As one Latino high school student put it, "Being a good student doesn't do anything for your social life"

(Gándara et al., 2004). Furthermore, as Steele (1997) has demonstrated, many students of color may not even try to excel in school for fear of confirming the stereotype that they are intellectually inferior if they fail. Given these realities, we are compelled to question if mentors from the same backgrounds as the students might be more adept than others at breaking through the walls of fear and self-doubt. We also wonder if there is not also an added measure of inspiration when a student's mentor has confronted the same barriers and overcome them. These are questions to be answered by future research.

Mentoring is also a high-stakes intervention. Given the kinds of interventions that programs may choose to incorporate, mentoring is labor intensive and relatively costly. Moreover, program effectiveness appears to depend on a number of factors: size, composition of students, length and strength of the mentoring relationship, ability to recruit appropriate mentors, training and supervision of the mentors, and quite possibly the degree to which mentoring supports other aspects of the program. McPartland and Nettles (1991) concluded from their study that smaller programs that targeted students who were not significantly behind academically were most likely to be successful. Of course, this limits greatly the potential impact of such programs. If only a few students can be effectively served, and these students represent the least at-risk among their peers, the impact of such a program is relatively narrow. Virtually all studies note the problems of recruiting mentors, and it is typical for students to have to wait up to a year to be matched with a mentor. If this relationship does not work out, often there will not be enough mentors to provide for a second chance. Mejorado (2000) found that only about one third of mentor matches endured for a year or more in her study. Careful studies have lamented the extent to which we do not know what happens in many of these mentor relationships, how often the dyads actually meet, or what kinds of activities prove to be most productive. We do know that a nonevaluative "friend" approach appears to result in the strongest relationships, but McPartland and Nettles (1991) remind us that "some of the student behaviors that appear most responsive to influence by outside adults, such as improved school attendance, may require adult monitoring and pressure that goes beyond the theoretical role of mentors or beyond the understandable preferences of some adults who actually fill these roles to avoid possible confrontations with their students" (p. 584). That is, mentors may not in fact be the best persons to help achieve the changes that will make the most difference to at-risk students *academically* over the long run. And as Perna (chapter 6) points out, academic preparation is the key predictor of enrollment and persistence in college. Providing a caring presence, a good role model, and someone to share life's challenges may be an important role that mentors can play, but this may not be the key to real substantial change in academic outcomes.

Rumberger and Brenner (2000) question whether, given the limited impact that mentoring seems to have on academic outcomes, such programs are really cost effective. Evidence suggests that good programs—and these appear to be programs that serve relatively small numbers of students—cost upwards of $1,000 annually per student in mid-1990s dollars. It is worth questioning if other strategies could conceivably result in greater increases in academic achievement for the same cost.

Another reason for the unanswered questions about the actual and potential effectiveness of youth mentoring programs for raising academic achievement and increasing college going is the absence of high-quality evaluations of these programs. There is a lack of specificity about what programs actually do. Many studies are vague with respect to the nature of the mentoring and the objectives of the programs. Student outcomes are not explicitly tied to the specific activities of the program interventions. It is not clear what the theory of action is in these programs. That is, it is hard to know which aspects of the program are likely to lead to the outcomes that program directors seek. Studies often fail to describe how much time students spend with mentors or what they do when they are together (Grossman & Tierney, 1998). Reviews of the empirical literature on youth mentoring reveal that the link between improved academics and mentoring is weak (Grossman & Tierney, 1998), and the majority of published articles consist of testimonials and data collected through surveys without appropriate controls or comparisons (Foster, 2001). As noted earlier, there is also a dearth of research on the role of mentors in the development of a high-achievement identity for underrepresented students who participate in these programs.

It is safe to conclude that good mentoring programs may have a positive impact on behavioral outcomes for at-risk adolescents under particular conditions. Whether such programs can have a significant and sustained impact on academic outcomes and college going, however, is much more difficult to establish. Without a more substantial research base, our conclusions must be tentative. Given the substantial cost, the great difficulty in recruiting sufficient numbers of mentors to serve individual students, and the small numbers of students who can be served effectively, programs would be wise to think twice about whether this represents the best investment of their funds. Mentoring may be a desirable intervention to stimulate college going, but it does not appear to be a critical one, at least as it has been conceived and studied in the literature to date.

The lack of a clearly articulated theory of action for mentoring has hampered researchers' ability to identify its specific effects on student outcomes. This problem is exacerbated by the fact that most mentoring programs include other interventions that no doubt contribute to program effects and are difficult to control for. Moreover, a lack of specificity about the personal characteristics of the mentors, the nature of the mentoring activities, and the length and intensity of the mentoring relationships has prevented many studies from illuminating our understanding of the potential for these programs. The literature on college access programs—and mentoring programs often fall in this category— suggests that such programs often have different rates of success with different kinds of students (Gándara & Bial, 2001), yet we know little about student– program interactions within mentoring programs—for whom do they work best, and under what conditions? What are the cultural considerations that must be taken into account in designing and implementing these programs (see chapter 1)? The research agenda for the study of mentoring is clear: the field must develop better definitions of terms, a clearly articulated theory of action, and attend to the multiple influences, both internal and external to programs, that no doubt have an impact on their effectiveness but are seldom specified in program and study designs.

Part 2

Programmatic Elements

LAURA W. PERNA

Chapter Six

The Key to College Access: Rigorous Academic Preparation

INTRODUCTION

Sponsored by the federal government, state governments, not-for-profit organizations, and individual colleges and universities (Fenske, Geranos, Keller, & Moore, 1997; Perna, Fenske, & Swail, 2000), college preparation programs promise to increase the educational attainment levels of low-income and other disadvantaged groups of students by cultivating the skills, knowledge, confidence, aspirations, and overall preparedness that are required to enroll in and succeed in college. Although some research (Perna, 2002; Swail & Perna, 2002) describes the characteristics and components of such programs, few studies have focused on identifying the components of college preparation programs that most effectively promote college enrollment for low-income and other disadvantaged groups of students. As others (e.g., Perna, 1999; Perna et al., 2000) have noted, the ability of researchers and program administrators to identify the most critical component of college preparation programs has been limited by the great variation in program sponsors and other program characteristics. Perhaps in part because of the lack of empirical research, many college preparation programs offer a wide variety of components and services including college awareness, social skills development, campus visits, cultural activities, critical thinking skills, career counsel-

113

ing, leadership development, academic advising, and academic enrichment (Swail & Perna, 2002).

Determining the most essential component of college preparation programs is important for several reasons. First, although the federal government has been involved with college preparation programs since the establishment of the TRIO programs in the 1960s, individuals with low family incomes, African Americans, Hispanics, and American Indians continue to be underrepresented among both college and university enrollments and degree recipients. For example, the current 30% gap in college enrollment rates between low- and high-income students is the same size as the gap was in the 1960s (Gladieux & Swail, 1999). Second, in the context of scarce resources and competing priorities, administrators of college preparation programs need to know how to allocate their resources in ways that most effectively achieve their primary goal, namely to raise the college enrollment rates of historically underrepresented groups of students (see chapter 9).

Although little is known about the effectiveness of particular components of college preparation programs (Tierney, 2002), much is known about the predictors of college enrollment. Through a review and synthesis of prior research, this chapter demonstrates that college preparation programs will most effectively achieve their primary goal of raising college enrollment rates by ensuring that low-income, African American, and Hispanic high school students are academically prepared to enroll and succeed in college. This chapter shows that college preparation programs should focus on academic preparation not only because a high level of academic preparation is required to enroll in college but also because the groups of students who continue to be underrepresented in higher education are also the groups that are least likely to be academically prepared. The chapter concludes by identifying the ways in which college preparation programs should address the critical role of academic preparation. Only by focusing on ensuring that students are adequately academically prepared will college preparation programs effectively raise the college enrollment rates of groups of students who continue to be underrepresented in higher education.

ACADEMIC PREPARATION IS CRITICAL TO COLLEGE ENROLLMENT

The consistently strong relationship between academic preparation and college enrollment found in prior research demonstrates that academic preparation must be a central component of any college preparation program. Researchers have consistently shown that academic preparation and achievement are important predictors of both predisposition toward, or interest in, attending college and actual college enrollment (Alexander, Cook, & McDill, 1978; Hossler, Braxton, & Coopersmith, 1989; Manski & Wise, 1983; St. John, 1991; Hossler et al., 1999; Perna, 2000a; Cabrera, La Nasa, & Burkam, 2001).

Research on college enrollment uniformly demonstrates the contribution of academic achievement, a product of academic preparation. Academic achievement is typically measured by high school grades or test scores. Some research (Hossler et al., 1999) suggests that high school grade point average is positively related to predisposition toward college enrollment. A longitudinal study of 1986 ninth graders in Indiana suggests that students with higher high school grades consider attending a larger number of colleges, are more likely to consider attending selective colleges and universities, and continue to plan to attend college throughout their high school years (Hossler et al., 1999).

Research consistently shows that individuals with higher test scores are more likely to enroll in higher education (Sewell, Haller, & Ohlendorf, 1970b; Alexander & Eckland, 1974; Alexander, Pallas, & Holupka, 1987; Catsiapis, 1987; Hossler et al., 1989; St. John & Noell, 1989; Jackson, 1990; St. John, 1991; Kane & Spizman, 1994; Rouse, 1994; Kane, 1999; Perna, 2000a; Beattle, 2002). Comparing the predictors of college enrollment for the class of 1972 and the class of 1980, Alexander and colleagues (1987) found that the contribution of test scores to college enrollment increased over this period after controlling for socioeconomic status, sex, race, curricular program, and high school grades, and that test scores had a larger positive effect on the college enrollment of boys than girls. St. John (1991) found that the probability of college enrollment among 1982 high school seniors increased with test scores even after controlling for region, family social background, high school experiences (including curricular track and grades), and postsecondary plans. Using the same database, Beattle (2002) found that, while the probability of enrolling in a two-year or four-year college or university increased with test scores among both boys and girls after controlling for race, marital and parental status, educational expectations, and high school sector, boys with high test scores tended to enroll in higher education even if they expected low economic returns. Examining a more recent cohort of students, Perna (2000a) found that the likelihood of enrolling in a four-year college increased with test scores among 1992 high school graduates after controlling for sex, race, curricular program, financial resources, and cultural and social capital. Using the same database, Kane (1999) found that 94% of high school graduates with mathematics test scores in the highest quartile enrolled in college within two years of graduating from high school, compared with only 52% of high school graduates with mathematics test scores in the bottom quartile.

DEFINING RIGOROUS ACADEMIC PREPARATION

Rigorous academic preparation is sometimes equated with participation in an academic or college preparation track. Research consistently shows that college enrollment rates are higher among students who participate in an academic or college preparation curricular program during high school (Alexander & Eckland, 1974; Alexander et al., 1978, 1987; Alwin & Otto, 1977; Thomas, 1980; Borus & Carpenter, 1984; Hossler et al., 1989; St. John & Noell, 1989; Jackson, 1990; St. John, 1991; Altonji, 1992; Lucas, 1999; Perna, 2000a) and lower for students who participate in a vocational curricular program (St. John, 1991) even after controlling for other variables. A longitudinal study of students who were in the ninth grade in 1965 revealed that students who participated in a college curricular track were more likely than other students to plan, as high school seniors, to go to college, apply to college, and be accepted into college after controlling for background characteristics (Alexander et al., 1978). A comparison of the predictors of college enrollment for high school graduates in 1972 and 1980 showed that the positive effect of an academic curricular track on college enrollment declined over the period, particularly for Hispanics, girls, and students with the highest socioeconomic status (Alexander et al., 1987). Alexander and colleagues (1987) speculated that the reduced importance of curricular track in predicting college enrollment suggests a decline in the rigor of the high school curriculum. Although the magnitude of the effect may be smaller now than in the past, a more recent longitudinal study demonstrates that participation in an academic curricular track continues to promote college enrollment. Perna (2000a) found that, among 1992 high school graduates, participating in an academic curricular track increased the likelihood of enrolling in a four-year college within two years of graduating from high school even after controlling for test scores, financial resources, and measures of social and cultural capital. The positive effect was comparable in magnitude for African Americans, Hispanics, and Whites.

Other researchers have shown the importance of strong academic preparation regardless of racial/ethnic group or socioeconomic status. Alexander and colleagues (1987) concluded that, for students with "high" academic resources (defined as enrollment in an academic curricular track and test scores and grade point averages at least one standard deviation above the mean), college enrollment was a "virtual certainty." Although the level of academic resources was unrelated to the type of institution Black students attended net of other variables, White and Hispanic students with high academic resources were substantially more likely to enroll in a four-year than a two-year institution. Students with "low" academic resources (defined as test scores and grade point averages at least one standard deviation below the mean and enrolled in a nonacademic curricular track in high school) were unlikely to enroll in any type of institution. For the majority of students who were in the middle of these two ends of the continuum, academic curricular track was an important predictor of college enrollment. College enrollment rates were substantially higher for students in an academic curricular track than for their counterparts in nonacademic curricular tracks who had similar test scores, grades, race, and socioeconomic status. Moreover, socioeconomic status had a larger positive effect on college enrollment for students in nonacademic curricular tracks than for students in academic curricular tracks. Among students with both low and middle levels of resources who were enrolled in nonacademic curricular tracks, the likelihood of enrolling in college was substantially higher for students with the highest than for students with the lowest socioeconomic status (Alexander et al., 1987).

Nonetheless, research suggests that the label "academic track" may be an unreliable indicator of precollegiate academic preparation (Adelman, 1999). Using data from the High School and Beyond study of 1980 high school sophomores, Adelman (1999) found wide variation in the level of preparation among students in so-called academic curricular tracks. For example, 37% of high school graduates who had participated in an academic curricular track during high school had not completed algebra II, and 33% had completed no more than eight credits in core academic subjects. Similarly, using data from the National Educational Longitudinal Study of 1988 eighth graders (NELS:88/90), Stevenson, Schiller, and Schneider (1994) found that only 32% of high school sophomores in a college preparation track had studied algebra I and geometry or a higher level of mathematics, and only 27% had studied chemistry or physics.

Therefore, a more accurate definition of academic preparation describes the quality and quantity of courses that are completed in particular subject areas (Adelman, 1999). Research shows that taking at least one advanced mathematics course is associated with a higher probability of enrolling in a four-year college or university among students who are at risk of dropping out of high school (Horn, 1997), first-generation college students (Horn & Nuñez, 2000), and students who reported aspiring to earn at least a bachelor's degree as high school sophomores (Perna & Titus, 2001). Altonji (1992) found that the number of years of postsecondary education completed increased with each additional year of high school science, math, and foreign language that was completed even after controlling for curricular track, aptitude, and family background.

Recognizing the role of the quality and intensity of academic coursework, Berkner and Chavez (1997) developed a "college qualification" index using data from the NELS:88/94. Designed to reflect a student's qualifications to attend a four-year college or university, the index is based on a student's cumulative grade point average in academic courses, class rank during the senior year of high school, scores on the 1992 NELS aptitude tests, and SAT or ACT scores, with an adjustment for whether a student completed a rigorous program of academic coursework, defined as at least four years of English, three years of science, three years of math, three years of social studies, and two years of foreign language. Nearly all (87%) students who were very highly qualified according to this index enrolled in a four-year college or university within two years of graduating from high school, compared with only 15% of those who were marginally or not qualified and 36% who were minimally qualified (Berkner & Chavez, 1997).

Being academically prepared for college appears to be particularly important to the college enrollment decisions of students with low family incomes. Descriptive analyses of data from the 1980 sophomore cohort of High School and Beyond showed that 50% of sophomores in the lowest quartile of socioeconomic status but highest quartile of academic resources enrolled in a four-year institution, compared with only 14% of students in the lowest quartile of socioeconomic status and the lowest quartile of academic resources, where academic resources is a composite measure of students' abilities, high school class rank, and the quality and intensity of high school curriculum (Cabrera et al., 2001). One fifth of students with low socioeconomic status and low academic resources completed a bachelor's degree within 11 years, compared with more than half (58%) of those with low socioeconomic status but high academic resources.

WHY ACADEMIC PREPARATION SHOULD BE RELATED TO COLLEGE ENROLLMENT

The positive effects of academic preparation on college enrollment are consistent with both econometric and sociological theoretical approaches to college enrollment. According to the economic theory of human capital, an individual decides to enroll in higher education if the individual calculates the net benefits (i.e., the short-term and long-term benefits less the short-term and long-term costs) to be greater than the net benefits of all alternatives (e.g., full-time employment). Econometric approaches posit that academic preparation and achievement positively influence the individual's assessment of future earnings (Catsiapis, 1987). Specifically, an individual with low academic preparation and achievement is expected to be less likely to enroll in higher education because that individual knows that, because of low academic preparation and achievement, he or she is less likely to successfully complete the educational program and obtain a job that will produce the expected future earnings premium.

A limitation of econometric approaches is that the informational and computational demands that are associated with assessing the net benefits of all alternatives exceed an individual's information processing capacities. Consequently, econometric or rational models of decision making are generally regarded as normative rather than descriptive models (Hogarth, 1987). To manage cognitive decision-making demands, individuals adopt such strategies as satisficing or bounded rationality. McDonough (1997) has used Bourdieu's concept of habitus to explain that an individual's expectations, attitudes, and aspirations are not based on rational analyses but are "sensible or reasonable choices" (p. 9). Habitus, or the internalized system of thoughts, beliefs, and perceptions acquired from the immediate environment, conditions an individual's expectations, attitudes, and aspirations (Bourdieu & Passeron, 1977; McDonough, 1997). According to this perspective, the act of enrolling in rigorous academic coursework may shape a low-income or minority student's habitus to also expect and aspire to college enrollment.

In contrast to econometric approaches, sociological status attainment models focus on the predictors of educational and occupational aspirations. Such models posit that educational aspirations, a prerequisite to postsecondary enrollment, are determined by such behavioral variables as a student's academic performance and such demographic characteristics as socioeconomic status (Hossler et al., 1999). Status attainment models predict that individuals with higher levels of academic preparation and achievement receive greater encouragement from significant others, including parents, teachers, counselors, and peers, and that this encouragement promotes higher aspirations. Higher aspirations, in turn, are expected to lead to greater educational and occupational attainment.

Traditional status attainment models may be less appropriate for understanding the educational experiences of lower-income and minority students. Based on his review and synthesis of prior research, Stanton-Salazar (1997) argued that structural barriers limit the extent to which working-class minority students can gain access to the opportunities and resources that result in high levels of educational attainment. Specifically, working-class and minority children and their parents lack access to the social capital, defined as social support networks and institutional connections, that is required to acquire the opportunities and resources that are controlled by the dominant group (i.e., middle- and upper-class Whites) but that facilitate college enrollment. Stanton-Salazar (1997) argues that, to acquire the social capital that promotes college enrollment, low-income and minority students must develop a "bicultural network orientation." In other words, they must learn to cope with multiple settings and discourses.

ACCESS TO HIGH-QUALITY ACADEMIC PREPARATION IS UNEVEN

Although prior research clearly shows that enrolling in college requires becoming adequately academically prepared, a review of prior research also suggests that the groups of students who continue to be underrepresented in higher education are also less likely to be academically prepared for college. The level of academic preparation for college varies based on such individual characteristics as racial/ethnic group, family income, socioeconomic status, level of parental educational attainment, and educational expectations. Lower-income, African American, and Hispanic students are less likely to be academically prepared for college because of the characteristics of the schools they tend to attend and because of such practices as curricular tracking and ability grouping. Together, the importance of academic preparation to college enrollment and the lower levels of access to rigorous preparation among groups of students who continue to be underrepresented in higher education create a critical opportunity for college preparation programs to address continued gaps in college enrollment rates.

Low-Income and Other Disadvantaged Groups Less Likely to Be Academically Prepared

Although data describing gaps in the level of academic preparation are available for only 6 of the 50 states, data reported in *Measuring Up 2000* suggest that the quality of academic preparation for college varies within a state, with African Americans and Hispanics being less likely than Whites to have access to high-quality academic preparation (National Center for Public Policy and Higher Education, 2000). For example, the percentage of high school students enrolled in upper-level mathematics and science courses is twice as high among Whites as Hispanics in Arkansas (67% versus 36%) and about twice as high among Whites as African Americans in Connecticut (78% versus 39% for math and 74% versus 42% for science; National Center for Public Policy and Higher Education, 2000).

Descriptive analyses of national data from the NELS:92/94 also show that a smaller share of Black and Hispanic high school graduates than of White and Asian high school graduates are academically prepared for college (Berkner & Chavez, 1997). Only about half of Black (47%) and Hispanic (53%) 1992 high school graduates were at least minimally qualified to attend a four-year college or university, compared with more than two thirds of Whites (68%) and Asians (73%). Other analyses show that, among first-time, first-year students attending four-year colleges and universities nationwide in 1995–1996, only 8% of Blacks had completed a rigorous curricular program during high school, compared with 16% of Hispanics, 20% of Whites, and 31% of Asians (Horn & Kojaku, 2001). Moreover, 42% of Blacks had completed no more than a core curriculum, defined as four years of English, three years of mathematics, three years of science, and three years of social studies, compared with 29% of Whites and 27% of Asians (Horn & Kojaku, 2001).

Academic preparation also varies by family income (Berkner & Chavez,

1997). Descriptive analyses of the NELS revealed that only 53% of 1992 high school graduates from families with low family incomes were at least minimally qualified to attend a four-year college or university compared with 86% of high school graduates from high-income families (Berkner & Chavez, 1997). Analyses of the Beginning Postsecondary Student survey (BPS:95/98) show that, among students who were enrolled at a four-year college or university in 1995–1996, only 15% of those from low-income families and 17% of students from middle-income families had completed a rigorous curricular program in high school, compared with 27% of those from high-income families (Horn & Kojaku, 2001).

Also using data from the NELS:88/94, Cabrera and La Nasa (2000b, 2001) concluded that only 29% of high school seniors in the lowest socioeconomic status quartile were at least minimally academically qualified to enroll in a four-year college or university, compared with 70% of students in the highest socioeconomic status quartile. After controlling for parental involvement and academic ability, students with the lowest socioeconomic status were 15% less likely than their upper-socioeconomic status peers to be at least minimally qualified to attend a four-year college (Cabrera & La Nasa, 2000a).

Other descriptive analyses suggest that parental education is related to the level of academic preparation. For example, the share of 1992 high school graduates who had taken algebra in the eighth grade and any advanced mathematics courses in high school was substantially smaller among potential first-generation college students than among students whose parents had completed college (14% versus 34% for algebra I, and 22% versus 61% for advanced math; Horn & Nuñez, 2000). Using data from the same database (NELS), Choy, Horn, Nuñez, and Chen (2000) found that, although completing rigorous mathematics coursework in high school was associated with a greater likelihood of four-year college enrollment, potential first-generation college students were less likely to take such courses than students whose parents had attended college. The percentage of first-time, first-year students attending four-year colleges and universities in 1995–1996 who had taken a rigorous curricular program during high school ranged from 9% among those whose parents had completed no more than high school to 25% for students whose parents had completed at least a bachelor's degree (Horn & Kojaku, 2001).

Educational expectations may also influence the level of academic preparation. Based on their review and synthesis of prior research, Cabrera and La Nasa (2000a, 2000d) concluded that planning to attend college early in the educational pipeline is positively related to being academically qualified to enroll in college. Using data from the NELS:88/94, Cabrera and La Nasa (2000a) found that the likelihood of being at least minimally academically prepared to attend a four-year college or university increased with the level of parental involvement in the child's education and the student's 1988 postsecondary educational plans. The probability of being at least minimally qualified to attend a four-year college or university was also lower for students who lived in single-parent families, had siblings who had dropped out of high school, had changed schools, had poor academic performance, and had repeated a grade (Cabrera & La Nasa, 2000a).

Low-Income and Other Disadvantaged Groups Attend Schools
With Less Rigorous Courses

One reason low-income, African American, Hispanic, and other groups of students are less likely to be adequately academically prepared for college relates to the types of schools these students tend to attend. The likelihood of participating in a rigorous curricular program appears to increase with the affluence of the student body at the school attended. Among students nationwide who successfully enrolled in a four-year college or university in 1995–1996, the share who had completed a rigorous curricular program during high school ranged from only 11% for those who graduated from high schools with the poorest students (i.e., at least 25% of the students were eligible for free or reduced-price lunches) to 27% for those who graduated from high schools with the richest students (i.e., fewer than 5% of the students were eligible for free or reduced-price lunches; Horn & Kojaku, 2001).

Participating in rigorous academic coursework in high school depends on the availability of such courses. Both original research (Oakes & Guiton, 1995) and syntheses of research (Gándara, 2002a) suggest that schools that are located in more, rather than less, affluent areas are characterized by the availability of more rigorous academic coursework. Schools with predominantly African American and Latino student bodies have also been found to offer fewer college preparation courses than other schools (Oakes & Guiton, 1995). In an exploratory examination of the relationship between social class and course offerings at six high schools, Spade, Columbda, and Vanfossen (1997) found that schools that were located in more affluent school districts offered higher numbers of advanced mathematics and science courses than schools that were located in working-class districts. Schools with above-average gains in students' mathematics and science test scores offered more advanced math and science courses than schools with average gains in student achievement even after controlling for the social class of the school (Spade et al., 1997). Schools with above-average gains in student achievement and schools in more affluent districts offered smaller numbers of non–college preparation courses in math and science than schools with average gains in student achievement and schools in less affluent districts (Spade et al., 1997).

While descriptive analyses suggest that course-taking patterns and course availability vary based on the demographic characteristics of the school and school curricular offerings, multivariate analyses suggest that neither the demographic composition of schools nor school curricular offerings are related to students' achievement test scores. In an examination of data from the 1980 sophomore cohort of the High School and Beyond longitudinal study, Gamoran (1987) found that, after controlling for student background characteristics and schooling effects, measures of school composition and measures of school offerings were largely unrelated to student achievement on each of six different achievement tests. School composition was measured by the mean achievement of students attending the school, the mean socioeconomic status of students attending the school, the percentage of Black students enrolled at the school, and the percentage of Hispanic students attending the school. School offerings included the share of students in an academic curricular track, the number of mathematics and science course offerings, and whether the school offered a program for gifted and talent students.

Other research suggests that a more important school-level predictor of academic preparation is the academic climate. Goddard, Sweetland, and Hoy (2000) found that the reading and mathematics test scores of fourth grade students varied across schools and that part of the variation was attributable to differences in the "academic emphasis" of schools. Academic emphasis was a factor composite measuring teachers' perceptions of the extent to which students respect others who earn high grades; students work to improve their performance; the learning environment is ordered; students are able to achieve academically; students complete their homework; and students seek extra help from teachers. The analyses also suggest that attending a school with an academic emphasis may be particularly effective in raising the achievement of lower-income and minority students (Goddard et al., 2000).

Low-Income and Other Disadvantaged Groups Are Less Likely to Be Placed in Rigorous Courses

A second reason why low-income, African American, Hispanic, and other groups of students are less likely to be adequately academically prepared for college is because these groups tend to be placed in lower curricular tracks and lower academic ability groupings. Although schools seem to be shifting from placement of students in particular curricular tracks (i.e., curricular tracking) to placement on a course-by-course basis (i.e., ability grouping; Lucas, 1999), both result in relatively homogeneous groupings of students (Yonezawa, Wells, & Serna, 2002). Proponents of curricular tracking and ability grouping assume that students learn more when they are grouped with students of comparable academic ability, thereby increasing aggregate levels of achievement (Gamoran, 1993; Gamoran, Porter, Smithson, & White, 1997). Opponents argue that, contrary to promoting educational opportunity for all students, tracking promotes educational inequality since research generally shows that students in upper-level classes learn more and students in lower-level classes learn less, thereby increasing achievement differences over time (Gamoran & Mare, 1989; Gamoran, 1992; Gamoran et al., 1997). Although ostensibly classifying students into various curricular tracks and ability groups based on academic ability and achievement, tracking serves to segregate students by both race and socioeconomic status, with minority and poor children concentrated in the lower tracks (Oakes, 1985, 1995; Gamoran et al., 1997; Yonezawa et al., 2002).

Both qualitative and quantitative studies show that students from lower-class families are disproportionately represented in nonacademic curricular tracks and ability groups. Among students who were in the ninth grade in fall 1965, Alexander and colleagues (1978) found that those with lower socioeconomic status were less likely than those with higher socioeconomic status to be enrolled in a college preparation track after controlling for other characteristics. About two thirds of the effect of socioeconomic status on track placement was exerted indirectly, through academic ability and achievement, educational goals, curriculum plans, and parental and peer social supports (Alexander et al., 1978). In a longitudinal study of 2,000 seventh grade students attending 17 public and private elementary and middle schools in two Midwestern cities, Hallinan (1996) showed that, after controlling for other variables, students with higher family incomes and higher parental education were more likely than other students to be in a mathematics course sequence that included algebra II and geometry. Using data from the High School and Beyond longitudinal study of 1980 high school sophomores, Gamoran and Mare (1989) found that the likelihood of being in a college preparation track increased with socioeconomic status after controlling for prior academic achievement, sociodemographic characteristics, and school characteristics. Moreover, Gamoran and Mare (1989) concluded that tracking contributed to the gaps in both 12th grade achievement and high school graduation rates between those with low and high socioeconomic status. Using the same database, Lucas (1999) concluded that students with lower socioeconomic status were less likely than students with middle- and upper socioeconomic status to be enrolled simultaneously in college preparatory mathematics and college preparatory English and that curricular tracking was more common at schools characterized by greater socioeconomic diversity among the student body.

Findings from research regarding racial/ethnic group differences in curricular track placement are mixed. Descriptive analyses show that, during the 1970s and early 1980s, African Americans and Hispanics were relatively overrepresented in "educable mentally retarded" classes and underrepresented in gifted and talented classes (England, Meier, & Fraga, 1988). African Americans were also overrepresented among students in "trainable mentally retarded," "specific learning disabled," and "seriously emotionally disturbed" classes. In contrast, multivariate analyses of data from the High School and Beyond longitudinal study of 1980 high school sophomores show that, while Hispanics were as likely as Whites to be in a college preparation track net of other variables, African Americans were more likely than Whites to be in a college preparation track (Gamoran & Mare, 1989; Lucas, 1999). Gamoran and Mare (1989) cautioned, however, that only a small share of African Americans was comparable to Whites in terms of all other variables in the model. Qualitative analyses typically show that African Americans and Hispanics are not only overrepresented in low-ability classes, but also less likely than their White counterparts to be placed in high-ability classes (Oakes, 1995).

As described by Tierney and Auerbach (chapter 2) and others (Oakes, 1995; Oakes & Guiton, 1995; Lucas, 1999; Yonezawa et al., 2002), one likely explanation for the concentration of African Americans, Hispanics, and students from lower-income families in nonacademic curricular tracks and low-ability classes is that their parents are less likely to know the ways in which parental input is considered in the placement process. Based on her examination of the use of tracking in two school systems, Oakes (1995) concluded that the criteria for placing students in a particular track are applied inconsistently, with parental requests having greater weight than other measures of student performance and ability, including achievement and teacher recommendations. Using data from the NELS:88/90, Stevenson and colleagues (1994) concluded that African American students and students with low family incomes were not only more likely to be initially placed in lower curricular tracks, but were also less likely to have parents who were able to work with school personnel to change the initial placement.

In an exploratory study of the process by which students were placed in courses at six high schools, Spade and colleagues (1997) found that course placement processes varied based on the social class of the district in which the school was located. The process included a more comprehensive and objective assessment of student abilities and more active input from teachers and guidance counselors at more affluent compared to less affluent schools and at schools with above-average gains in student math and science achievement compared to schools with only average achievement gains. In contrast, parents and students played the primary role in the course placement of students at working- and middle-class schools with average gains in student achievement (Spade et al., 1997). In their examination of the reasons why offering "freedom of choice" did not successfully "detrack" six high schools, Yonezawa and colleagues (2002) found that information about the open access policy was unevenly distributed across family income and racial/ethnic groups and that schools responded differently to placement requests. White, Asian, upper-income, high-achieving, and high-track students were more likely than African American, Latino, lower-income, lower-achieving, and lower-track students to have information about placement policies and were more likely to receive their requested placement.

Although the prevalence of grouping, and the effects of grouping on achievement, appear to be greater for mathematics than science (Hoffer, 1992), movement across tracks is generally limited (Oakes, 1985), particularly movement from a lower to a higher ability track or course (Oakes & Guiton, 1995; Lucas, 1999) and for students with lower family incomes (Hallinan, 1996). Teachers may be especially hesitant about moving students from a remedial class or other low ability track to a higher track (Oakes & Guiton, 1995). Hallinan (1996) found that students who received free- or reduced-price lunch were more likely than other students to move from a higher to a lower curricular track in English and that students with low socioeconomic status were more likely to drop out of an English or mathematics sequence.

The degree of mobility across curricular tracks appears to vary by academic subject (Hallinan, 1996; Stevenson et al., 1994; Lucas, 1999). Regardless, mobility across curricular tracks may be particularly important to academic preparation and achievement. Some research suggests that achievement gaps across curricular tracks are smaller at Catholic than public schools (Gamoran, 1992, 1993), possibly due to differences between Catholic and public schools in the structure of tracking. At Catholic schools, tracking is characterized by greater flexibility and by more frequent mobility between tracks (Gamoran, 1993).

Although an imperfect measure of academic preparation, as described above, curricular tracking negatively influences the academic preparation of students in low-ability groups. Opportunities to learn are smaller for students in lower compared to higher ability groups (Oakes, 1985, 1995; Hoffer, 1992), as reflected by their restricted access to knowledge, inferior instructional resources, and less qualified teachers (Oakes, 1994). Based on her examination of 297 mathematics and English classes, Oakes (1985) concluded that students in low-track math and English classes were exposed to less rigorous course content, were generally not expected to learn the types of skills required to succeed in college, spent less time on instructional activities in class, and were expected by their teachers to spend less time on their homework. An examination of tracking in two school districts revealed that, regardless of initial level of academic achievement, achievement gains were lower for students in low-ability classes than for students in high-ability classes (Oakes, 1995). These findings are confirmed in larger-scale quantitative analyses. Analyzing data from the Longitudinal Study of American Youth, Hoffer (1992) found that gains in mathematics and science test scores were higher for students in high-ability groups and lower for students in low-ability groups relative to their counterparts in nongrouped schools. The negative effect of low-ability grouping was larger in magnitude than the positive effect for high-ability grouping (Hoffer, 1992).

Despite the negative consequences of tracking on academic preparation and other outcomes, social, cultural, and political challenges limit the extent to which detracking or mixed ability grouping can be achieved (Oakes, 1994; Lucas, 1999; Oakes et al., 2002; Yonezawa et al., 2002). Lucas (1999) concluded that, although the end of formal tracking in 1975 resulted in substantial changes in course-taking patterns, placement in particular courses (e.g., college preparatory English) among students who were high school sophomores in 1980 was not completely explained by prior achievement in that academic area. Yonezawa and colleagues (2002) concluded that an open access policy did not detrack six high schools because the policy did not address institutional barriers, students' tracked aspirations, or students' need to learn in "safe spaces." For example, students in lower-ability classes were unlikely to choose to move to higher-track classes at least in part because their aspirations had been "leveled"; because of past low-ability placements these students identified themselves as being "low track" (Yonezawa et al., 2002). Enhancing the caliber of the low-track curriculum is also unlikely to be effective because students in lower ability groups will continue to understand that they are segregated to a lower level (Oakes, 1994).

Some efforts are being made to identify viable alternatives to curricular tracking and thus improve the academic preparation of students in lower ability groups, a disproportionate share of whom are students with lower family incomes, African Americans, and Hispanics. "Transition" courses, such as those adopted in California and New York, may be one type of bridge to college preparation courses for lower-achieving students. Nonetheless, research suggests that such courses are only moderately effective in promoting mathematics preparation and achievement among lower-achieving students (White, Gamoran, Smithson, & Porter, 1996). After controlling for sex, race/ethnicity, and final math grades during the previous academic year, the growth in math achievement was comparable for students in the transition courses, college preparation tracks, and general curricular tracks. But while students participating in the transition courses completed more college-preparation mathematics during subsequent years of high school than students in general curricular tracks (White et al., 1996; Gamoran et al., 1997), a smaller share of students in transition courses than of students in regular college preparation courses completed two or more years of college preparatory math (Gamoran et al., 1997).

IMPLICATIONS FOR COLLEGE PREPARATION PROGRAMS

This literature review shows that rigorous academic preparation is required to enroll in higher education and that access to high-quality academic preparation is uneven. The groups of students that continue to be less likely to enroll in and graduate from college are also the groups that are less likely to be adequately academically prepared: namely, individuals with low family incomes, African Americans, and Hispanics. Moreover, curricular tracking and ability grouping, practices that disproportionately disadvantage low-income, African American, and Hispanic students, persist despite the documented negative consequences of these practices. Therefore, as others have concluded based on their own research (e.g., St. John, 1991; Cabrera & La Nasa, 2000a) and their reviews and syntheses of other research (e.g., Choy et al., 2000; Oakes et al., 2002), efforts to increase college enrollment rates must focus on raising the level of academic preparation of groups of students that have lower levels of academic preparation, that is, the groups that continue to be less likely to enroll in higher education.

Although the elimination of curricular tracking and ability grouping in the nation's schools may not be feasible, and such alternatives as transition courses are still being developed, one seemingly possible and essential school-level systemic reform is to eliminate general, non–college preparation mathematics courses at all schools (White et al., 1996). Research shows that lower-level mathematics courses are a dead end, in that they are unlikely to lead to enrollment in college preparation mathematics courses (White et al., 1996). School-level systemic reform should also focus on ensuring the availability of well-qualified teachers who engage students in learning, addressing the finding from prior research that low-ability classes are characterized by lower-quality instruction (Gamoran, 1993).

Nonetheless, school-level systemic reforms are unlikely to eliminate the negative consequences of ability grouping. As Oakes and colleagues (2002) argued, efforts to increase the resources that are devoted to underachieving groups, thereby equalizing educational opportunities across groups, are likely to be met by actions that serve to maintain class distinctions. Specifically, middle- and upper-income parents (i.e., those whose children are overrepresented in high-ability groups) are likely to respond to such initiatives by securing additional resources that benefit their children and by identifying ways to raise standards, thereby maintaining class stratification (Lucas, 1999; Oakes et al., 2002). Whereas schools with predominantly middle- and upper-class student bodies will likely embrace efforts to raise standards, schools with more socioeconomically diverse student bodies are likely to respond, as they have in the past, with initiatives that maintain class distinctions among students (Lucas, 1999). As long as college admissions is a competitive process, students in high-ability groups (and their parents) will feel entitled to, and consequently will likely work to maintain, their status at the top of the academic hierarchy (Yonezawa et al., 2002).

In the context of such barriers to school-level systemic reform, college preparation programs offer a promising approach to raising the level of academic preparation, and thus the college enrollment rates, of groups that continue to be underrepresented in higher education. Academic preparation is a central component of many existing college preparation programs (Jun & Tierney, 1999; Tierney & Jun, 2001; Perna & Swail, 2001). College preparation programs may address the role of academic preparation and achievement in the college enrollment process through such components as preparatory, supplemental, accelerated, and college-level academic courses, summer bridge programs, tutoring and remediation in high school courses, and activities designed to develop study and test-taking skills (Chaney et al., 1995; Swail & Perna, 2000; Gándara, 2002a). To address the inadequacy of academic and college counseling in the schools that is described by McDonough (chapter 4), college preparation programs may provide academic and career counseling to ensure that students are aware of their options and make appropriate curricular choices during high school. Some programs may stimulate higher levels of academic achievement by requiring a minimum level of academic performance in order to receive financial assistance (Perna, 1999).

Nonetheless, although much more needs to be learned about the effectiveness of particular components of college preparation programs (Gándara, 2002a; Tierney, 2002), descriptive analyses suggest that the majority of programs do not focus enough attention on improving the academic preparation of participants (Laguardia, 1998; Perna, 2002). Only two thirds of the administrators of 16 partnerships between K–12 schools, community colleges, and four-year colleges that had among their stated goals to improve the academic performance of students and improve the college entry rates of minority and disadvantaged students reported that their program adequately improved the academic preparation of minority high school students (Laguardia, 1998). Although the extent to which college preparation programs may directly influence curricular or course placement in a school may be limited, Perna (2002) found that encouraging students to take rigorous coursework is among the least frequently reported goals of college preparation programs that are targeted to low-income students and historically underrepresented minority students.

By focusing on improving academic preparation, college preparation programs will not only increase the likelihood of college enrollment of disadvantaged groups of students, but also generate other desirable outcomes including higher high school graduation rates (Cabrera & La Nasa, 2000b), higher college entrance examination scores (Horn & Kojaku, 2001), higher representation at more selective colleges and universities (Horn & Kojaku, 2001), higher rates of transfer from a two-year to a four-year institution (Cabrera et al., 2001), greater progress toward earning a bachelor's degree by age 30 (Adelman, 2002), higher college persistence rates (Horn & Kojaku, 2001), and higher college completion rates (Cabrera & La Nasa, 2000b; Cabrera et al., 2001). Cabrera and La Nasa (2000b) found that, when high school students are at least minimally qualified to attend a four-year college or university, high school graduation rates are unrelated to socioeconomic status. Analyses of data from the 1995–1996 Beginning Postsecondary Student Survey suggest that students who have taken a rigorous program of coursework during high school are more likely to be continuously enrolled within a three-year period either at the college or university of initial enrollment or at any four-year institution after controlling for demographic characteristics, college entrance examination scores, and college experiences (Horn & Kojaku, 2001). A rigorous program of academic coursework in high school (at least four years of English, three years of foreign language, three years of social studies, four years of mathematics including precalculus, three years of science including biology, chemistry, and physics, and at least one honors or advanced placement course) also appears to increase the likelihood of college persistence indirectly, as students with a rigorous high school curriculum transfer less frequently to another college or university, attend more selective four-year colleges and universities, and have higher grade point averages during the first year of college (Horn & Kojaku, 2001). Completing a rigorous curricular program during high school appears to be a more important predictor of college persistence than test scores (Horn & Kojaku, 2001), particularly for African American and Latino students (Adelman, 1999). After identifying nine different pathways to a bachelor's degree, Cabrera and colleagues (2001) concluded that the most certain route is becoming highly academically prepared and enrolling in a four-year college or university immediately after graduating from high school.

The research described in this chapter suggests that, in order to raise college enrollment rates of traditionally underrepresented groups, college preparation programs must meet a need that is not being fulfilled by the nation's elementary and secondary school systems and focus on ensuring that all students are adequately academically prepared to enroll in and succeed in college. To achieve this goal, college preparation programs must (1) ensure rigorous academic preparation; (2) begin efforts to improve academic preparation before students enter high school; (3) deliver academic preparation activities in culturally appropriate ways; and (4) coordinate with K–12 and college educators.

Ensure Rigorous Academic Preparation

Most important, to ensure that students are academically qualified to enroll in college, college preparation programs must improve the academic preparation of low-income, African American, Hispanic, and other disadvantaged groups of students. Although such services as tutoring, admissions test preparation, academic assistance, academic counseling, and instruction in note taking and study skills may be beneficial components of student-centered academic development programs, these activities should be used only to support successful completion of high-quality, rigorous academic coursework. Based on their analyses of the effectiveness of three college preparation programs in California, Hagedorn and Fogel (2002) found that enrollment in advanced academic coursework (e.g., algebra, geometry, biology, chemistry, foreign languages, advanced placement, honors classes) was the single most important predictor of college enrollment after controlling for grades, time spent studying, academic self-efficacy, goal orientation, ego anxiety, and participation in a college preparation program.

By focusing on improving the level of academic preparation of low-income and other disadvantaged groups of students, college preparation programs move beyond the traditional emphasis of econometric models on the costs and benefits of college enrollment to recognize the importance of academic preparation, that is, the initial level of human capital. By emphasizing high levels of academic preparation, college preparation programs may also shape an individual's habitus by creating an expectation for college enrollment.

Begin Efforts to Improve Academic Preparation Before
Students Enter High School

Second, as noted by Bonous-Hammarth and Allen (chapter 8), to most effectively ensure adequate academic preparation, college preparation programs should initiate efforts to improve academic preparation prior to high school. Observers (e.g., Gándara, 2002a; Levine & Nidiffer, 1996; Swail & Perna, 2002) have concluded that the most effective college preparation program strategies are those that focus on long-term student involvement. Based on their review and synthesis of prior research, Cabrera and La Nasa (2000b, 2001) concluded that the process of becoming academically qualified to enroll in college begins as early as the eighth grade. Therefore, college preparation programs should begin to work with students during middle school and junior high school to ensure that students and their parents are informed about the academic requirements for college and the sequencing of the college preparation curriculum (Cabrera & La Nasa, 2000d; Perna, 2002). By beginning early, college preparation programs will likely not only improve academic preparation but also raise educational expectations, another predictor of both academic preparation and college enrollment (Cabrera & La Nasa, 2000a, 2000d).

Perhaps because of limited resources, only about one third of college preparation programs that are targeted at low-income students, historically underrepresented minorities, and potential first-generation college students currently begin working with students prior to the eighth grade (Perna, 2002). Research shows the benefits of promoting high-quality academic preparation prior to the high school years. Specifically, students are more likely to take advanced mathematics courses in high school, an important predictor of college enrollment, when they have taken algebra in the eighth grade regardless of parents' level of education or math proficiency (Horn & Nuñez, 2000; Choy et al., 2000; Stevenson et al., 1994).

Deliver Academic Preparation Activities in Culturally Appropriate Ways

Third, as concluded by Villalpando and Solorzano (chapter 1), to most effectively promote high-quality academic preparation, college preparation programs should deliver academic preparation activities in ways that recognize the context of students' families and neighborhoods and that affirm students' cultural integrity (Ascher, 1985; Tierney & Jun, 2001; Gándara, 2002a). This recommendation addresses a limitation of status attainment models as described by Stanton-Salazar (1997). According to Stanton-Salazar (1997), working-class minority students are challenged to cope with multiple and disparate worlds. In order to gain access to key resources and opportunities, they must learn to "decode the system" that has been established by the dominant group and establish relationships with key institutional agents.

From her review of prior research, Ascher (1985) noted that, compared with Whites, Hispanic high school seniors are likely to have greater financial concerns, more extensive family responsibilities, and less support for their education from their parents. Yonezawa and colleagues (2002) concluded that efforts to detrack six high schools were unsuccessful, at least in part, because they failed to address students' need to learn in safe spaces, or spaces in which lower-income, African American, and Latino students would not only have supportive peer networks, but would also have teachers and peers who respected and valued their knowledge, perspectives, experiences, and culture. Based on their evaluation of one college preparation program, Tierney and Jun (2001) concluded that, although the central program activities focused on academic preparation in such areas as mathematics, English, and computer literacy, along with study skills, the program was successful because of the ways in which the program affirmed the identities of the participants. The program, which served primarily African American and Hispanic first-generation citizens or immigrants in Los Angeles, sought to link program experiences with students' lives by developing relationships with students' parents and neighborhoods (Jun & Tierney, 1999; Tierney & Jun, 2001). College preparation programs should consider the ways in which academic preparation can be provided to students to build on the cultural wealth or the assets and resources that participants possess (chapter 1).

Coordinate With K–12 and College Educators

Finally, as recommended by Gándara (2002a), administrators of college preparation programs should coordinate with both K–12 and college educators to ensure not only that the type of academic preparation that is needed to gain access to college is what is provided, but also that the systemic changes that will ultimately eliminate the need for college preparation programs are identified and achieved. College preparation programs should also share expertise and resources with other educators, particularly with regard to the effectiveness of various strategies (Weinstein, 1996). Greater collaboration may promote the development of alternative methods of demonstrating the potential to succeed in college, and ultimately yield the type of reconsideration of the definition of merit for which Oakes and colleagues (2002) call. Oakes and colleagues (2002) concluded that continued reliance on traditional indicators of merit, namely test scores and grades, will continue to limit access to postsecondary educational opportunity for certain groups and that only by engaging in the politically difficult task of reconceptualizing merit will equal access to college be ensured.

CONCLUSION

This chapter is not meant to diminish the importance of other efforts that are designed to increase college access for traditionally underrepresented groups, particularly federal and state-sponsored student financial aid programs, but to highlight the critical importance of academic preparation to the process of enrolling in college. While necessary, high-quality academic preparation is not sufficient to ensure college enrollment. Berkner and Chavez (1997) showed that, although the majority of students who were academically qualified to attend a four-year college enrolled in a four-year institution within two years of graduating from high school, four-year enrollment rates were lower among academically qualified students from low-income families than high-income families (52% versus 83%).

The negative effect of lower family incomes on the likelihood of enrolling in college appears to be greater for students with lower levels of academic preparation. Kane (1999) showed that the difference in the likelihood of enrolling in some type of postsecondary education within two years of graduating from high school between students in the lowest and highest family income quartiles was 12 percentage points for those with mathematics test scores in the highest quartile but 18 percentage points for those with mathematics test scores in the lowest quartile after controlling for parents' education and racial/ethnic group. Among students attending similar high schools and with similar class ranks, the income gap in postsecondary enrollment rates was larger for those with class ranks in the lower half than for those in the upper half of the distribution. After controlling for mathematics and reading test scores, parents' education, and racial/ethnic group, the gap in postsecondary enrollment rates between those in the lowest and the highest family income quintile was 17 percentage points for those with class ranks in the bottom half of the distribution and 12 percentage points for those with class ranks in the top half of the distribution (Kane, 1999).

Therefore, the federal and state government-sponsored student aid programs that Swail describes (chapter 9) must continue to provide need-based financial aid to ensure that a lack of financial resources does not limit the ability of low-income but academically qualified individuals from enrolling in a four-year college or university and persisting to degree completion. Nonetheless, as others (Gladieux & Swail, 1999) have noted, financial aid is not enough to ensure equal postsecondary educational opportunity, particularly since not all individuals are equally likely to be academically qualified to attend a four-year college or university. Therefore, policy interventions designed to increase college enrollment must address not only inadequate financial resources, but also inadequate academic preparation. Federal and state-sponsored student financial aid programs are useful only to those who are academically qualified to enroll and succeed in college.

College preparation programs can play a critical role in increasing the postsecondary enrollment rates of groups of students that have been historically underrepresented in higher education by recognizing that rigorous academic preparation is required to enroll in college, that the groups of students who are underrepresented in higher education are the same groups who are less likely to be academically prepared for college, and that institutional and structural barriers limit the extent to which schools can address differences in academic preparation across groups. Only by focusing on ensuring high levels of academic preparation will college preparation programs effectively reduce the continued income and racial/ethnic group gaps in college enrollment and degree completion.

JAMES C. HEARN
JANET M. HOLDSWORTH

Chapter Seven

Cocurricular Activities and Students' College Prospects: Is There a Connection?

Some factors' effects on college attendance are rather straightforward. For example, it is no surprise that students' academic experiences in high school relate closely to their eventual college attendance plans and outcomes (see chapter 6). But what about activities that on the surface would be considered nonacademic, or at least largely irrelevant to academic outcomes? Interestingly, substantial research suggests that participation in certain voluntary nonschooling activities, such as student government or athletic teams, can positively affect high school students' academic attitudes and accomplishments and therefore, indirectly, their prospects for enrollment in a college or university.[1] Evidence is less clear, however, about the role of other nonschooling activities. Because participation outcomes are increasingly important for improving college readiness from both an individual and societal perspective, it is also important that analysts address the relative lack of knowledge about the nature and extent of nonschooling activities' effects on attendance.

Of particular interest for this chapter are the various cocurricular activities taking place in programs directed toward fostering college attendance. Youth in college preparatory programs tend to be from socially and economi-

The authors gratefully acknowledge the helpful comments of Julia Colyar, Cynthia Hudley, Bill Tierney, and authors of other chapters in this volume. For all communications, please contact the first author.

cally disadvantaged backgrounds, and thus tend to be among those most likely to forego postsecondary attendance and its lifespan benefits (Gándara & Bial, 2001). Can the cocurricular activities embedded in college preparatory programs significantly offset students' initial disadvantages in college prospects? For example, what advantages might accrue from programs' commitments to sports, games, physical exercise, and various team-building exercises? Similarly, what is to be gained from structured field trips to local museums, cultural events, and colleges?

This chapter was undertaken to provide answers to those specific questions. The directly relevant evidence, however, is sparse. For that reason, the chapter examines the evidence on the effects of high school students' cocurricular and social activities in general, with the intent of inferring some implications for the effects of cocurricular activities in college preparatory programs. Included in the broad array of activities considered here are on-campus activities outside regular school hours and activities taking place in the larger community. Are such activities irrelevant, or do they in fact shape students' likelihood of entering a college or university? And for our purposes here, what do the effects of such activities suggest about the potential effects of cocurricular efforts in college preparatory programs? Addressing those questions is at the heart of this chapter.

The chapter is structured in three parts. First, we develop a conceptual framework for the wide range of social activities in high school students' lives, taking into consideration how various aspects of the framework might affect postsecondary participation. Next, we review the literature on the attendance effects of formal, school-based cocurricular activities, formal cocurricular activities in community-based college preparatory programs, and other formal and informal community-based activities. We conclude the chapter with some implications of the review for practice and for further research.

CONCEPTUALIZING THE ROLE OF COCURRICULAR ACTIVITIES IN POSTSECONDARY PARTICIPATION

The primacy of grades, test scores, and high school curricula in college attendance has been well established by decades of educational attainment research in sociology and economics (e.g., see Sewell, 1971; chapter 6, this volume). Yet schools do not operate outside the unequal distribution of social and cultural capital valued in the society. Values, norms, and access to sociocultural and educational resources vary across socioeconomic statuses in the society, and these differences help shape students' academic performance (see Bourdieu, 1977; chapter 4, this volume). As this volume suggests, a focus on academic performance alone oversimplifies the college attendance process. Similarly, a focus on socioeconomic factors alone does not fully explain attendance. Socioeconomic factors influence academic performance and also exhibit direct effects on attendance, but much of the variation in college attendance remains unexplained by simple statistical models containing only academic and socioeconomic indicators. In fact, a complex web of interrelated influences permeates the lives and decisions of high school students, and the workings of those influences are inadequately understood.

With that in mind, analysts have increasingly begun to examine the possible role of nonschooling experiences in enrollment. Some have found the evidence for such influences extraordinarily compelling. For example, Swail (2000) has noted that, "although public education is a significant component of the learning and maturation process, what happens outside of school is where the real learning takes place. What happens during non-school time is key to the aspirations and motivations of our youth" (p. 86). Not every observer attributes such power to the role of nonschooling factors, but these factors merit serious attention by those concerned over postsecondary enrollments. Among the nonschooling factors researchers have begun to consider in recent years are having a sibling in college, parental involvement in school-related activities, the availability of learning-related resources in the home, and the nature of peer-group influence (McDonough, 1997; Horn, 1997; Brown & Theobald, 1998; Cabrera & La Nasa, 2000a, b, d; Krei & Rosenblaum, 2001; Terenzini, Cabrera, & Bernal, 2001; chapters 2 and 3, this volume).

Of greater relevance for this chapter is another nonschooling factor: the social activities of high school students. In its most basic form, social activity occurs when two or more people get together for a purpose.[2] Social activity can range along a continuum from the most informal interactions (e.g., gathering with friends to watch a movie or "hang out") to the most formal and structured (e.g., participating in school-sponsored cocurricular activities). Students engage in activities such as high school sports and special interest clubs for both intrinsic and extrinsic reasons. Often, the rationale for participation boils down to the simple appeal of doing something fun after the school day ends.

Regardless of the motivation, involvement in these activities may play a role in whether and where students attend postsecondary institutions. Because U.S. high schools are so similar in curricular and structural characteristics, students and the colleges that evaluate them for admissions value individual differentiation and cultivation of individual talents and interests. Thus, social activities of various kinds may not only help shape students' attitudes toward further education but may also shape their attractiveness to institutions where they apply. Unfortunately, little is known about how different kinds of social involvement might influence students' choices and opportunities across types and selectivity levels of higher education institutions.

To redress that problem, a framework for considering potential influences of social activities may be useful. Such activities vary in levels of personal interdependency (highly individualized activities versus activities requiring significant collaboration among group members), organizational structure (formal or informal), and location (school based or community based).[3] Using these three dimensions, Table 7.1 presents a typology of high-school social activities potentially influencing eventual postsecondary enrollments.

Among the most familiar and most studied social activities are extracurricular high school sports. The media and popular culture pay significant attention to, and place significant value on, students' participation and achievement in interscholastic athletics. In the terms of Table 7.1, such activities exhibit high interdependency, take place within a formal structure, and are school based. Social offerings in the form of cocurricular activities provided through community-based organizations serve as additional learning contexts for students outside of school day hours. These social activities, formal or informal in nature, can influence students' school achievement, socialization, and broader personal and social development (Brown & Theobald, 1998). Other social activities are less publicly visible, but are potentially quite important for further educational opportunities, especially when the activities focus directly on the goal of fostering college attendance. Notably, college preparation programs are devoted directly to that goal and pursue it in a variety of ways (i.e., with high or low interdependency, under formal or informal structure, and in school or community sites).

As Table 7.1 suggests, the range of social activities potentially affecting college-going plans and behaviors is broad and diverse. It follows that the causal mechanisms for such influences are most likely broad and diverse, as well. The purpose of this chapter is to review the evidence on the effects of high school students' involvement in various kinds of cocurricular activities on their prospects for college attendance, with particular attention to implications for college preparatory programs. We therefore do not consider here the ways young people involve themselves informally and independently (e.g., meeting at a recreation center for pickup basketball or skateboarding, participating in a car or book club, obtaining individual academic counseling, and so forth). We do consider formalized social activities taking place as part of a school's extracurricular activities, a community-based youth program, or a college preparatory program. Because the literature is inconsistent in its operationalization of the terms "cocurricular," "extracurricular," and "social" activities, we use "cocurricular" here as an umbrella term encompassing all but those activities in Table 7.1 that are informal with low levels of interdependency.

Clearly, high school students' wide-ranging cocurricular activities are rather difficult subjects for analysis. One might even be tempted to ask, "Why bother?" After all, the nature of these activities is highly differentiated. What is more, the organizational structures and processes involved vary notably across

TABLE 7.1.
A Typology of Social Activities Among High School Students

	School Based		Community Based	
Interdependency	*Formal Structure*	*Informal Structure*	*Formal Structure*	*Informal Structure*
High	Student government Football, basketball, softball Choir/band Drama School-based college preparation program with cohort focus	Club sports Latino/a club Multiplayer computer games over school networks Intramurals	Boy and Girl Scouts, 4-H, Big Brothers/ Big Sisters, Boys' and Girls' Clubs Youth group at church, synagogue, or mosque Community-based college preparation program with cohort focus	Multiperson activities (e.g., team sports) at neighborhood or religious center
Low	National Honor Society Debate School-based college preparation program with individualized focus	Individualized college counseling Car club	Community-based college preparation program with individualized focus	Spontaneous play at community recreation center Book club Skateboard areas/parks

localities, as do participation patterns and levels. In this light, prospects seem dim for unearthing influences on college enrollment anywhere near as powerful and verifiable as those of socioeconomic and academic factors. Still, it is important to bear in mind that, even after years of research, we lack sufficient evidence on the actual mechanics of the undeniably fundamental influences of socioeconomic and academic factors. We especially lack sufficient evidence on policy-manipulatable factors encouraging college participation. That is, we lack information needed to shape effective public and private investment in educational equity. It seems logical to suggest that nonacademic activities may be intertwined in significant ways with the influences of socioeconomic and academic factors. Exploring the effects of cocurricular activities and their connections to students' family, school, peer, and community contexts may contribute to the design of potentially effective approaches to encouraging postsecondary attendance.

REVIEW OF THE LITERATURE

The existing research regarding the relationship between high school students' participation in specific cocurricular activities and postsecondary attendance is relatively sparse, is mainly focused on the effects of involvement in formal, school-based activities such as interscholastic athletics, is too often based in flawed research designs, and (perhaps as a consequence) is less than ideally consistent. In a comprehensive review published in 1988, Brown found serious deficiencies in the then-existing research on the effects of formal high school extracurricular programs. Although research in that area is perhaps the most developed of all the areas covered in Table 7.1, Brown concluded that "studies of extracurricular participation in secondary school have been surprisingly bereft of a conceptual framework, rife with methodological problems, and prone to include overstatements or 'overinterpretations' of findings" (p. 107).

Our review suggests that Brown's conclusions still ring true. Researchers have failed thus far to uncover strong, direct causal links between social activities and college attendance, although the hypothesis of a positive relationship between the two seems quite sensible. Nevertheless, in the past 15 years more sophisticated and convincing research has been conducted, and the literature continues to grow (e.g., see Broh, 2002; Guest & Schneider, 2003). This newer research tradition suggests that the effects of cocurricular activities on students' attainments are significant but indirect rather than direct. In the following pages, we review findings from more recent research studies on these kinds of social activities.

We organize the literature review in three sections: formal school-based cocurricular activities, formal cocurricular activities in community-based college preparation programs, and other formal and informal community-based social activities. Under this framework, we explore what the literature suggests concerning the effects of potential college enrollment and students' participation in these kinds of cocurricular activities.

Formal School-Based Cocurricular Activities

Most of what we know about students' social activities and the effects of those involvements comes from research on their involvement in formal school-based cocurricular activities. The focus of these activities varies in level of interdependency (e.g., chess club members must perform largely individually in competition, while members of the student government must collaborate on student issues and policies). Regardless of the level of interdependency, formal cocurricular activities provide forums for students to interact socially with peers sharing similar interests as well as with adults serving as supervisors and perhaps mentors. Conceptually, traditional high school extracurricular activities would seem likely to have indirect rather than direct effects on students' college prospects, through such mechanisms as shaping youths' self-concepts and providing venues for accomplishment.

Specifically, despite the controversial evolution of the extracurriculum over the past 50 years toward a more competitive and expertise-driven model, analysts have noted numerous academic benefits potentially deriving from participation in formal cocurricular school-based activities in contemporary high schools (Brown & Theobald, 1998). Among those potential benefits are higher academic achievement, development of social skills, increased levels of career aspirations and educational attainment, decreased likelihood of high school dropout, greater feelings of self-efficacy, and higher self-esteem (Hanks & Eckland, 1976; Lindsay, 1984; Camp, 1990; Holland & Andre, 1991; Marsh, 1992; McNeal, 1995; Gerber, 1996; Mahoney & Cairns, 1997; McNeal, 1998; Brown & Theobald, 1998; Guest & Schneider, 2003). Viewed as a whole, research on the effects of formal high school extracurricular activities in general suggests positive effects of various activities on academically related outcomes, and those academic characteristics have in turn been shown to affect college prospects.

There are some inconsistencies in these results, however, suggesting that the positive effects of activities are contingent on the nature of the activities and students involved (Marsh, 1993; Lisella & Serwatka, 1996). Melnick, Sabo, and Vanfossen (1992) and Eitle and Eitle (2002), for example, provide convincing evidence that not all racial or ethnic groups reap the same benefits from sports participation, and that benefits may be different for different kinds of students and different kinds of sports. More recent work by Guest and Schneider (2003) extends that conclusion to different kinds of schools and communities as well.

A number of studies suggest that sports and other extracurricular activities can raise students' commitment to their school and thus promote continuing enrollment. These findings contradict the views of critics who have long suggested that participation in high school sports may have a zero-sum effect on academic achievement: the time a student spends participating in school sports may represent time and energy taken away from his or her academic work, to detrimental effect. An examination of the national High School and Beyond data by Marsh (1993) suggests, however, that the hypothesis does not hold: he found significant, positive effects associated with athletic involvement in the last two years of high school. Similar results were found by Mahoney and Cairns (1997): in their study, involvement in formal school-based cocurricular activities was found to be linked to a decreasing rate of dropout for high-risk boys and girls because "participation provides an opportunity to create a positive and voluntary connection to the educational institution" (p. 248).

More recent and ambitious analyses featuring multivariate modeling and national databases refine and qualify these earlier findings in important ways. In an analysis of high school academic achievement, Broh (2002) found that participation in certain formal school-based cocurricular activities (notably interscholastic sports and student council, plus to a lesser extent music, journalism, and drama) improves achievement on various college-related indicators like grades and test scores. Broh's results suggest, however, that participation in other activities (notably vocational clubs and intramural sports) diminishes achievement on those indicators. Guest and Schneider (2003) found that nonsports extracurricular activities produced positive effects on grades across different school and community settings, while the effects of sports participation varied by the extent to which a student, school, and community valued an athletic identity among students. That is, sports participants who identified themselves as athletes in social contexts valuing that identity received especially positive grading benefits from their sports participation. Although the data sets employed in these two studies allowed no opportunity to assess cocurricular activities' effects on longer-term educational attainment, including college enrollment, it is logical to posit a benefit in college attendance as an indirect consequence of the improved academic performance.

Some studies have moved toward investigating that hypothesis, linking cocurricular activities to postsecondary aspirations and expectations, if not actual attendance. Brown, Kohrs, and Lazarro (1991) found that 42% of students in their representative sample were involved in at least one extracurricular activity and that those involved had higher levels of educational expectations and aspirations than their nonparticipating peers. These expectation and aspiration levels increased with a greater rate of involvement and involvement in a diverse array of activities, especially among Whites and females. Guest and Schneider (2003) found that nonsports extracurricular activity was associated with higher educational expectations across a wide range of school and community contexts, while athletic participation's positive effects on expectations were more notable among students identifying themselves as athletes and attending school in a context favoring athletic identities among students.

Studies that statistically associate high school students' activities with their educational aspirations and expectations are valuable, but multivariate modeling focused on students' actual postsecondary attendance is especially informative. Using a multivariate model, Snyder and Spreitzer (1990) found positive attainment effects of formal, school-based cocurricular participation. These analysts used the national High School and Beyond data set from the 1980s to examine whether athletics involvement related to male high school students' college attendance patterns, with special attention to the potentially related factors of race/ethnicity, strength of parental relations, and cognitive development. Overall, the results suggest that student athletes attended college at higher rates than their nonparticipating peers. Interestingly, sports participation had more positive effects among students exhibiting lower levels of cognitive development. The only exception to these patterns was for Hispanics from higher-SES backgrounds, good parental relations, and higher cognitive development: these athletes were less likely to attend college compared to their Hispanic peers who were not involved in sports.

Horn (1997) examined college attendance patterns in conjunction with a somewhat wider range of cocurricular activities than those considered by Snyder and Spreitzer. Her multivariate analysis of national data related to high school students' involvement in traditional extracurricular activities suggested that involvement in "two or more extracurricular activities increased the odds of enrolling in any postsecondary education by about 59 percent over not participating in any activities" (p. 13). Interestingly, Horn found that if moderate-to high-risk students were involved in two or more activities, they were two times as likely to enroll in a four-year institution.

One study addressed the activities/enrollment question over a longer term than earlier studies. Shieh (2002) used logistic regression modeling (controlling for race, gender, SES, and standardized test scores) on data from the National Education Longitudinal Study (NELS) of the eighth graders of 1988 to explore the relationship between extracurricular participation and the eventual attainment of a four-year college degree. The results suggest empirical benefits of both athletic and nonathletic extracurricular activities. Of particular interest is Shieh's finding that students participating in athletic activities were two times more likely than their nonparticipating peers to obtain a four-year college degree or a higher degree within 10 years of high school graduation.

Assuming the positive results of cocurricular involvement, the challenge may be in finding ways to engage high-risk students, including those in college preparatory programs, to participate in formal cocurricular activities. The question of equitable access to relevant, varied and quality cocurricular activities looms large. Holland and Andre (1991) have noted, "Students with higher ability, or more encouraging families, or more desirable social/personal characteristics may select themselves into activities" (p. 7). Shieh (2002, p. 6), in the course of discussing his positive findings for cocurricular activities, notes:

> Despite availability of activities offered by schools, students from low SES backgrounds participated less than their counterparts from high SES backgrounds, and low achievement students participated less than did high achievement students. This participation gap may be a cause for concern, in particular if extracurricular activities can be a means of bringing those students more into school engagement and increasing their chance of future school success . . . those activity programs may

foster important personal, interpersonal, and intellectual skills in students that can help them remain in school and successfully advance in postsecondary educational studies.

This participation gap may be particularly significant regarding involvement in interscholastic athletics. Although Fejgin's (1994) analysis of longitudinal data from a nationally representative sample of high school sophomores suggested positive effect of sports participation on grades, self-concept, internal locus of control, and educational aspirations, the data shows there is an unequal distribution of sports participation by socioeconomic status and gender. The students most likely to participate in school-sponsored sports programs are males from high-SES backgrounds and individuals attending private and/or smaller schools.

In a similar vein, McNeal (1998) explores the question of equity in access to participation in traditional, formal school-sponsored cocurricular activities. Proposing a status-based continuum of activities ranging from interscholastic athletics (higher status) to vocationally related clubs (lower status), he notes that students tend to be sorted along the continuum based on their socioeconomic backgrounds. Perhaps this sorting is purely a matter of individual choice, he notes, but it may be that teachers formally or informally shape students' access to certain activities:

> The popular conception is that the extracurriculum is unique in comparison with other facets of school because participation is voluntary. The notion that participation in extracurricular activities is voluntary and open to all is based on the rule that participation is generally not governed by administrative allocation procedures (as is academic track) or by explicit teacher actions (as are language skills and teacher attention). However, recent empirical evidence indicates that teachers, peers, and performance criteria may systematically select students into these activities, and participation may not be as voluntary or open as previously believed. (McNeal, 1998, p. 184)

The selection patterns noted by Holland and Andre, by Fejgin, and by McNeal pose difficulties for researchers. For example, research conducted specifically on interscholastic athletics has produced mixed results regarding whether or not student involvement in sports positively influences student academic achievement or simply correlates with achievement because of preexisting differences between participants and nonparticipants (Eitle & Eitle, 2002). Eitle and Eitle (2002) suggest that whether there are indeed causal connections between athletics participation and college attendance remains a question for further work.

More broadly speaking, establishing why certain students do or do not participate in cocurricular activities, and how students from different backgrounds can benefit from participation, is important but analytically challenging. From the research protocols and designs employed thus far in the field, it is unclear whether it is the cocurricular activities themselves or something predisposing students to participate in them that accounts for any positive outcomes uncovered.

McNeal (1998) and, in earlier work, Fejgin (1994) have found that students' access to sports teams differs in an important way from access to other cocurricular activities in school, such as yearbook/newspaper and student government-related activities. Students' access to the latter activities appears to be more open than their access to sports activities. Specifically, students who are not involved in sports before high school appear to have limited opportunities to participate in sports activities once they enter high school. In contrast, those who were able to be involved in formal sports activities through clubs and association before high school are more likely to be involved in such activities in high school.

These patterns may reflect the increasing emphasis in school athletics on expertise, and on the weeding out of inexpert participants. Brown and Theobald (1998) suggest that extracurricular sports programs have transformed over the past few decades into highly competitive enterprises focused almost entirely on developing high levels of expertise in athletes. This emphasis, they argue, has brought limitations in access to these activities for students, as well as declining attention to the personal and social development of participants.

These findings become more troubling in the context of findings in other studies that various cocurricular activities tend to be associated with each other: a lack of opportunity in high school sports may affect students' likelihood of participating in other high school activities (Melnick et al., 1992; Lisella & Serwatka, 1996). The finding may apply especially to students of color attending urban schools, because the sports association with other cocurricular activities is especially strong in those settings. That is, students in those schools appear more likely to be involved in additional extracurricular activities if they are participating in school-based athletics programs (Lisella & Serwatka, 1996).

In sum, students with resources to participate in sports activities before high school have an advantage in access to sports activities later when they have entered high school. In turn, that engagement in high school sports facilitates engagement in other cocurricular activities. All those activities, in concert, appear to increase chances of academic achievement and eventual attainment. The causal chain is long and undeniably tenuous given the varied evidence, but the implications are troubling.

Formal, school-based cocurricular activities such as athletics and student government appear to have significant indirect influences on postsecondary prospects, and may also have some more direct influences. Still, the connections of these results to effective college preparatory programs are unclear. While this review of the literature provides no firm evidence on the college-going effects of the cocurricular activities provided in school-based college preparatory programs, what is available instead is evidence of the effects of other cocurricular activities taking place in high school.

Sports are among the activities found especially beneficial, for example, yet there is no practical way to assign students in college preparatory programs to participate involuntarily in formal high school sports. Similar limitations apply to student government activities. What is more, even if such assignments could be made, the effects of the assigned cocurricular activities may in fact not extend to those students participating in the activities involuntarily. What we do know from the literature focusing on formal cocurricular involvement in schools is therefore somewhat broader and less precise: there are academically beneficial effects from these kinds of nonschooling activities, and analysts should continue to explore ways to extend this knowledge into successful structures and offerings in college preparation programs.

Formal Cocurricular Activities in Community-Based
College-Preparation Programs

Many communities, particularly urban communities, are home to college preparation programs taking place outside of formal school settings. Designed to help academically disadvantaged, low-SES, and generally at-risk students prepare for and aspire to postsecondary education attainment (Perna & Swail, 1998; Swail, 2000; Hagedorn & Tierney, 2002; Center for Higher Education Policy Analysis, 2002), community-based college preparatory programs are prominent topics of interest for those concerned over unequal educational opportunities in the society.

There is some evidence that these programs are working. McLaughlin, Irby, and Langman (1994) studied large representative samples of at-risk and non–at-risk youth and found that at-risk youth participating in community-based organizations generally held higher expectations for graduating and attending college. Many of these participants also achieved at higher levels academically in comparison to their average peers. McLaughlin et al. noted, "Youths actively engaged in community-based organizations also reported greater confidence and optimism about what the future would hold and a strong sense of civic responsibility and commitment to give back to their communities" (p. xii). Reviewing this evidence, McLaughlin et al. stress the importance of community programs in the development of young people, especially at-risk young people from low-SES, minority, rural, and urban communities:

> Community organizations cannot and do not fulfill all of young people's
> needs. But they provide broad support for youth development and inten-

tional learning environments that complement those usually created by schools. They occupy critical hours that are, as the Carnegie report notes, "times of increased risk or opportunity" and extend learning and personal growth into the nonschool hours. And, for many, they become caring communities that help young people navigate adolescence and explore their identities, their communities, and their commitments. (p. ix)

McLaughlin et al. (1994) note that social activities and support of the right kind appeal to youths and help keep them engaged in their community organizations. In that vein, they note, "effective youth organizations look very much like gangs in the kinds of supports and recognition they provide to their members, but the outcomes of the two groups could not be more dissimilar. The gangs lead to violence, crime, and quite possibly death; the effective youth organizations enable youth to take a different road that leads to life and a productive future" (p. 213).[4]

In general, community-based college preparatory programs tend to be student centered rather than school centered and tend to target students of color and urban youth. In most cases, a primary agenda is expanding participants' cultural and academic capital (College Board, 2000; Swail, 2000a; Gándara, 2002; Hagedorn & Fogel, 2002). Community-based outreach programs "are frequently similar to those in school-based programs, but they can also incorporate elements that are specific to a particular community, including cultural experiences that help students to develop healthy self-concepts" (Gándara & Bial, 2001, p. 19). As in the case of high-school cocurricular activities, understanding who participates in the various types of community-based programs is important, especially in light of the possibility that participants are self-selected rather than selected based on academic risk status.

College preparation programs based in the community vary notably in their home locations and sponsors, which can be local organizations, postsecondary institutions, governments, and K–12 systems as well as private corporations and foundations. Programs also vary appreciably in their specific approaches, and can emphasize numerous different outcomes, including student persistence and dropout prevention, improved study skills, better academic performance, raised educational aspirations and expectations, and increased levels of postsecondary attendance (Gándara, 2002a; Hagedorn & Tierney, 2002). Some privately funded community-based college outreach or preparation programs focus on preparation for life beyond college as well as for postsecondary education itself (Swail, 2000).

Assessing whether desired outcomes are being achieved by these programs, and by the cocurricular aspects of the programs in particular, is challenging. Many programs do not engage in effective program evaluation activities (Gándara & Bial, 2001; Gándara, 2002a; Tierney, 2002). Although most college preparation programs represent a useful step toward greater postsecondary access for underrepresented youth, there are problems in speaking with confidence about the cost effectiveness of these efforts (see chapter 9). This has ramifications for justifying resources spent on the cocurriculum.

Taking the analytic challenge beyond evaluations of individual college preparation programs toward the generation of broader conclusions is even more difficult, because of the extraordinary diversity in programmatic features. College preparation programs vary widely in their goals and in the experiences and opportunities they offer their participants. Programs vary in instructional processes (i.e., in-school activities or after-school offerings), organization (i.e., formally or informally structured), and modes of delivery (e.g., tutoring, workshops, campus visits, mentoring, etc.). Programs may offer a range of academic and nonacademic services to participants, including field trips, seminars, social skill development, college fairs, preparation for standardized tests, and remedial education (Hagedorn & Tierney, 2002).

This comprehensive and multidimensional nature of programming may pose a challenge in practice, however, and most college preparation programs offer distinctive combinations of various components. The common elements of most programs include some form of counseling, academic and personal enrichment, parental involvement, social integration, mentoring, and scholarships (Gándara & Bial, 2001). In a 2001 report of the National Postsecondary Education Cooperative (NPEC) Working Group on Access to Postsecondary Education, Gándara and Bial found that majority of the K–12 intervention programs for underrepresented youth consisted of counseling and academic enrichment components. Counseling, in particular, is an essential part of most intervention and preparation programs because underrepresented students have typically received inadequate counseling regarding postsecondary education (Oakes, 1985; McDonough, 1997; Gándara & Bial, 2001; chapter 4, this volume).

Of particular interest for the present review, only 18 of the 33 programs reviewed for the NPEC report had a personal enrichment and social integration element. Social activities conducted through these programs involved students serving in the community together, going on field trips, and visiting with speakers or role models from colleges or universities, local businesses, or the community. The conceptual foundations of these activities are not always clear from external literature, suggesting that academically focused programs may need to better communicate the logic and importance of the cocurricular involvement built into their programs (Coles, 1999).

Gándara (2002a) provides a provocative discussion of the importance of peer groups in college-preparation programs (also see chapter 3). Clearly, some level of social interaction and integration is inevitable among participants in even the most loosely organized programs. For example, social integration may occur in an informally structured program mainly on field trips to college campuses, in courses, or workshops. In more structured programs, peer group influence is recognized and activities are specifically designed to create opportunities for students of similar abilities and backgrounds to positively influence one another. Of particular importance is the development of peer groups that support academic achievement. Unfortunately, most programs do not attend to "the issues that students face when they choose to excel in a peer culture that is not supportive of academic achievement" (Gándara, 2002a, p. 91). Chapter 3 reviews peer group issues in great detail, and we defer further discussion of that topic here.

Other Formal and Informal Community-Based Social Activities

Community-based groups and organizations can provide positive social integration, socialization, and broader developmental opportunities for students and may play a role in college preparation as well (Brown & Theobald, 1998). Not-for-profit entities, such as youth groups associated with local places of worship, community-based outreach programs, community recreation centers, and local units of larger national organizations such as the Girl Scouts, 4-H, Boys' and Girls' Clubs, and Big Brothers/Big Sisters can in theory be quite helpful to youth as they consider life plans and goals. For example, in an chapter on community involvement and disadvantaged students, Nettles (1991) suggests conversion, mobilization, allocation, and instruction are among the critical personal change processes potentially derived from involvement in structured and unstructured community-related activities.

Nettles notes, however, that "although the literature is sprinkled with anecdotes about students who suddenly began to achieve or who suddenly ceased to behave in destructive ways as the result of exposure to a powerful message or charismatic person, systematic research on this kind of phenomenon with disadvantaged students is rare" (1991, p. 380). It may well be that youth who have been marginalized inside and outside their schools stand to make particularly strong gains when exposed to well-conceived community-based activities. It may also well be that youth of particular social and cultural backgrounds are more likely to value and be involved in community-based social activities as opposed to traditional, school-sponsored extracurricular activities. Unfortunately, evidence on these hypotheses is simply not available thus far.

Many who discern more fundamental, formative processes at work when examining students' involvement in after-school activities emphasize that personal investment and exposure to significant others may be important factors in eventual college enrollment patterns. Jordan and Nettles (1999) note that students who spend substantial after-school and weekend time involved in enrichment activities in their communities or with their parents and families have more opportunities to interact with positive adult role models as well as like-minded peers. They argue that these activities also facilitate social, moral, and intellectual development.

Involvement in community-related social activities in and of itself is not sufficient to influence youths' college-going behaviors, of course. Instead, the particulars of the involvement seem significant. According to Roffman, Pagano and Hirsch (2001), positive social integration with like-minded peers and the strength and type of relationships with adult supervisors, mentors, and staff members appear to affect a variety of participants' behaviors relating to academic progress.

Despite these findings, there may be very real limits on the attainment effects of youths' involvement in community-related activities. Guidance counselors and teachers are gatekeepers to college information: they select scholarship nominees, write letters of recommendation, and provide leadership opportunities, and may not be aware of a student's involvement in community activities. If certain groups of students are heavily involved in cocurricular activities outside of school and less involved inside the school, counselors and teachers may be unaware of those students' nascent aspirations. Greater opportunities linked to educational attainment may be communicated and afforded to those involved in school-based, formal activities. This could place the externally engaged students at a disadvantage relative to their internally engaged peers. If the externally engaged students tend to come from socioeconomically disadvantaged backgrounds, existing societal inequalities may be reinforced.[5]

CONCLUSION

Because of the paucity of research on the effect of social activities in college preparatory programs on college prospects, this chapter focuses mainly on evidence from studies of high school students' social activities in general. Much of the research reviewed has been on the effects of traditional activities such as high school athletics and student government participation. The review suggests that students' involvement in cocurricular activities of this kind can influence their prospects for college attendance. That is, there is no reason to accept the null hypothesis that cocurricular activities are irrelevant to enabling students to get into a college or university. It should be stressed, however, that the influences of the traditional cocurriculum on attendance prospects appear to be modest and largely indirect, that is, mediated through other factors such as student attitudes and academic performance.[6] The path from these findings to the particular question of designing effective cocurricular activities in college preparatory programs is not at all clear, because the topic has simply never been adequately examined. Although the precise causal mechanisms for cocurricular effects are not clear, the findings of the review are intriguing and suggest a number of questions for further theory development and research.

The question of equal access to cocurricular activities was raised by many of the studies reviewed. Who has access to traditional, highly valued, school-sponsored cocurricular activities not associated with college preparation programs? That is, which students are allowed to participate and thus to benefit from involvement in such activities? If participation in cocurricular activities of various kinds can have positive academic effects on students, and possibly play a positive role in their postsecondary access, then access to those activities themselves is an important question for theory, research, and practice.

Although few research studies attempt to link activity involvement to postsecondary education access, the evidence that does exist raises some notable concerns about obstacles to disadvantaged groups' involvement and the status placed on specific activities that too few from disadvantaged backgrounds can access. Formal and informal social activities provide a context for sociability, a sense of belonging, and opportunities to enhance personal competencies (Hultsman, 1992). Socially and culturally constructed barriers may exist that prevent individual students or groups of students from involvement. Further research should consider the individual and group-level characteristics that shape participation of different kinds. Such research, by definition, should include students varying in socioeconomic background, gender, race, and ethnicity.

Obstacles to access may include the inability to pay financial costs for participation, lack of transportation to and from the cocurricular activity, and lack of understanding and support from parents. Financial, social, and cultural barriers to participation can emerge in early adolescence, potentially constraining students' decision to participate in these activities later in high school. Failing to participate may affect postsecondary attainment indirectly, via weaker performance in classes and lower educational aspirations. Failure to participate may also affect access directly in that many institutions consider students' involvement in activities as evidence of motivation and accomplishment. Thus, it seems important for future research to explore who participates in what types of social activities, and what barriers may exist to participation by students from different backgrounds.

It will be important in such studies to thoroughly integrate theory and existing research evidence into research designs. Too many of the studies of social activities in high school are purely descriptive, with few or no references to social science theory or prior research. Grounding future research in theory and research evidence will provide more nuanced and generalizable understanding of the effects of activities on postsecondary attendance, choice, and attainment.

It is also important that research reflect multiple methodological traditions. The quantitative analytic traditions of attainment research in sociology and economics are valuable, and have formed the basis of some of the best research in this arena. National survey-based databases such as High School and Beyond and NELS have been invaluable to the generalization of results regarding cocurricular activities. More than quantitative work is necessary, however. Because of survey limitations, little attention can be paid in the national databases to the social status associated with particular activities, the selection process for the activities, and the type of interaction with adult supervisors in the activities. As Quiroz, Gonzalez, and Frank (1996) note, survey data are limited in that they cannot completely capture the broader social processes associated with activity involvement. By going beyond easily answered questions such as which students are involved and to what extent, qualitatively framed studies may help build understanding of the nuances in the experience of student involvement.

Another limitation of existing research is the small number of voices being heard and the limited number of cocurricular activities being studied. On the former point, a wider array of actors should be included in future research—guidance counselors, students, parents, teachers, preparation program staff, community leaders, and college admissions personnel.[7] By casting a wide net, researchers may be able to illuminate some of the complex connections between high school students' cocurricular involvements and college admissions and enrollment at different types of institutions. Regarding the nature of the cocurricular experiences studied, our inability to find empirical research on the potential college-going effects of many of the activities appearing in the Table 7.1 typology is telling. A number of authors have written on the benefits of various youth development programs in promoting high school persistence and the avoidance of risky behaviors (see Grossman & Tierney, 1998; Roth, Brooks-Gunn, Murray, & Foster, 1998; Vandell & Posner, 1999; McLaughlin, 2000). Little of this work has examined effects on college attendance, however, and that lack should be addressed.

Further research and theory clearly needs to attend to the question of contingency. Early work on cocurricular influences by Spady (1970), Otto (1975), and others has been questioned along these lines in recent years (see Chen, 1997). The extent to which cocurricular participation mediates SES and academic ability and performance in affecting attendance is a question of vigorous debate, as is the extent to which participation and effects vary by student background and context (for recent work in this vein, see Guest & Schneider, 2003). Additional research should more closely examine the potentially important roles of different kinds of peer influence and different socialization processes.

Again, social science theory may help sort out the complex relationships among the many factors associated with these processes. Among the theoretical perspectives that may prove helpful as lenses through which to examine the relationship between social activities and postsecondary participation are status allocation theories (Bidwell & Friedkin, 1988, Quiroz et al., 1996), institutional theory, and social reproduction theory (Bourdieu, 1977). Anchoring future research in these theories will provide a broader basis for inference, through consideration of such factors as the formal and informal opportunity structures in schools, the social organization of school-based and community-based social activities, social-psychological processes at work in participation, informal and formal mechanisms working to open or block access, and ways in which social and cultural capital may be reinforced and distributed through cocurricular involvement.

Research using these ideas can extend into the domain of college choice. There is some evidence that participation in high school social activities may influence not only whether students enroll in postsecondary education but also the nature of the institutions attended by those students who do enroll. For example, in multivariate analyses of postsecondary attendance patterns in a national sample of high school graduates, Hearn (1984, 1991) found that participation in such cocurricular activities as high school student government had significant (albeit limited) positive influences on attendance in selective colleges and universities, even in the context of controls for students' academic and socioeconomic characteristics. What factors of cocurricular activities might predispose students to attendance in certain kinds of postsecondary institutions? To the extent certain kinds of institutions may benefit students' life chances in particular ways, notable equity issues may be embedded in this research question.

One can also extend the research beyond postsecondary access and choice to include the related constructs of postsecondary educational persistence and degree attainment. Nora (2002) notes that precollege psychosocial attributes may influence social involvement in college and therefore increase college persistence and achievement. Students "who have held high school leadership roles or who have been involved in civic activities during their high school years are better prepared to engage their social environment during their college years" (Nora, 2002, p. 72). Nora's point is that there may well be a consistent relationship between involvement and persistence for the degree. The literature suggests that this is the case at both the high school and postsecondary levels (Pascarella & Terenzini, 1980, 1983, 1991; Mahoney & Cairns, 1997).

From a more practical perspective, policymakers and educational leaders should consider the existing evidence of the effects of cocurricular activities, and encourage research in pursuit of further understandings. As leaders of college preparation programs, policymakers, and others evaluate the effectiveness of programs for curricular, funding, performance, and accountability reasons, it is essential that more data become available to ascertain the impacts of cocurricular offerings on participants' educational plans, hopes, and attendance patterns.

Such work will bump against the reality that cocurricular activities, and activities within college preparatory programs in particular, are not a straightforward subject for analysis. Because the outcomes of cocurricular activities are partly dependent on what participants bring into them from the start, discerning the activities' consistent influences across large samples of students and programs is difficult. The point is especially valid for activities provided through college preparatory programs: without multivariate longitudinal studies including young people who do and do not enter these programs, there is no way to discern the distinctive influences of these programs and their programmatic features.

Still, research in this domain is well worth pursuing. This chapter began by noting the growing social and economic importance of postsecondary attendance to individuals and the nation. Analysts and advocates of college access, including providers of college preparatory programs, have long commented on the poorly understood "black box" of interlinked socioeconomic and academic effects on postsecondary attendance.[8] Despite extraordinary efforts, talented high school graduates from disadvantaged backgrounds continue to attend college at lower rates than other, equally talented graduates.[9] We thus are confronted with an important national problem about which we have insufficient information. It seems increasingly necessary that we better understand the significant remaining mysteries in college attendance decisions.

NOTES

1. See the literature reviews and empirical analyses by Broh (2002) and Guest and Schneider (2003).

2. That purpose can be negative or positive in nature. For example, a young person involved in a street gang is involved in a form of social activity but one that is unlikely to lead to positive, long-term outcomes such as postsecondary attainment. Our focus here is on activities with potentially positive outcomes.

3. It is important to note that, although we focus in this chapter on nonschooling activities, such activities can and quite often do take place on school grounds and under school auspices. The distinction is that the activities of interest to us are not part of the school-day curriculum (i.e., the "schooling") pursued by all students.

4. For more in the literature on how needs for belonging, status, and safety are connected to involvement in gangs, see Vigil (1993).

5. Interestingly, Buckhalt, Halpin, Noel, and Meadows (1992) note that participation in interscholastic athletics decreases across grade level, while student involvement in community-related activities such as church youth groups tends to remain constant over time. This finding suggests that students involved in community-related activities may accrue distinctive personal benefits over time, but may not be linked into the formal system associated with the communication of college-related information.

6. This chapter focuses on recent high school graduates entering higher education. It may be that involvement in cocurricular activities has more influence on college choice and persistence than on entering higher education, but those topics are beyond the scope of this review.

7. For example, Noeth and Wimberly (2002) report that 75% of African American and Hispanic seniors in college preparation programs reported the extracurricular activities in those programs were helpful in the college planning processes, but these findings alone do not suggest firm conclusions on the most helpful specific mechanisms in those programs.

8. E.g., see Jackson (1982), Grant Commission (1988), Hearn (1991), Horn & Chen (1998), and Gándara and Bial (2001).

9. See Hearn (2002) for a review of this attendance gap.

MARGUERITE BONOUS-HAMMARTH
WALTER R. ALLEN

Chapter Eight

A Dream Deferred: The Critical Factor of Timing in College Preparation and Outreach

INTRODUCTION

The comedian's lament that timing is everything is clearly relevant when discussing college preparation. The college preparation process for students brings to mind images of commuters who trek to jobs and other destinations each morning. Imagine that students are these commuters, arriving at the Long Island Railroad's Port Jefferson station or some other first stop of a railway line en route to a major city. It's not unusual to see the first train of the morning waiting for its commuters, so those planners who have arrived early can peruse newspapers or drink coffee while they wait. Some commuters may arrive just as the conductor announces the train's imminent departure and quickly hop on. Others, unaware of or unable to meet the train's schedule, miss it altogether. Akin to these commuters, regardless of how much planning each student may need to successfully meet all the deadlines and preparation points for college readiness, the fictitious train will depart on its own schedule for a specific college destination.

The researchers extend their thanks to the representatives at the Andrew W. Mellon Foundation for their support to make the CHOICES: Access, Equity and Diversity in Higher Education Research Project study possible.

What happens to those commuters who arrive late and miss the first train altogether? These students certainly have options to reach their proposed destinations—similar to the late commuters who meet the same train at later points in a journey, those who take trains scheduled at other times throughout the day, or those who use different transportation. These students also may select to postpone their travel. In the case of students already labeled at risk of leaving the academic pipeline, postponement or delays in college preparation may result in plans that exclude college and professional education entirely.

The question of timing remains an important consideration for youth simply because effective learning synchronizes environmental resources to meet student readiness in ways that foster agency and growth (Piaget, 1991, p. 12). In the case of high school students preparing for college and careers, issues of timing correlate with a period during the life course when maturation and previous developmental stages coalesce and enable students to acquire new skill sets. Timing also reflects points during that period when school and family structures provide different resources to facilitate student understanding about future roles such as that of college student.

This chapter examines the timing of college preparation within the context of students' college choice processes and specifically with reference to the structure of college outreach programs. The specific sequence of activities and behaviors that students engage in to prepare for college becomes increasingly important because essential tasks such as completing algebra or actually filing a college application must occur within prescribed deadlines set by colleges, high schools, and other agents. Students have four years during high school to focus intently on college preparation, and the earlier they begin this process, the more knowledge they have to complete the maximum activities possible to remain prospective college applicants.

Our discussion draws upon sociological frameworks related to college choice, stratification of educational opportunities, and life course development models that describe the formal and informal timelines when key decisions are made by students to (1) attend college, (2) research college choices and the completion of college prerequisites, and (3) apply to and select a specific college for enrollment. We then discuss several aspects of college preparation: developing aspirations to attend college, completing the required high school curriculum, and developing communications networks to inform students about specific college options, costs, and admissions processes. We discuss how, by identifying college aspirations early in their academic lives, students have better chances to complete the rigorous coursework required for college entrance and to garner information about colleges and the college application process from teachers, counselors, peers, and other social contacts. Next we discuss timing and components of structured college resources—school-organized programs that provide specific information about the college admissions process, cultivate student interest in college, and improve student preparation for postsecondary participation. These partnership programs and interventions all occur during the course of high school (some even prior to high school), with the goal of having students complete coursework, research colleges, and apply to specific institutions by college deadlines during senior year. We conclude with recommendations to address achievement disparities among college-bound students in hopes of strengthening curricular and outreach efforts for a sector of students who typically access college preparation advising and key activities later than their peers, for example during the last two years of high school. Interventions that can help students to develop college aspirations, access necessary curriculum, and build their knowledge about college opportunities from the first year of high school will increase the likelihood of student participation in college.

UNDERSTANDING TIMING AND HOW CONTEXTS SHAPE COLLEGE PREPARATION

Educators reported good news that the number of high school graduates in the year 2000 transitioning directly from secondary education to college increased by 14% during the course of a decade (National Center for Education Statistics [NCES], 2002, p. 74). In this sense, the students who travel these more direct routes to postsecondary enrollment reaped the benefits of counseling, academic preparation, and enrichment programs at particular times in their life courses to boost their respective college readiness. However, race, gender, and social class disparities in the academic preparation of graduating high school seniors suggest that additional programmatic and structural changes are needed to provide equitable college access (Table 8.1).

While focusing on specific aspects of timing and structure of college preparation during the high school years, educators must understand the fac-

TABLE 8.1.
Participation of California Public High School Graduates in College Preparatory Curriculum in 1990 and 1996

Race/Ethnicity	1990	1996
African American	25.4	27.9
Asian	48.0	53.6
Caucasian	33.1	39.7
Hispanic/Latino/Chicano	19.1	22.3
Native American	19.5	24.0

Source: California Postsecondary Education Commission (1997).

tors that contribute to students' academic competence and knowledge about college. In this respect, it is essential to consider the context in which such learning occurs. Researchers describe a college choice process that includes: (1) student decisions to attend college, or the predisposition stage; (2) student information gathering about prospective colleges, or the search stage; and (3) student application and/or matriculation in specific colleges, or the selection stage (Attinasi, 1989; Hossler et al., 1989; Hossler & Gallagher, 1987; McDonough, 1997; Stage & Hossler, 1989). However, it should be recognized that students in the academic pipeline experience different learning opportunities, given diverse cultural backgrounds and values, inequitable resources available in their learning communities, and specific student experiences with sorting processes such as tracking.

It is also important to remember that each student develops along an individual trajectory while sharing a schooling process, and that this individual maturation plays a role in learning outcomes. As suggested by developmental psychologists, students in the high school age group are able to approach strategizing in inherently different ways than their younger peers and to grasp subjects more abstractly and deductively to engender effective agency (Piaget, 1991; Singer & Revenson, 1996). In this respect, further learning stems from the interactions between students with respective high school and home resources. And it may be that the timing of these resources may or may not match the needs of these students to facilitate their college preparation.

In his examination of the college choice process for Chicanos/Latinos, Attinasi (1989) found that relational factors (e.g., fraternal and teacher mentoring, anticipatory socialization and other identification with college-going peers) positively influenced the abilities of students to view college as a feasible time investment (p. 269). The access students have to key resources and experiences is further complicated by the use of institutional tracking (or ability grouping) to determine placements in courses that are college prerequisites (Garet & DeLany, 1988; Oakes, 1985). Understanding college preparation, then, entails not only examining the factors that influence student agency in a college choice process, but also addressing contextual barriers and facilitators that influence student academic cache (e.g., the type of academic preparation, career counseling, and information networking that occurs prior to college).

As college choice does not occur in a vacuum, studies of college preparation and decision making must consider the formal and informal aspects of precollege life that contribute to student readiness and potential for success in college. Formal components to study include variables associated with the structure of schools, families, and communities, such as the high school curriculum, student skill set, and guidance and career counseling that influence academic standing and marketability for college admission. Informal components to examine include information networks or ways that students gain understanding about steps in the college admissions process, roles and expectations about college and its outcomes, and student, teacher, and family values and perceptions about postsecondary education. The formal and informal components of college preparation enable students to compete with varying success for college admittance. While the formal components may provide students with explicit cues on the types of credentials necessary for college admission, the informal components provide students with resources and support strategies to identify and navigate the college choice process effectively.

Theories on the life course in general, and on student development in particular, suggest how formal and informal preparation components influence development during and across key years or stages in life. From a life course perspective, a major life transition such as moving from high school to college must include study of the dynamic connections among individual biography and sociohistorical factors that influence life changes and transitions (Elder, 1985; Spencer, Brookins, & Allen, 1985). Such theories generally explore at least one of five major themes related to: (1) historical time and place; (2) the timing of life events; (3) "linked lives," or the network of shared relationships; and (4) individual human agency (Elder, 1998, p. 4). From this sociological perspective, a focus on student preparation for college relates to understanding how critical transition points in a student's life culminate to influence participation in college and subsequent transitions in career and family. For example, a study of college preparation with attention to the life course would identify factors that influence individual change and changes across and within generations of students and key actors (e.g., parents, peers, teachers) at the point of transition to college.

Student development theories focus specifically on the level of student academic and social preparation for transition to higher education. Specifically, these theories suggest connections among student characteristics and other precollege factors, college environments, and learning outcomes (Astin, 1993; Pascarella & Terenzini, 1991). Findings from several independent studies related to college impact, or the ways in which college participation influences student outcomes, show that although postsecondary environments and peer groups have dominant influence on college outcomes, precollege factors such as strong analytical training in high school, degree aspirations for the baccalaureate, and parental college completion positively influence student transition to college (Allen, 1992; Astin, 1993).

Taken together, the preceding perspectives frame this examination of college outreach components to highlight the temporal factors and other important influences that shape student academic preparation, information gathering about higher education opportunities, and effective student agency in diverse learning communities. The lenses used to examine college preparation enable us to see student preparation for college as a major juncture in individual development, when students' cognitive growth and interactions with their environment and support networks of family, teachers, and counselors are approached differently than in preceding years. Concurrently, we must examine student strategizing and decision making for college tied to environmental resources across the life course—in particular, how resources absent in previous years or those that never manifest to a level required by students at this point in time affect student plans for college attendance. In the next section, we discuss timing and resources from the primary domain of the student, family, and school before considering a focused discussion on the role of intervention/ college preparatory programs in the preparation process.

TIMING AND SUPPORT

Students gain insight about college preparation from a number of informants, including family, teachers, counselors and peers (see chapters 2, 3, and 4). These mentors offer support, timely information about the college search process, and advisement that aid student decision making about college (see chapter 5).

Parental support plays a major role in motivating students to articulate intentions to enroll in college and to develop "cultural capital," or specific knowledge and strategies for the college choice process (McDonough, 1997, p. 111). It makes intuitive sense that parents who graduated college have more experience with and knowledge about college preparation activities than parents with no traditions of college attendance. The development of a student's aspiration to attend college prompts a second step—a review of various college options to make college application and enrollment the reality. Students who, by design or by circumstances, have effective support from parents—and for that matter, siblings, teachers, and friends too—expedite their college preparation by strengthening their self-concepts and aspirations and by garnering tried and true strategies to facilitate college enrollment.

Research shows that parental support in some form is related to student engagement and advancement in the educational pipeline—whether the support is explicit information sharing and actions such as visiting prospective campuses or implicit in verbal or nonverbal cues (chapter 2, this volume; Conklin & Dailey, 1981; Stanton-Salazar & Dornbusch, 1995; Hossler & Vesper, 1993). Student concerns over college costs, parental savings for college, and parental socioeconomic status suggest student perceptions about parental support in regard to college financing disproportionately limit the college participation of students from economically disadvantaged backgrounds (Gladieux & Swail, 1998; Hossler & Vesper, 1993).

With respect to the ultimate goal of student participation in college, parental support provides measurable benefits and exerts unique influence on students, if such support occurs consistently over time. High school seniors reporting consistent parental encouragement (college participation was "taken for granted" in 9th through 12th grades) had higher probabilities of enrolling in higher education than peers receiving parental support only in their senior year or for peers receiving no parental encouragement (Conklin & Dailey, 1981, p. 259). Thus, it makes intuitive sense to provide ways for parents to engage in activities with college-bound students to develop their own values about college participation and to foster these values in their children.

Research also suggests that students who develop information and advocacy/support networks with multiple rather than singular sources of information during the critical predisposition and search phases of their college planning have better opportunities to clarify their thinking and strategies concerning course plans and potential college choices (Stanton-Salazar & Dornbusch, 1995). For example, Chicano/Latino students who identified themselves as "highly bilingual" and exhibited larger networks with friends, family, and school contacts reported higher grades and held significantly higher educational expectations than Spanish-dominant-speaking peers (Stanton-Salazar & Dornbusch, 1995, p. 129). These multiple sources of information allow students to develop and confirm their strategies for college participation at critical points when missteps (e.g., selecting vocational or noncollege preparatory courses) could reduce their competitiveness and marketability as college applicants.

TIMING AND SCHOOL RESOURCES

The issue of timing is also a factor for students using school resources for information gathering and academic preparation for college. While students complete college applications within similar timelines (fall through winter of the 12th grade), they need to identify themselves as college bound at earlier points in the academic pipeline to learn about anticipated careers and related college choices. In fact, high school students who identified college aspirations by the eighth grade were 17% more likely than those who did not to complete minimum college requirements by the close of their senior year (Cabrera & La Nasa, 2000a, p. 37). This early planning ensured a positive trajectory for students toward college completion over time.

Depending on the numbers of students and credentialed staff available, counselor-to-student ratios in secondary school academic and college advising may range from 1:323, the national average for public high schools, to 1:848, the average for public high schools in California (McDonough, 1997, p. 92). In organizing academic counseling, high school representatives make assumptions about the level and frequency of counseling needed by students for their vocational and college preparation, and specific college advising may occur as early as middle school or as late as senior year in high school (McDonough, 1997; chapter 4, this volume). In cases where assumptions were miscalculated (students did not receive information and guidance from parents on college opportunities since parents did not attend college), the late timing of formal advising played a role in the resulting low numbers of four-year college attendees (McDonough, 1997, p. 106). Successful college enrollment results when students gain the combined advantages of early academic guidance, broad access to rigorous curricula (courses that enhance knowledge and abilities), and strong college aspirations.

Academically, the students most likely to leave high school without degrees and thus not immediately enter a pool of college applicants were those who did not complete academic qualifications such as the college prerequisites outlined in Figure 8.1 (Cabrera & La Nasa, 2000b).

FIGURE 8.1. Academic Preparation and Outreach During the High School Years

Family and Social Contacts			
9th Grade Decision to attend college	10th Grade College search	11th Grade College selection	12th Grade Application/ admission
Attend to: College prerequisite courses (gateway math and science), college savings, search for potential college choices	*Attend to:* College prerequisite courses (gateway math and science), college savings, information on specific college "matches"	*Attend to:* College prerequisite courses (advanced math and science), prep/tests, college savings, applications for college choices	*Attend to:* College prerequisite courses (advanced math and science), college savings, application submissions
Testing: PSAT	*Testing*: PSAT	*Testing*: SAT/ACT	*Testing*: SAT/ACT
Typical college prerequisites: 4 years English, 3 years mathematics, 2 years lab science, 2 years foreign language, and 2 years college electives			

School Culture

Since students at risk of dropping out tended to come from households with limited traditions of college attendance, they were less likely to have mentors who advised them about career options and the college search process (Cabrera & La Nasa, 2000a, p. 32). The more rigorous the academic preparation in high school, the more likely that students enroll in college, persist to degree completion, and subsequently participate in advanced education (NCES, 2002). However, the greatest challenge for students to access early college advising and rigorous academic preparation as the norm is an overriding assumption that high school students universally have the same experiences and receive the same opportunities to make informed decisions about college. In fact, a severe dichotomy exists between the college choice process as it unfolds for the pool of students who typically access college opportunities and for the pool of students whose social or academic backgrounds place them at a disadvantage in completing high school and attending college.

Although high school students with limited resources and limited access to counseling may experience negative repercussions from late college planning, no other structural component at the high school level is as damaging for students as academic tracking. Tracking is the sorting practice in place at many high schools of grouping students by abilities within subject courses. Research shows that support for tracking is often based on fundamental beliefs that students have different and fixed capacities to learn and need to be grouped accordingly to maximize school resources (Oakes, Quartz, Ryan, & Lipton, 2000).

In their examination of how 16 schools implemented a Turning Points initiative supported by the Carnegie Foundation, Oakes et al. (2000) identified how tracking debates reflected perspectives on social class and race and ethnicity as well:

> Grouping and its consequences have meaning and exchange value beyond school. After all, homogeneous grouping accompanied by public labels and status differences, signals which students should gain access to the university and the status and life changes that higher education can bring. Thus, tracking became part and parcel of the struggle among individuals and groups for comparative advantage in distributing school resources, opportunities and credentials that have exchange value in the larger society. Therefore, it is not surprising that there were those with a clear personal stake in maintaining homogeneous grouping. . . . In all of the racially mixed schools with significant numbers of middle-class or more affluent white families, these parents battled heterogeneous grouping. (p. 116)

In this light, even if students share the same learning environments, they may not share the same learning experiences or the same learning outcomes.

In their study of course placement probabilities, Garet and DeLany (1988) found that students who ranked high for math were not enrolled at corresponding levels for respective science placement (p. 72). The structure of school offerings (e.g., availability of feeder/advanced math classes vs. fewer math course options) and the composition of students at school sites (many students competitive for top-ranked math and science courses vs. few competitive students) influenced access to and enrollment in college-bound curricula. This observation mirrors similar discussions in the literature on status attainment about a "social distribution of opportunities," where individual access to information and valuable resources vary given their social standing and relationships with institutional agents in authority (Stanton-Salazar & Dornbusch, 1995, p. 116).

In many respects, the course placement process for advanced math and science courses remains controversial because research on "curriculum membership" shows the strong correlation between course placement and all subsequent academic outcomes for students (Alexander et al., 1978, p. 48). Track placement is most notably related to student goal orientations beyond high school, with college track enrollment increasing one's probability for continued participation in education by 30% (Alexander et al., 1978, p. 60).

Although on the surface these findings suggest a match between school resources and student abilities, the data foreshadow several drawbacks, particularly in resource-poor schools with few advanced placement or other college-bound offerings. Access to rigorous academic curricula, such as science and mathematics, may vary across institutions, presenting disadvantaged students opportunities for advanced courses in science and mathematics only in specific situations where low competition opens access to fill college preparatory classes (Garet & DeLany, 1988, p. 73). These opportunities may be erratic rather than regularized, occurring only under infrequent conditions specific to either students or the high schools.

As discussed in chapter 6, knowledge about and enrollment in collegiate-track courses as high school freshmen enable students to remain competitive for the college applicant pool. The early completion of introductory algebra by eighth grade places students in the queue for capstone calculus or other fifth-year math course completion by 12th grade (Flanders, 1987; Useem, 1992). Additionally, research findings that the highest math courses taken correlate with undergraduate degree completion prompt both students and college admissions directors alike to include rigorous academic preparation among college selection criteria (Adelman, 1999).

STRUCTURED EDUCATIONAL INTERVENTIONS AND COLLEGE OUTREACH

Thus far, our discussion has focused on how the timing of family and school resources influences college preparation outcomes for students. However, students spend large parts of their days in structured school activities that may include academic interventions to motivate and help them to organize their college plans. Structured college outreach activities, such as university–high school partnerships, can be viewed as effective collaborations that improve information dissemination and academic advising about college opportunities for all students. Outreach and intervention programs focused on college preparation address specific course and academic advisement issues and typically target students at local high school sites.

These interventions may vary by type and duration, but they share common elements that focus on counseling, academic enrichment, parental involvement, personal enrichment, social integration, mentoring, and scholarships (Barela, Christie, & Alkin, 2001; Eisenberg & Martin, 2001; Gándara, 2001; Hayward, Brandes, Kirst, & Mazzeo, 1997; chapter 2, this volume). Findings from one study on the specific components of 33 intervention programs suggested that the majority of these "pipeline programs" included a primary focus on counseling, perhaps both to overcome inadequate services in resource-poor schools and to address minority student concerns that high school counseling tracks most minorities into low-level classes without information on college preparation (Gándara, 2001, p. 21). In addition, these programs typically structure mentoring opportunities. Assessing the impact of mentoring on student academic achievement has been inconclusive (Gándara, 2001, p. 28). In essence, pipeline programs address major challenges that limit student college access. They aim to increase college participation by including academic counseling for college prerequisites, providing formal mentoring and support, focusing on esteem- and skill-building experiences, involving parents to build cultural and social capital about college, and providing monetary incentives/scholarships to actualize college attendance (Gándara, 2001, p. 32). As is discussed in chapter 2, while high schools and intervention program representatives may view family involvement as critical, there is often a limited range of opportunities for parents to participate in their children's college preparation programs.

While most pipeline interventions have goals of increasing student interest, eligibility, and participation in college, evaluative data often remain uncollected or unavailable to assess program performance (Eisenberg & Martin, 2001; Gándara, 2001; Hayward et al., 1997). However, Gándara (2001) suggests that the most successful college preparation programs featured several components that addressed mentoring for long periods/multiple years, high-quality instruction, long-term partnerships with schools, programs that reflected or considered student cultures and backgrounds, and scholarship assistance (p. 36).

Findings by Hayward et al. (1997) support a focus on the timing and timeline for outreach programs, suggesting that successful interventions share elements such as student socialization to college and career roles, strategic timing of interventions, extensive integration in the K–12 environment and program sustainability over time (pp. 14–15). Successful college outreach activities enhanced the resources already available in the secondary school environment, building name recognition, support from parents, students, and administrators, and an academic track record with students over the course of multiple-year involvement. These programs also provided sustained coordination between the secondary and postsecondary sectors that made possible a reasonable division of labor among professionals and potential whole-school reforms. Similarly, the programs ensured effective timing and consistency of interventions.

Timing specific pipeline interventions on academic preparation, test preparation, and college financing to begin at least by ninth grade has the potential to positively improve student preparation for college enrollment. This early timing enables parents to develop the necessary savings and financing options for college participation, and to assist their children in test preparation and review. Moreover, these early interventions enable students to access counseling and develop long-term mentoring relationships to support their college search activities.

A 1990 eligibility study found that in addition to 12.3% of the public school students who were fully eligible with courses, grades, and achievement tests to apply to the University of California, an additional 6.5% of public school students had met all admissions criteria except standardized tests (California Postsecondary Education Commission [CPEC], 1992). As researchers suggest,

> For this group of students, the barrier is the test. . . . Students should be encouraged to take the tests early and often perhaps as early as the tenth grade to receive detailed feedback so that they can make up any deficiencies by the twelfth grade. (Hayward et al., 1997, p. 22)

Standardized test preparation has long been a contentious issue for students and college admissions representatives alike. While many studies attack the validity of college entrance examinations to assess student potential for college persistence accurately, many studies support that these tests provide limited measures of generalized student abilities (Hanford, 1991; Lemann, 1999; Wilmouth, 1991). The popularity of these tests as part of the criteria for college admissions is supported by statistics of approximately 2 million students participating in the Scholastic Aptitude Test and the American College Testing Program (College Board, 2002; American College Testing Program, 2002). Immediate outreach activities starting early during the high school years will diagnose any outstanding academic deficiencies among students and enable a significant portion of students to complete standardized test prerequisites for college admissions. Further, these programs communicate important registration and fee waiver information to facilitate more students, particularly those from low socioeconomic backgrounds, to complete another requirement for college admissions.

In general, the literature suggests the importance of sustained intervention activities through college–high school partnerships and other pipeline interventions. For these programs to impact larger groups of students, their program elements must be institutionalized and provided from the early high school years through the completion of 12th grade. By doing so, college representatives will better understand the populations of students who will apply to their campuses, and students, their parents, and their teachers have opportunities to improve student performance and high school structures aimed at counseling and support.

THE CHALLENGE FOR SCHOOL–UNIVERSITY PARTNERSHIPS

Taken together, the literature discussed in this chapter supports structured college preparation programs that begin early, at minimum by ninth grade. These programs supplement the counseling and academic advising that may or may not exist in high school learning communities to inform students' college searches and career opportunities. Also, these interventions help students to develop foundational skills and subject knowledge, self-esteem and aspirations for college and graduate education, multiple and reliable contacts and mentors, test preparation strategies, and other skills to navigate the college admissions process. National and state statistics suggest continued problems with college access and retention (Allen, Bonous-Hammarth, & Teranishi, 2002; Wilds, 2000). Academic outreach programs and other pipeline interventions aim to improve opportunities for college access by working directly with students, parents, teachers, and school districts.

Several continuing challenges are faced by partnership staff and school administrators involved in intervention programming. In general, lack of reliable program data hinders formal evaluation connected to student outcomes such as high school graduation and undergraduate and graduate school participation. Moreover, program data would help staff to refine the intervention more appropriately for participants from year to year and would enable staff to measure student development throughout the course of the intervention. In addition, issues related to student attrition from voluntary programs suggest that timing programs too late during high school or for too brief amounts of time to benefit students, and at too superficial a level to benefit schools, impede greater program success (Gándara, 2001). In one study, program respondents suggested that outreach programs had the greatest impact on changing school cultures, fostering student identity, and providing intensive college-going support—items all related to the conditions they believed were necessary to create systemic educational reform (Barela et al., 2001, p. 29). However, in an era of frequently unstable budgets, program representatives face erratic funding that impacts staffing, program quality, and duration, and program ability to help high schools realize reform goals (Eisenberg & Martin, 2001, p. 25).

The emerging research discussed in this chapter suggests important ways that early academic interventions and sustained partnership efforts may improve student transitions from high school to college. The findings also raise questions for educators about the role of higher education institutions in sponsoring such initiatives by effectively engaging teachers, students, and parents in these interventions. It is also important to note the necessity of providing consistent teaching tools and curricula to reach academic targets for students that enable their immediate and postcollege success.

REVISITING STUDENT AND INSTITUTIONAL STRATEGIES FOR COLLEGE SUCCESS

This chapter examines several issues in the literature with reference to the timing of college preparation, development of aspirations for college, and completion of college prerequisites. Past research has identified a general three-stage process for college choice, with student predispositions to attend college developing during their elementary school years from parental influences and school engagement, and subsequent information gathering about college options and college choices occurring during high school (Cabrera & LaNasa, 2000c; Hossler et al., 1989; Hossler & Gallagher, 1987; Stage & Hossler, 1989). The literature suggests that high schools structure activities, such as college advising, based on assumptions that students at earlier stages in the pipeline have access to information about college opportunities (from parents) and are completing prerequisite coursework for college (McDonough, 1997). University partnerships and other pipeline interventions provide activities that range in terms of frequency, content, effectiveness, and involvement with middle schools, secondary schools, students, teachers, and parents (Barela et al., 2001; Gándara, 2001; Hayward et al., 1997).

The literature discussed in this chapter suggests that a majority of students—those from low socioeconomic backgrounds or from families where college attendance is not an established tradition—are insufficiently prepared to enter higher education directly from high school (CPEC, 1992, 1997; Wilds, 2000). However, underpreparation for college is by no means limited to these disadvantaged groups. College preparation programs and intervention efforts organized to target students in the later years of high school will do little to improve transition rates for students whose academic records and unfamiliarity with the Scholastic Achievement Test in middle school set them on paths away from higher education. In this sense, educators must recognize that these interventions must begin at, if not before, ninth grade and must aim at sustained programmatic activity.

As educators, we know that students need to develop aspirations for college and that their parents need to understand how elementary and high school coursework connects to college readiness, college opportunities, and potential career placements. To this end, we need to promote equitable means to inform students and to foster their college goals. We also need to be sensitive to the inequitable distribution of resources that occurs across K–12 schools. Instead of relying on traditional frames of reference—a focus and spending of resources on those "on track" in their articulation of college goals—we should structure learning opportunities to provide all students with access to college information and opportunities. This logic also supports an argument for providing greater resources to students and families with the least cultural capital about college preparation/attendance to improve their planning skills and financial resources for college.

Implicit in our proposition is an understanding that while students make decisions about whether or not to attend college and choose whether to seek information on potential colleges, these students of necessity rely on information from networks of parents, siblings, counselors, teachers, and peers. To return for a moment to our commuter story that opened this chapter: If students only receive scheduling information for the first train leaving the railroad station, they may never know about subsequent train departures from alternative sites or, in college preparation terms, the alternative paths to college and the variety of college options available to them. For students' college preparation to lead to successful college enrollment, educators must facilitate networking to provide information early and consistently about academic prerequisites and the process of college admissions.

RECOMMENDATIONS FOR RESEARCH, PRACTICE, AND POLICY

Our brief examination in this chapter suggests several ways that educators may think about research, practice, and policy differently to support early and consistent college preparation activities for students.

Research

Educational research remains an ever-evolving and increasingly complex endeavor, but allows us opportunities to examine a range of factors and their influences on student outcomes. Longitudinal research and cross-sectional studies on students at key points during the life course will provide us with helpful insights on how these students strategize and enact their educational progress. This type of research would be particularly effective in assessing the impact on college participation and retention among students at different preparation points across the life course (e.g., at the end of middle school, at the start of 9th grade, and perhaps later, at the start of 11th grade). As suggested by Hayward et al. (1997), it is critical to develop student information sources for outreach programs to enable current and future researchers to evaluate program effectiveness within and across the spectrum of activities offered. Similarly, it is important to understand the characteristics and issues faced by students in numerous college preparation programs and by those who leave these programs (Gándara, 2001). Considered in conjunction with institution-level data, these analyses will provide powerful insights on the roles that specific learning contexts played in influencing college participation and about the facilitators and barriers to success in various learning communities.

In general, the information examined by researchers should determine how soon specific college preparation activities should occur for students, and the impact of these activities for different types of students to obtain the maximum benefits of knowledge and skills to aid in their college applications. In addition to the assessment of specific partnership program data, researchers should examine the timing of parental involvement in college preparatory activities and the impact of all—versus several or a few—program elements in early academic preparation.

Practice

The evidence from several studies suggests contradictory findings on performance outcomes for students on homogeneous ability tracking (compared to facilitating mixed ability groups) but does suggest that these practices have discriminatory effects for poor and minority students (Lake, 1988; Mills, 1998). Tracking impedes deep learning for many students and circumvents the development of values related to democracy and social justice in a multicultural classroom. Students need to engage in the broadest possible spectrum of learning experiences in order to gain information about the college and admissions process. Student learning experiences should be designed to foster agency and esteem, resiliency, and effective college/postcollege academic practices. Since curriculum is often developmental, requiring students to engage in foundational courses before graduating to more complex knowledge courses, high school counseling is needed from ninth grade to advise students about college prerequisites and other courses that will aid their holistic development.

The consideration of the student's role in college preparation is just one piece of the puzzle, given the many factors and relationships (e.g., with teachers, counselors, parents) that influence student interest in college. Educators should examine the learning paths of their students relevant to educational opportunities available in their schools. Specifically, district and school coordination should encourage resource-rich schools (ready access to credentialed teachers, professional development, teaching facilities, and other resources) to coordinate with resource-poor schools to facilitate teacher development, organize joint school research and curricula, and implement early and consistent college counseling. Teachers should also develop effective peer programs that provide students with different opportunities across social class and ability groupings for collaboration in the learning process.

Practice also needs to focus on independent and community efforts to engage parents and students in networking about college concerns. Whether this activity involves self-organized student/parent meetings to share information on college resources, or structured activities and workshops for parents about preparing their children for college, family involvement and high school organization should be weighed. Also, the timing of specific events—financial aid application workshops, test preparation strategies, and other information sessions, for example—should occur early and consistently across the student's high school years to positively impact the social capital for college preparation. In all these activities, the general timelines for assessing student progress and readiness for college should be identified clearly and built into teacher and district evaluations.

Policy

Appeals for additional resources in education often reflect concerns about money. However, the expertise of policymakers—their national and international understanding of student learning outcomes based on knowledge about the many programs currently operating in high schools and colleges to improve educational preparation/achievement—would be a key resource to provide at the institutional and district levels for high schools. Without an understanding of the policy tensions relied upon to assess and evaluate educational practices and interventions, few helpful dialogues and alliances are likely to develop between educators and policymakers. Finally, where the evidence suggests that funding and key state mandates have hindered college access for students, there should be immediate action to remedy these problems.

Policymakers bear a large responsibility for assessing the mechanisms by which students access college—specifically, what financial aid information is available to parents, when this information is available, and how the process for financial aid may be streamlined to improve student participation. It is important to change the policies that have constricted the grant aid for the most needy students and, by so doing, have fueled the perception that higher education is available to only a very few in our society. Moreover, it is important to provide sustained funding to support comprehensive and specific outreach programs that augment and in some cases are the sole sources of college advisement to an increasingly diverse high school population.

In examining the corollaries of strong college preparation for students from diverse academic and cultural backgrounds, we need to be aware of our tendency to articulate a limited model. Too often models of the trajectory of college-bound students fail to recognize that many students stop out or defer college enrollment or traverse alternate paths (e.g., work or transfer enrollment) before completing professional education. We need to recognize that our arbitrary expectations about suitable criteria for college admissions or appropriate measures for student evaluation do not necessarily suit all students. Given that students experience different influences over time and develop at different rates, we need to retarget resources and emphases. Students should be provided options at several points over the life course to continue on a path to college. At the same time, however, we must assure that these interventions are accompanied by early and consistent efforts to familiarize students with the possibilities and to equip them with the skills to achieve.

WATSON SCOTT SWAIL

Chapter Nine

Value Added: The Costs and Benefits of College Preparatory Programs in the United States

INTRODUCTION

A mentoring program in Detroit, Michigan, provides services to 300 low-income students each year. A tutoring program in Olympia, Washington, serves over 1,200 students across the district. And a mathematics intervention in El Paso, Texas, helps 230 students complete algebra I by the end of the eighth grade. Each of these programs offers a public good by helping students overcome barriers to educational progress. These programs typify thousands of similar but different efforts across the country, some supported by public funds, others privately. While the prevailing notion is that these programs play an important role in the preparation of at-risk and other underrepresented students for college, there is little empirical evidence related to the actual success of these programs (Gándara & Bial, 1999; Swail & Perna, 2002). Moreover, we have little concept of the true impact of funding on service delivery and long-term program impact.

Previous chapters offer much to the discussion of strategies to ameliorate the conditions facing our most needy students. As evidenced in these chapters, there are a plethora of programs using these techniques. However, rarely do we ask about the effectiveness of these programs or whether they are an efficient use of tax dollars and philanthropic funds.

The following pages consider issues related to the complex proposition that the cost of program delivery is directly and positively tied to the ability of programs to successfully enable students to get into college. As part of this discussion, I touch on some background information on the funding of these programs and the competition for limited fiscal resources, and introduce cost analysis as a method of answering these questions. Cost analysis can be an extremely complex analytical process, which is one reason why it is seldom used in the education arena. However, when used properly it can be a very powerful tool in defining the true social and economic impacts of programs.

BACKGROUND

The Returns of Education

This discussion is predicated on the belief that the returns of a college education far outweigh those of not attending a postsecondary institution, and are measured in terms of the development of fiscal and social capital. From a purely financial standpoint, bachelor's degree recipients earn, on average, almost $30,000 per year more than individuals with only a high school diploma (Mortenson, 2002). Over the course of a lifetime, this translates into a net differential of approximately $1 million, before consideration of investment dividends. And graduate and professional students earn about three times as much as high school graduates.

Individuals who attend and graduate from college realize a number of short- and long-term benefits. The short-term consumption benefits of attending college include enjoyment of the learning experience, involvement in extracurricular activities, participation in social and cultural events, and enhancement of social status. Long-term or future benefits include higher lifetime earnings, more fulfilling work environment, better health, longer life, more informed purchases, and lower probability of unemployment (Bowen, 1980; Leslie & Brinkman, 1988; McPherson, 1993).

Over the course of the 20th century, more people enrolled and completed a postsecondary degree than ever before. Today, over 14 million students attend a postsecondary institution in the United States, due in part to the understanding that a college degree is the key to economic and social success in American society. This growth is not isolated. All groups, regardless of background, are going to college at higher rates. However, participation rates for students from low-income backgrounds and students of color significantly lag behind those of White and Asian students (Gladieux & Swail, 1999).

Public Policy

Public policy has long concerned itself with the experiences of individuals from lower socioeconomic levels. At the federal level, the 1940s GI Bill and the 1960s "War on Poverty" are landmark examples of government safety net programs to ensure that individuals on the lower rungs of society are given some type of public support. The Higher Education Act of 1965 (HEA) provided student aid and academic support programs targeted to low-income families and students of color. Today, HEA provides over $40 billion to students in direct financial aid each year, plus several billion dollars more in special programs for targeted groups. Additionally, state and local governments spend millions of dollars on special programs to facilitate academic preparation and college access for underrepresented students.

The federal government spends over $1 billion each year on two intervention initiatives to help students overcome social and cultural barriers to higher education. The largest appropriation ($802 million in fiscal year 2002) is through TRIO, which includes the precollege programs Upward Bound and Talent Search. A second federal initiative and program, GEAR-UP (Gaining Early Awareness and Readiness for Undergraduate Programs), was created during the 1998 reauthorization of the Higher Education Act. GEAR-UP differs from TRIO by targeting a cohort of students in public schools for services and following them through to graduation.[1]

Individual states have also created their own programs, such as Florida's CROP (College Reach-Out Program) and California's CalSOAP (California Student Opportunity and Access Program). The private sector, through a variety of non-for-profit entities, is responsible for programs like the California-based MESA (Mathematics, Engineering, and Science Achievement) and the national I Have a Dream Foundation. A few corporate foundations have created their own programs, such as College Bound, sponsored by the GE Fund.

Each year, programs like these compete for funds in both governmental and philanthropic arenas. Slicing the federal, state, or local budget pie is fraught with difficult choices of competing interests. For instance, only 1 in 6 dollars of federal spending are considered discretionary in nature, meaning only 17% of the federal budget is beyond the jurisdiction of the main departments of federal authority. Within this discretionary area, health services programs (e.g., NIH), research and evaluation (e.g., NSF), arts and humanities (e.g., NEA), and programming and research through the Department of Education each compete for a slice of the pie. Programs must annually make their case for funding through the appropriations process, but in a shrinking economy, the stakes are greater.

Although the federal government is a primary example, the story is no different at any other level of government. Programs must compete for funds in an environment where the competition can be fierce. Those who do well during an appropriations campaign often do so for two reasons: they effectively motivate their grassroots organizations and stakeholders to pressure the appropriations committee, and they effectively illustrate the importance and value of their program. Programs funded by philanthropic organizations also find themselves in a fix during tough times. The recent fall of the stock market has forced many large philanthropic organizations to reduce funding due to decreases in endowments. Thus, a poor economy invariably affects all programs, regardless of funding source.

Half of all precollege intervention programs receive federal funding, one quarter receive state funding, and 20% receive funding from philanthropic organizations (Swail & Perna, 2000). Therefore, the issues discussed above do impact programs.

Linking Program Costs With Effectiveness

In an era when budgets are constricted and new sources of funding seem less apparent, the cost effectiveness of public programs is more important than ever. Interestingly enough, this seems to have had little impact on public policy. A number of studies have shown that several large-scale public programs, including Head Start, Upward Bound, and Success for All have had marginal impact on students from an empirical standpoint. Still, each program has been rewarded with an increasing commitment of federal funds because people understand how these programs change lives, even if the research does not necessarily support this conclusion.

We must also consider that the constriction of public funds will increase as time passes. Our aging population will further constrain budgets at all levels of government, and it is plausible that public focus will shift to the elderly. So the competition for program funding is likely to intensify, not decrease, even given a recovered economy.

In answering the proposition this chapter begins with, practice and theory must lead us to assume that increased program funding is associated with a greater chance of postsecondary access and success for participating students enlisted in these programs. Almost all programs rely on significant face-to-face contact with students, the most expensive type of intervention. Borrowing from Levine and Nidiffer (1996), at-risk and underrepresented students require "one arm around one child" in order to succeed. At the ConnectED precollege program conference in 2000, one of the success story participants, a first-generation college student from rural Virginia who graduated with honors from Harvard, commented that it took several pairs of arms to get her through. Thus, interventions to support traditionally underrepresented students are costly and rely heavily on personnel.

On a simplistic level, we can understand that a change in personnel funding or service delivery can have a net impact on student outcomes. Increased funding allows more of everything, while a reduction reduces the flow of services to students. Most practitioners will testify that staffing is critical to their efforts to serve students, and most acknowledge that their ability to impact students relies heavily on services provided through project staffing. However, we must also consider cost efficiency in the analysis of the effect of program funding, staffing, and services on student outcomes. In an economic sense, a dollar spent on staffing may not yield one dollar's worth of impact with regard to student outcomes. Similarly, that same dollar spent on Web development, books and supplies, or transportation may not translate efficiently to the program's primary outcome. Thus, we cannot guarantee that increased program resources have a direct 1:1 ratio of spending versus impacts. In some cases the ratio may be higher (more efficient) or sometimes lower (less efficient).

Efficiency is a paramount concept for consideration. While educators are raised on the notion that program cuts are the antithesis of progress, the corporate world has operated on much different rules mandated by a competitive, global market. The 1990s were a decade of downsizing for corporations and businesses. The business/industry sector found that strategic or surgical workforce cuts may generate a leaner, more efficient system capable of producing greater profits. It is possible that this phenomenon occurs in education as well, but there is little or no evidence substantiating this fact. Approximately 80% of public school budgets are spent on personnel. Intervention programs are no different, because they also work in the business of direct services to students and families. Thinking in more pragmatic terms, funding for programs and strategies as discussed in this book has a direct impact on the following:

- The number of students served
- The number of teachers or instructors involved in a program
- The hiring of administrative support, including a director
- The coordination of volunteers
- The rental of space for programming
- The use of transportation (e.g., buses)
- Special programming (e.g., plays, etc.)
- Coaching materials for SAT/ACT test taking
- Counseling materials

Because we rarely focus on cost analysis in education, we similarly rarely focus on efficiency. We talk often about the impact of programs, usually through test scores or other concrete, tangible measures, but we seldom take the extra step to look at long-term issues and program accountability. Perhaps we focus on services and process because we do not have the political longevity, inclination, or resources to focus on outcomes, cost, and effectiveness.

MOVING FROM BELIEF TO EMPIRICISM

The difficulty in accepting our proposition resides in the fact that there is little empirical evidence for us to hang our collective hat on. For us to move from the theoretical to the practical world, we must build tangible, empirically based models to measure program impact and efficiency. Without models, our policymakers will be forced to make prudent policy decisions based on limited information. As well, we cannot assume that more money allocated to education will have a significant impact on student outcomes unless we have proof of the linkage between the two (Hummel-Rossi & Ashdown, 2002, p. 1).

Three questions must be answered to produce the information desired. Does the program produce the desired impact that it was designed to produce? Does the benefit of the program outweigh program costs? Third, does the program offer the most cost-effective and appropriate way of reaching the desired goals?

Unfortunately, the ability to answer these questions within the scope of precollege intervention programs is severely hampered by our lack of data and our unsophisticated research methodologies (Gándara, 2002a; Gándara & Bial, 1999; Swail & Perna, 2002; Tierney, 2002). According to Gándara, "college interventions suffer from a serious lack of rigorous evaluation, in spite of the millions of dollars that are invested in them annually" (2002a, p. 97). Our first question, that of impact analysis, is the foundational question for all analysis. We simply must know how the program impacts students. The reality is that we often cannot answer this question because (a) resources are rarely applied to evaluation and analysis, and (b) we do not deem it as a priority. When we do travel down the evaluation road, we typically default to the more simplistic measures of student outcomes, such as test scores, attendance patterns, and retention in school. By doing so, we step away from the more difficult work of addressing other potential benefits of intervention programs, including medium- and long-term effects that are often less tangible. Many programs designed to help students get into college do not collect accurate data on student outcomes (Gándara & Bial, 1999; Swail & Perna, 2002), and information about program costs is often not reported or collected from programs, even in large-scale educational evaluations (Karoly et al., 2001).

Cost analysis is rarely used in education, despite significant expenditures within an environment that is significantly more interested in program outcomes and effective use of taxpayer dollars than any previous generation (Hummel-Rossi & Ashdown, 2002). As well, understanding the role of cost is an important factor in program design, population targeting strategies, and implementation (Karoly et al., 2001).

Cost Analysis Defined

Cost analyses provide a mechanism to compare program costs to the benefits due to the program, and can be used to promote fiscal accountability, set priorities when resources are limited, and act as an effective tool to persuade legislators and potential funders of the importance of the program (Sewell & Marczak, 2002). Additionally, cost analysis can help policymakers and program directors estimate a program's costs and benefits before implementation, improve the understanding of program operation and underscore the most cost-effective components, and identify unexpected costs. Disadvantages include the high level of technical skill required, disagreements over the benefit of these types of analyses, and the difficulty in assigning monetary values to qualitative goals. Important to note is that, in the end, cost analyses cannot determine whether a program or strategy exhibited a desired impact. It can only describe the costs associated with that impact (Rice, 1996).

Cost-benefit and cost-effectiveness analyses are forms of efficiency analysis that attempt to define the benefit of a program or policy versus the cost (Rossi & Freeman, 1993). Although the two forms of analysis are different in scope, the lines between the two sometimes get blurred in the literature. A cost-benefit analysis evaluates the costs and benefits of a program in dollars and then compares the two, and is essentially interested in answering the question, "Is this program worth doing?" Three analytical steps make up a cost-benefit analysis, although there are many considerations that must be made within each of these steps. The first step is to evaluate the costs of running the program. Second is the evaluation of program benefit. Third is the determination of whether the calculated benefit outweighs the accounted program cost. This is usually done in the form of a cost-benefit ratio, which is nothing more than the product of dividing the benefit by the cost. For example, if program cost is accounted at $10,000 and the determined benefit is $40,000, then:

$$\text{CB ratio} = \frac{\$40,000}{\$10,000} = 4.0$$

Thus, the cost-benefit ratio is 4.0, meaning that the program benefit outweighs program costs by a 4 to 1 ratio. Put another way, the returns to the program are four times the investment.

Cost-benefit analysis is generally used to determine the cost versus benefit of a single program, and may be used to determine either the fiscal benefit to the program or institution (e.g., cost savings) or the fiscal/societal benefit to the individual and society (e.g., lifetime earnings). With respect to precollege outreach programs, we can utilize a cost-benefit analysis to determine whether the individual and societal benefits of a community youth mentoring program outweigh the costs of program delivery.

A cost-effectiveness analysis differs from a cost-benefit analysis by considering the relative costs and benefits of a number of alternative programs (Rice, 1993). With cost-effectiveness analysis, we are generally interested in answering the question, "Which of these interventions is more efficient in terms of its use of resources?" Benefits are assumed in a cost-effectiveness analysis, such as when we compare the cost effectiveness of Program A versus

Program B. We assume that both have about the same impact, but are interested in knowing which program does so in a more efficient manner.

Cost analysis is, on a simplistic level, an example of proper use of program budgeting and accounting practices (Kettner, Moroney, & Martin, 1990). Instead of credits and debits, we work with costs and benefits. The cost side of the equation involves the allocation of dollar values to all program inputs and resources, such as staffing, logistics, and materials. The benefit side is infinitely more complex due to the difficulty in allocating resources to future situations.

Depending on the scope of the study, calculating costs and benefits can be either simple or complex. For instance, to calculate the costs associated with a precollege program, one would sum up tangible program costs such as staffing, overhead charges associated with program space, materials, transportation, and perhaps additional costs for special events, such as field trips. One could also add the opportunity costs associated with participating in the program, such as immediate earnings that could be earned during program hours.

On the benefit side, one would sum up the tangible and less tangible benefits, immediate and future oriented. These may include increased earnings for students who persist and earn a bachelor's degree, increased tax revenue, and reduction in incarceration rates and recidivism. Table 9.1 illustrates the items used in a 1971 cost-benefit analysis of Upward Bound participants.

Variables such as foregone earnings, unemployment and welfare costs, and after-tax lifetime income involve complex calculations. Because the identification of costing of benefits can be subjective to a certain degree, the outcomes of a cost-benefit analysis are often debated.

TABLE 9.1.
Description of costs and benefits associated with Upward Bound cost-benefit analysis
(1971, Garn)

Costs	Benefits
• Additional tuition costs required of Upward Bound students due to higher rates of post-secondary attendance. • Additional expenses of Upward Bound students while in college. • Earnings foregone by Upward Bound students while in college. • Transfer income over the lifetime fore-gone by Upward Bound students (e.g., unemployment and welfare).	• Increased after-tax lifetime incomes. • Stipends paid to participants during the program. • Scholarships and other grants received by Upward Bound students in college.

(Rossi and Freeman, 1993, p. 385)

Cost analysis takes many forms and is peculiar to the type of program being assessed. Again, many of these analyses are very complex. The scope of this chapter does not allow for an in-depth investigation into specific cost-analysis treatments. However, to provide a better understanding of how cost analysis works in the real world, it is worth reviewing a few examples from the research literature.

Case Study I: The Supplemental Instruction Experience

The Supplemental Instruction (SI) program, developed at University of Missouri–Kansas City (UMKC) in 1974, provides academic support to students through specific course work. While not labeled as a tutoring program, SI contributes tutoring-like experiences for students on campus. The UMKC SI program, currently in use at over 1,100 institutions nationwide, provides three weekly sessions of academic support for students beginning the first week of class and is open to all students on a voluntary basis.

Participation in SI at UMKC has been equal across all levels of students, with the same number of students from low and high ACT composite score quartiles enrolling. Still, the program targets classes with 30% or higher rates of D and F grades. By developing the students' concepts of how to learn with knowing what to learn, the SI program has been known to reduce the number of Ds and Fs in addition to the number of course withdrawals by up to 50%.

Following the 1995–1996 academic year, SI conducted an internal cost-benefit analysis of their program (UMKC, 1997). Of the 3,655 students enrolled in 41 selected courses at UMKC in 1995, 40% (1,454) of the students participated in SI at an average cost per student of $46.89. According to their analysis, SI students reenrolled in school and graduated at rates 10 points higher than those of students who could not take SI due to scheduling conflicts. Based on this rate, SI infers that 145 students would have dropped out if not for SI (1,454 students × 10% = 145). Given that the average undergraduate student spends $1,750 on tuition, fees, and other expenses each semester, those 145 students provided a revenue increase of $253,750 to the university (145 × $1,750 = $253,750). This analysis only accounts for one cohort of students. Taking into consideration the full impact of four annual cohorts of freshman students (5,302 students in total), the net retention impact at any one time is argued to be 530 (using the 10% retention rate) additional students due to SI. The financial impact resulting from SI is almost $1 million each year ($1,750 × 530 = $927,500). What is not accounted for here are the costs associated with recruitment and admissions services that must be applied to each admitted student.

Case Study II: The Perry Preschool Program

The cost-benefit analysis of the Perry Preschool program is a benchmark case in the research literature (Karoly et al., 2001; Borman & Hewes, 2001;

Schweinhart, Barnes, & Weikart, 1993). Based in Ypsilanti, Michigan, the program served 58 African American children from low socioeconomic status backgrounds and with low IQ scores between 1962 and 1967. Program participants beginning at age three received two years of services, while four-year-olds received one year. The Perry Preschool program provided high-quality staffing and learning opportunities, with low pupil-teacher ratios. Although the program was small, a good portion of the interest generated by this study stems from the fact that participants from the experimental and control groups were followed through age 27. Impact of the program was measured through several variables. Program participants realized IQ scores 12 points higher than control participants, and academic achievement was also significantly enhanced through program participation. Although there were no differences in postsecondary participation, the final follow-up (age 27) found lasting differences in employment, welfare, and crime.

In his original cost-benefit analysis of the program, Barnett (1993) found that benefits to society exceeded program costs by a factor of 7:1. Karoly et al. (1998), in a reanalysis of the program data, found that the program reduced use of special education, reduced grade retention, increased taxes due to higher employment and less reliance on welfare programs and funding, and reduced justice system costs (Karoly et al., 2001). Table 9.2 shows Karoly et al.'s cost-benefit comparison of a program cost per child of $12,148 to a total benefit of

TABLE 9.2.
Costs and Benefits: The Perry Preschool Program

	Dollars per Child		
	Due to Mother	Due to Child	Total
Program cost			12,148
Savings to government			25,437
Reduction in education services	*	6,365	
Reduction in health services	*	*	
Taxes from increase employment	*	6,566	
Reduction in welfare cost	*	2,310	
Reduction in criminal justice cost	*	10,195	
Additional monetary benefits			24,535
Increase in participant income net of welfare loss	*	13,846	
Reduction in tangible losses to crime victims	*	10,690	
Total benefits			49,972
Net benefits			37,824

(Karoly, Kilburn, Bigelow, Caulkins, Cannon & Chiesa, 2001).
Note: * = not measured. All amounts are in 1996 dollars and are the NPV of amounts over time where future values are discounted to the birth of the participating child, using a 4% annual real discount rate.

$49,972, for a net benefit of $37,824. While not reaching Barnett's claim of a 7:1 benefit, Karoly et al.'s calculation still manages a 4:1 cost-benefit ratio.

Case Study III: Success for All

Success for All (SFA) is an early childhood reading program implemented in more than 1,500 schools throughout the United States (Matthews, 2002, p. 33). A cost-effectiveness analysis of the program (Borman & Hewes, 2001) focused on answering two research questions: what is the relative impact of the program on student success, and what is the cost of program delivery?

With regard to the former, Borman and Hewes tracked the educational outcomes of entering students (grades 1 through 5) through the eighth grade, using program data plus data from two norm-referenced standardized tests: the California Achievement Test (CAT) and the Comprehensive Test of Basic Skills (CTBS). Using a quasi-experimental approach, the researchers were able to discern the academic impact of SFA to students in a control group (thus making it a cost-effectiveness analysis).

For program delivery, the researchers collected several cost estimates. Basing their analysis on Levin and McEwan's (2001) Ingredients Model, the analysis summarized the total and marginal costs for program delivery. Marginal costs were limited to training, materials, and professional development. Costs associated with personnel costs within the Baltimore school system were also estimated.

The researchers acknowledged that SFA is an expensive reform model to implement. However, the purpose of the analysis was to determine whether SFA was any more expensive than the alternatives of having students repeat grades or enroll in special education. The researchers concluded that the mean cost of reaching the eighth grade for SFA students was $70,428.03, compared to $68,850.65 for control students—not statistically different.

Based on further adjustments and calculations, the authors found that SFA had a larger impact based on the cost of the program than published studies of other programs (Table 9.3). However, a reanalysis found that the average

TABLE 9.3.
Per-Pupil Expenditures (PPE) and Sustained Effect Sizes for Four Educational Interventions

	Annual PPE (in 2000 dollars)	Years of Intervention	Total PPE (in 2000 dollars)	Sustained Effect Size	Effect per $1,000
Success for All	603	4.56	2,749.68	0.27	0.1
Class size reduction to 15					
Nye et al.	998	4	3,992.00	0.32	0.08
Finn et al.	998	4	3,992.00	0.22	0.06
Perry Preschool	8,929	2	17,858.00	0.51	0.03
Abecedarian, preschool only	10,496	4.5	47,232.00	0.53	0.01

(Borman & Hewes, 2001)

SFA student failed to reach grade-level performance by the end of the third grade, and students continued to fall further behind national norms through SFA. By the end of the fifth grade, they were almost 2.4 years behind (Matthews, 2002, p. 35). Given that the original Borman and Hewes (2001) analysis found the program to be cost effective and have desirable results, these new findings suggest a different conclusion, and also illustrate how findings from alternative cost analyses can be debated and contradictory.

COST ANALYSIS AND PUBLIC POLICY

Focusing exclusively on cost can also have negative ramifications. According to Rice (1996), while cost analysis can help determine feasibility within a limited resource pool, it provides no information on the effectiveness of the program in meeting the desired needs. "To the degree that an intervention is ineffective, adopting it exclusively on the basis of its relative cost may be a waste of valuable resources, potentially translating into exceedingly high long-term costs" (p. 34).

Policymakers often look at per-pupil expenditures (PPE) as a simple default for cost analysis. As we know, there are great disparities in PPE across counties, states, and regions. For example, the median average PPE for U.S. public schools in 2002 was $6,657 (NEA, 2002). North Dakota spends $4,426 per student, compared to $12,345 in the District of Columbia. Valuing Rice's (1996) statement of the break between feasibility and effectiveness, we find that, although the District of Columbia spends almost three times as much per pupil as North Dakota, that does nothing to explain why the latter scores significantly higher on NAEP tests, on average, than DC students (NAEP, 2001). Nor can we assume that DC spends three times as much as North Dakota on student learning. Therefore, we must be careful when using a single number, such as a PPE, in a costing model without taking other factors into consideration.

Much damage can be done when cost-analysis data are misused. For instance, to suggest that a program is inefficient or too costly to maintain based solely on the number of individuals who meet the final program criteria, without consideration of those who benefit from the program but do not reach the final stated goals, is a careless use of data. One must always attempt to build into the analysis all unintended positive impacts of the program. A simple example is the program participant who does not complete a bachelor's degree but does complete an associate's degree. This individual may lead a productive, tax-paying, community-serving life. Not considering these benefits negatively skews the cost-benefit ratio.

We must also be mindful of misinterpreting a positive cost-benefit analysis as an implication of program feasibility or effectiveness, or the opposite, that a positive impact suggests that the program is cost effective. These misconceptions are common in the literature, where research articles point to the "cost effectiveness" of a program, with no evidence of evaluating program inputs as they relate to outputs. Just because a program has a positive impact does not infer that it is cost effective or efficient. It only implies a positive impact.

Finally, cost and impact analyses may be largely ignored in the public policy arena (Anderson, 1993). When an evaluation has a negative finding on a program, it is common for organizations and individuals to critique the evaluation on methodological grounds and attempt to negate the evaluation. This was illustrated when a 1999 study of Upward Bound was released with findings that did not paint an overall positive picture of the large-scale federal program (Myers & Schirm, 1999). Critics quickly pointed to methodological problems associated with the choice of control group participants, putting the evaluation into question. Another federal program, Head Start, has traditionally battled with poor research findings. As with Upward Bound, critics quickly lambasted these evaluations.

Thus, even thoroughly and appropriately conducted evaluations and assessments rarely determine the final outcome for a program. Anderson (1993) suggests that he is unable to think of a governmental program that was terminated "solely as a consequence of an unfavorable systematic evaluation" (p. 292).

SUGGESTIONS FOR IMPROVING THE QUALITY OF INQUIRY

For those who are deeply interested in cost analysis as a tool to better understand their program and to provide evidence of their program's social impact, I strongly suggest reviewing Barnett's (1993) nine-step process for cost-benefit analysis and Rice's (1997) template-driven model for unpacking costs and weighting benefits. It is worth reminding readers that these can become very complex, and outside expertise may be required.

Whether actively pursuing a cost analysis or reviewing information from a cost analysis, four issues are worthy of keeping in mind:

1. *Quality of information.* An analysis is only as good as the data. For the cost side, taking numbers directly from budget information may not be accurate. Researchers may have to determine actual costs associated with program operation from a variety of sources. On the benefit side, the further we get from the program (in terms of time), the more difficult it is to predict data that accurately depict program benefits. The benefit portion of the analysis can require subjective

decisions about the weighting or valuing of data and thus must be considered carefully.

2. *Short versus long-term impact.* Do we know what happens to students well after the intervention is complete? Given that a number of studies find that the effect of interventions often fades over time (Borman & Hewes, 2001; Currie & Duncan, 2000), it is important to understand this phenomenon, as it could impact the design and delivery of program services. Unfortunately, long-term analysis often requires longitudinal analysis of participants, which is tremendously costly. Additionally, defining the scope of the study at the outset will determine whether this is a short-term look or a long-term perspective.

3. *Tangibles versus intangibles.* Counting who completes, who graduates, or who scores well is generally not difficult work in itself. Calculating the impacts or defining the costs of seemingly intangible items, such as the "cost" of volunteers, or the societal benefit of an intervention, is much more complex. "Although it is often difficult to assign a value to many of the inputs and outputs of educational interventions, their inclusion in the total cost and effectiveness estimates is essential. This gives policymakers a realistic sense of the overall cost of the intervention, not just to the budget but to the community" (Rice, 1996, p. 37).

4. *Micro versus macroeconomics.* Researchers are generally looking inward rather than outward. Sometimes limited research budgets are responsible, but we must consider other external factors in our analysis. Otherwise, our research is encapsulated by our protected notion of "what is," with little regard for the impact of the program on other parts of society. Thus, the researcher must first define whether the interest is in determining the immediate, internal program effectiveness and benefits, or whether the long-term impact on the individual and society must be brought into the analysis.

CONCLUSION

With accountability the catchphrase of the day, knowledge of program effectiveness and impact is becoming more critical, especially in light of recent budget crunches at all levels of government. The need to produce evidence of program impact is important for sustained fiscal support.

Precollege programs often provide meaningful, individualized contact between a youth and an adult that is not typically available in the communities or schools from which they hail. For public policy, this is the most difficult type of policy to craft. As Levine and Nidiffer (1996) state, getting poor people into college "is retail, not wholesale, work in the sense that it requires intensive involvement with individuals" (p. 143). That type of effort requires a personnel-driven budget, which, as discussed, is the most expensive budget item in a program. Therefore, increases in funding almost assuredly impact the level or scope of service provided.

In the final analysis, costs matter. Interventions that expend $4,500 per student undoubtedly offer more robust services than those that average $300. All programs could stand a little efficiency testing, and perhaps we will find better, more efficient ways to help needy students prepare for and access college. For now, we need to redouble our effort to uncover the findings from current programs and promote continuous improvement of these efforts. For this to be realized, governmental agencies and policymakers must demand more information about how these programs operate and back it up with the necessary funding to make that happen. Unfunded mandates won't cut it. Philanthropic organizations, too, must demand a higher level of empirical evidence and support the needs of programs to that end, and also provide the financial support to make that happen. And program practitioners must push beyond current knowledge and practice and begin thinking and practicing high-level analysis and program management well before it comes to them in stated policy.

Of course, we must continue to be cautious about the use of numbers and statistics in defining social interventions. Einstein once said that not everything that can be counted counts, and not everything that counts can be counted. The use of cost analysis to explore the effectiveness of programs is an important tool, but results used out of context or in a truncated fashion can be more dangerous to the development of prudent public policy.

NOTE

1. See Swail and Perna (2002) for a more complete discussion of these and other programs.

ROBERT RUEDA

Conclusion: Making Sense of What We Know—From Nine Propositions to Future Research and Interventions

The current federal and national emphasis on education has placed a major focus on early education issues. Research clearly shows the importance and value of early intervention and its impact on later school achievement. Yet the current volume serves as a needed reminder that there are critical issues involving equal access to higher education later in the educational pipeline that merit attention as well. If early intervention efforts are thwarted later in the process, those efforts will have been in vain.

One by-product of the current national focus on education has been to direct public and professional attention to issues of accountability and "making a difference" in a cost-effective way. The push is toward taking or developing "reliable, research-based" interventions and trying to standardize, package, and mandate them, and then monitor the implementation for accountability purposes. The underlying assumption is that these types of intervention approaches are universally applicable in all settings. One problem is that this approach tends to ignore the effects of context—differences in subgroups, communities, and even individuals. What works in one place and with one group may not work elsewhere with different groups.

In thinking about issues of access, it is possible to fall into the same trap. That is, one could attempt to design and develop universally transportable interventions based on a small number of program elements or design principles that have been proven "to work." However, the efforts in the present volume should not be mistaken for an example of this approach. While the volume sets out to synthesize what is known about the parameters of effective college out-reach programs that seek to improve access to higher education for underrep-resented students, the attempt is not to highlight fixed, universal laws that might govern the creation of specific ready-made interventions or models in rigid ways. Rather, the focus is on examining the robustness of a small number of overarching principles and trying to synthesize what is known in a system-atic and comprehensive fashion. One advantage of the current approach is that it permits taking a fine lens to the oversimplified and global question, "What works?" It seeks to unpackage this complex question so that specific compo-nents can be examined in greater detail.

HOW DID THE PROPOSITIONS FARE?

Having qualified the nature of the effort represented in these chapters, what can be said about the propositions that framed the project? It will be recalled that the basic propositions guiding this project for enabling students to get into col-lege were as follows:

1. It is helpful, but not critical, to emphasize the culture of the student.
2. Family engagement is critical.
3. Peer groups are helpful, but not critical.
4. Programs need to begin no later than the ninth grade and have struc-tured activities throughout the year.
5. Having knowledgeable, available counselors at the core of the pro-gram is critical.
6. Access to a college preparation curriculum is the most critical vari-able.
7. Cocurricular activities are irrelevant.
8. Mentoring is helpful, but not critical.
9. There is a positive relationship between the cost of program delivery and achieving college readiness.

The following paragraphs summarize the key findings regarding the var-ious propositions.

The Role of Culture

It is not accidental that the chapter on culture (chapter 1) is one of the first in the book or that a cultural emphasis was a central feature in the conceptualiza-tion of the project. In fact, the book revolves around a "cultural integrity" framework that recognizes the cultural underpinnings of the personal, social, and institutional factors that interact in complex ways to mediate access to col-lege (chapters 1 and 3). In general, this argument and similar arguments (Gonzalez, Andrade, Civil, & Moll, 2001; Moll, Amanti, Neff & Gonzales, 1992) stress the value of preexisting knowledge, values, and beliefs as a foundation for promoting educational goals and designing intervention efforts. To reinforce the importance of this position, syntheses of the knowledge base governing learning and development have come to recognize the central role played by culture (Bransford, Brown, & Cocking, 1999; Lambert & McCombs, 1998; Shonkoff & Phillips, 2000). Nevertheless, like other reviewers (e.g., Swail & Perna, 2002) who have looked at this issue, Villalpando and Solorzano find that most outreach and college preparation programs do not attend to students' cultural identities or cultural needs. They also document that the literature in this field that does address culture draws heavily on Bourdieu's (1986) notion of cultural capital. While this is a useful theoretical construct that helps explain variance in educational outcomes, there is also the danger of treating it as a commodity, which by definition systematically relegates some to the "have" category and some to the "have not" category, as the authors appear to be well aware.

In the context of their discussion of the issue, they point to the complex interrelationships among culture, SES, ethnicity, race, class, and so on. They critique the deficit-oriented ways that culture is sometimes used to propose a model of "cultural wealth." This helps reframe the question from "How do we get students of diverse backgrounds to think and act like middle-class Anglo students?" to "What existing features of home and community cultural practices can be appropriated to further academic achievement?" (see Figure C.1). Unfortunately, while there is a good deal of theoretical support for such an approach, there is not extensive empirical evidence, as the authors correctly contend. They also note the importance of flexibility of models and program components to particular communities and contexts, and the need to couple cul-

FIGURE C.1.   A Hypothetical Model of Key Components for Academic Success

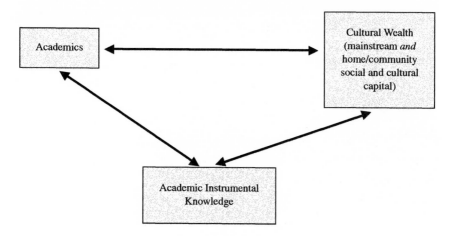

tural accommodations with rigorous academic preparation as opposed to stand-alone efforts. In short, we have very good theoretical reasons to postulate a central role of culture, but the research has not been as strong as might be expected.

Family Factors

Chapter 2 is very useful in documenting how structure, function, and conceptualization of the family have changed over time, and what the consequences are for thinking about college access issues. Not surprisingly, the chapter finds that few programs include a family component, and when families are included it is often in a trivial fashion. Consistent with the framework of the book, the authors go on to recommend a "cultural integrity" approach to considering the role of families and the ways in which program activities might be conceptualized and implemented.

The Role of Peers

Chapter 3 finds that similar to many of the other constructs investigated, the definitions and theoretical approaches to the role of peers are many and have changed over time. While the chapter emphasizes the different theoretical approaches taken to study and explain the role of peers, they conclude that in general the research does not provide a clear-cut answer about the effects of peers on college access for the population under consideration. Even so, the authors correctly maintain that it is clear that there are some effects, and also that peers and the out-of-school learning opportunities they provide are not elective; they are a part of life. The recommendations focus, then, on making them into more strategic tools.

The Role of High School Counselors

McDonough (chapter 4) points out that while college attendance is an important goal at almost every school, there is rarely if ever an identifiable staff member whose job includes direct responsibility for college advising and support in terms of opportunities and access to college. Not surprisingly, she documents the fact that counselor/student ratios are much larger than is considered advisable, and that a significant portion of counselors' days are not spent on direct service to students. While the evidence suggests that having knowledgeable and accessible contact with a college counselor over time is important in eventual college enrollment, the chapter also points out the obstacles: unmanageable caseloads, competing responsibilities, training focused more on psychological counseling than college preparation issues, and so on. This raises the chicken-and-egg question: If more well-prepared counselors were available, would there be a more extensive research base documenting the effects of counselors on eventual college outcomes?

The Role of Mentors

In light of previous work (e.g., Gandara, 1995) as well as at an intuitive level, one might suspect an important role for mentors in the overall picture of college access. Nevertheless, Gándara and Mejorado (chapter 5) find in their review that there is not a lot of research documenting strong effects for the role of mentors. Moreover, they argue that the theoretical mechanisms for understanding how mentors might facilitate college access are not well developed or studied. The typology found in Table C.1 is very helpful as a conceptual tool in bringing together the components of academic success and the propositions presented in this book. As with a discussion of mentors, this synthesis demonstrates how the research has left many issues understudied or unstudied.

The Role of Academic Preparation

The review by Perna (chapter 6) addresses the issue of whether academic achievement is a critical variable for gaining access to a postsecondary education. It is probably the area with the clearest empirical support in terms of its relationship to outcome measures such as college enrollment, and is acknowledged by virtually every other author.

The Role of Cocurricular Activities

In their review of the available research, Hearn and Holdsworth (chapter 7) find that the relationship of social activities to college success effects are modest and mostly indirect. Like some of the areas addressed by the propositions, there are good theoretical reasons to consider such factors, but the existing studies are few and tend to show the correlates but not the process by which they impact access. The authors do make a useful distinction between cocurricular activities that take place within college preparation programs and those that take place outside of them. Unfortunately, they find themselves having to rely on the only available research, which focuses on such activities in general. Like many of the issues addressed in other propositions, this provides a good example of how a comprehensive model is needed that looks at all of the critical factors and their complex and interactive interrelationships.

Timing and the Role of Structured Activities in College Preparation and Outreach Programs

Bonous-Hammarth and Allen (chapter 8) address the issue of timing—does it matter if outreach is done earlier rather than later? The question implies that there is a developmental process rather than one single critical incident that determines college access issues. The authors correctly note that student choices do not occur in a vacuum—there are issues of student agency, but also contex-

TABLE C.1.

Aspects of Intervention across the Domains of the Nine Propositions

Key Components of Academic Access and Success	Domain							
	Culture of the Student	Family Engagement	Peer Groups	Knowledgeable, Available, Counselors	Mentoring	College Prep Curriculum	Cocurricular Activities	Timing and Structured Programs
Academics	Academics can be enhanced with culturally relevant curriculum and delivery	Programs should provide families with information about the college-going process	Ensure that peers are academically oriented	Counselors should encourage rigorous course work	Mentors should encourage academic achievement and link academics to career	Schools should provide rigorous, challenging course work		Academic intervention should be targeted early in student's career
Academic instrumental knowledge			Ensure that peers have access to appropriate social networks	Counselors should be a source of social capital for students that provide access to networks and relevant knowledge	Mentors should build on the mentoring relationship to foster relevant instrumental knowledge		Programs should provide a forum for building community and engaging family	Provide access to knowledge and activities that facilitate college access early
Cultural wealth	Schools should incorporate culturally sensitive approaches in intervention design and implementation	Take into account family structure and dynamics in intervention activities	Ensure that peers provide a foundation for personal and cultural identity	Counselors should affirm identity and cultural pride	Mentors should provide high-status, culturally appropriate models that facilitate access	Curriculum should be challenging and culturally relevant	Social activities should provide socially and culturally appropriate outlets	

tual and institutional issues as well. The sociological perspective taken by the authors looks at student preparation for college through an understanding of critical transition points in a student's life and how these influence participation in college and subsequent transitions in career and family. It focuses on change as a dynamic process and the roles that key actors play, such that college is one part of a longer life history. The analogy to a train leaving the station is a good one, however, in terms of summarizing the review. While a commuter who has missed the train still has options to get to his or her final destination, they become fewer and more difficult over time. In general, then, in their review, the authors find strong support in the literature for programs that are both implemented early (at or before ninth grade) and structured and targeted.

The Costs of Program Delivery

In his chapter examining the relationship between the cost of program delivery and student success, Swail (chapter 9) presents some of the complex technical issues involved in cost analyses. It is possible that the complexities involved, the myriad ways of investigating the issue, and the large number of intangibles lead to the fact that more program evaluation data are not available. While the chapter gives the reader a sense of the issues, it would perhaps have been more informative to have used examples and specific studies from college access programs from the small number that exist (e.g., Fountain & Arbreton, 1999; Rumberger & Brenner, 2000; Sipe, 1996). It is difficult to evaluate the proposition given the data presented.

SUMMARY OF THE FINDINGS AND ADDITIONAL CONSIDERATIONS

What do the studies tell us as a group? Virtually no area is closed in terms of research needed. There are unanswered questions in each of the areas, although some have more of a foundation that might be used to guide policy. The factors that appear to be strongly supported by the evidence are academics, timing, and structure, while the roles of culture, mentoring, peers, and counselors are less strongly related to college access. The two areas where the least is known are extracurricular social activities and cost-benefit analyses. Given these summary statements, what are some of the issues raised by the preceding chapters, taken together?

Evaluating the Evidence: How Does One Make Sense of the Studies?

Many of the domains do not have sufficient evidence for a definitive answer—so while a particular proposition might be supported or not, in many cases we still do not know enough about the topic to guide intervention. To draw from an analogy in the testing world, in essence we should treat the reviews in these chapters more as ability tests than as achievement tests. That is, the "scores" (findings the chapters yield) are best seen as a measure of achievement rather than as indicators of potential. They tell us what is known at the present time, but do not tell us about what we might know or need to know in the future. There are many unexplored areas that might make for a new set of propositions at a future time when a more complete research base exists. Thus there is danger in the scorecard approach to examining the impact of the factors considered because it ignores the complex interrelationships and interactions that might mediate what works when.

Conceptual and Theoretical Frameworks

One observation regarding the topic of college access is that there does not appear to be an overarching conceptual and theoretical model that attempts to lay out the interrelationships of all the relevant variables. Almost every author makes reference to the other variables under consideration, but there is not a widely agreed-upon model that one might draw on to do so. This should not be mistaken as an argument to impose rigid or inflexible disciplinary, theoretical, or conceptual boundaries on future work, but rather as an argument for building toward a coherent and comprehensive synthesis of accumulating knowledge and how it relates both to what is known and to what remains to be investigated.

The Complexity of the Constructs and the Underlying Mechanisms

Many of the constructs are not as simple or one-dimensional as might be thought by their conceptual label. For example, Table 5.1 on mentoring shows the various complex factors that might be considered under the deceptively simple one-word label "mentoring," and the same can be said of many of the others—peers, families, counselors, and so on.

Another issue has to do with the mechanisms underlying specific observed effects and relationships. While the chapters related to social support networks (families, peers, mentors, counselors), for example, can be considered as related conceptually, do they operate through the same underlying mechanism or mechanisms? For example, do the factors under social networks influence access through more knowledge, social support leading to more self-efficacy or motivation, or providing access to more powerful social networks? Or is it a combination of all of these or some other uninvestigated factor? It may be necessary to consider them separately in order to unpackage the factors for analytical purposes, but conceptually an effort should be made to understand whether or how they embody the same facilitating mechanism.

What Are the Correct Outcome Measures?

In terms of outcome measures, it is possible to look at access in terms of equality of opportunity. However, it is necessary to consider more distal outcomes as well, such as college performance and graduation rates. If access and opportunity alone do not guarantee eventual positive outcomes, as Oakes et al. (2002) suggest, a reasonable issue should be what it takes to achieve them.

In addition, there is a significant level of difficulty related to unpacking all of the nested factors with low-SES students of color in terms of their relationship to outcome measures. These include factors such as ethnicity, SES, language, and cultural capital, which are all related. From a research perspective, how does one unpack these and determine the individual impact on outcome measures? A common yet problematic practice is to refer to or measure one of these factors and use it as if it indexed another—for example, defining a sample by ethnicity and then using that as an indicator of culture or cultural practices. Such practices should be avoided in research in this area.

The Role of Context

While universally applicable models, programs, or practices are desirable, the mediating influence of specific social contexts is critical to consider. As one example, in discussing tracking, Oakes et al. (2002) show that just raising academic preparation by itself likely will not work. As she suggests, remedies cannot be addressed in isolation; they occur in specific sociocultural contexts that have their own histories and dynamics which are powerful mediators of attempts to intervene (Lucas, 1999; Oakes, 2002; Yonezawa, Wells, & Serna, 2002). The "ecological fit" to specific contexts needs to be a strong consideration.

UNADDRESSED ISSUES: WHAT ELSE IS NEEDED?

Unexamined Factors

While the book gives primacy to the cultural underpinnings of college access, as the introduction indicates, there are aspects of the issue that were not addressed. These include, for example, cultural factors, structural and institutional inequities, and sociopolitical factors that characterize the educational contexts of many urban settings for large numbers of low-income students of diverse backgrounds. The complexity of these factors within those settings are not addressed in detail. While factors such as teacher preparation, access to print materials, quality of curricula, and economic constraints can be seen as noise that muddies the analytical waters, they do mediate efforts to improve access to higher education. Ultimately college is about access to resources and political power, and therefore factors related to these need to be incorporated in future work. For many students, the simple issue of financial aid is the difference between going to college and not. These factors deserve investigation.

A Comprehensive Theoretical Model

The very fact that nine propositions are needed suggest that multiple causal and mediating factors govern access for different groups and individuals. There is no simple package, or we would not need such an extensive list. Such a model would be extremely useful in designing and interpreting research on specific aspects of the problem.

The Role of Context

While universally applicable solutions to differential college access might be desirable, specific contexts mediate any intervention effects unless they are implemented under highly controlled conditions. Rather than pursuing the question, "What works?" it might be more useful to ask, "What works where, with whom, under what conditions, and why?"

Research Design Issues

A great deal of the research relevant to the propositions investigated in this book is correlational, and it should be acknowledged that such research is useful in providing empirical support for hypothesized relationships among various factors. What needs to be avoided, however, is falling into the well-known trap of attributing causality to correlational phenomena. Correlational analyses do not provide information regarding the multitude of questions related to how all the different program elements work or why they work. As an example, it is valuable to know that mentors or peers or families are correlated with later college enrollment, but how do these effects occur? What are the day-to-day processes that serve to create and mediate these relationships? These mediating effects are ultimately made up of specific interactions and encounters in specific contexts around specific issues. While we search for generalized patterns and relationships for purposes of theoretical and conceptual clarity, simplification, and generalization, it is important to also understand the myriad events that serve to define the larger patterns observed.

Two kinds of research seem underrepresented in the current body of literature. These include qualitative, in-depth studies of the processes by which observed effects occur and/or how different variables are related to one another (see, for example, Auerbach, 2002). In addition, consideration might be given to controlled studies that go beyond correlational assessments.

The Unit of Analysis Issue

A basic question in the line of research looking at the issue of college access for underrepresented groups is where does one look analytically and conceptually in thinking about this issue? That is, what is the appropriate target of intervention? What does one focus on in designing studies? As the chapters strongly indicate, the problem is multifaceted. Clearly one must look beyond individual factors for explanatory power or for a target of intervention.

One potentially helpful possibility is based on attempts to develop and elaborate sociocultural views of learning and development. Recent extensions of sociocultural theory propose that phenomena related to learning and development, which certainly include college access, occur in a dynamic process of transformation of participation in a specific sociocultural community. Further, participation in any sociocultural activity occurs on several planes or levels of interaction. Rogoff's (1994, 1995; Rogoff, Baker-Sennett, Lacasa, & Goldsmith, 1995) framework proposes that there are three levels to consider:

1. The *personal plane* involves individual factors such as cognitive processes, emotional factors, individual behavior, values, and beliefs.
2. The *interpersonal or social plane* includes interactional processes involved in specific social contexts such as classrooms, counseling encounters, or family interactions.
3. The *community or institutional plane* involves shared history, languages, rules, values, beliefs, and identities of entire groups.

This last plane of development, often overlooked in behavioral and social science, focuses on factors such as past and current power relationships among various groups under consideration, including (a) how they are embedded in social institutions, and (b) how they are perceived and experienced by individuals and their communities. This is sometimes addressed in studies of entire schools, districts, professions, neighborhoods, or cultures, and the ways that these "common sociocultural inheritances" interact with the other levels of development. In general, sociocultural theory emphasizes the interdependence of the three planes. While one plane might be foregrounded for analysis and the other planes backgrounded, a complete account of learning and development considers all three simultaneously.

While it is critical to focus on individual factors like motivation, interests, and ability, the other factors are critical to investigate as well. These might focus on the mediational history of an individual as manifested in specific interactional contexts such as counseling sessions, time with peers and other actors in available social networks, and finally the sociopolitical contexts of specific communities and institutions. Clearly, a great deal is known about how to facilitate college access for underrepresented groups. Future efforts might profitably focus on more comprehensive frameworks that explicate general principles as well as providing context-specific examples of how these operate in specific sociocultural contexts.

References

Adelman, C. (2002). The relationship between urbanicity and educational outcomes. In W. G. Tierney & L. S. Hagedorn (Eds.), *Increasing access to college: Extending possibilities for all students* (pp. 35–64). Albany: State University of New York Press.

Adelman, C. (1999). *Answers in the tool box: Academic intensity, attendance patterns and bachelor's degree attainment.* Washington, DC: U.S. Department of Education, Office of Educational Research and Improvement.

Alexander, C. N., & Campbell, E. Q. (1964). Peer influences on adolescent educational aspirations and attainments. *American Sociological Review, 29*, 568–575.

Alexander, K., & Cook, M. (1979). The motivational relevance of educational plans: Questioning the conventional wisdom. *Social Psychology Quarterly, 43*, 202–213.

Alexander, K. L., Cook, M., & McDill, E. L. (1978). Curriculum tracking and educational stratification: Some further evidence. *American Sociological Review, 43*(1), 47–66.

Alexander, K. L., & Eckland, B. K. (1977). High school context and college selectivity: Institutional constraints in educational stratification. *Social Forces, 56*, 166–188.

Alexander, K. L., & Eckland, B. K. (1974). Sex differences in the educational attainment process. *American Sociological Review, 30*(October), 668–682.

Alexander, K. L., Pallas, A. M., & Holupka, S. (1987). Consistency and change in educational stratification: Recent trends regarding social background and college access. *Research in Social Stratification and Mobility, 6*, 161–185.

Allen, W. R. (1992). The color of success: African American college student outcomes at predominantly white and historically Black public colleges and universities. *Harvard Educational Review, 62*(1), 26–44.

Allen, W. R., Bonous-Hammarth, M., & Teranishi, R. (2002). *Stony the road we trod: African Americans in California higher education.* Los Angeles: CHOICES Project, Institute for Social Science Research, UCLA.

201

Altonji, J. G. (1992). The effects of high school curriculum on education and labor market outcomes. *Journal of Human Resources, 30*(3), 409–438.

Alwin, W. F., & Otto, L. B. (1977). High school context effects on aspirations. *Sociology of Education, 50*, 259–273.

American College Testing Program. (2002). *Facts about ACT.* http://www.act.org/news/facts.html.

American Council on Education. (2002). *Minorities in higher education 2001–2002: 19th annual status report.* Washington, DC: Author.

American Counseling Association. (1999). *ESEA reauthorization provides chance to boost school counseling.* Alexandria, VA: ACA, Office of Public Policy & Information Advocacy Kit.

American School Counselor Association. (1999). The role of the professional school counselor. Retrieved 2/12/2002 from: http://www.schoolcounselor.org/content .cfm?L1=1000&L2=69.

Anderson, J. E. (1993). *Public policymaking* (3rd ed.). Boston: Houghton Mifflin.

Anderson, K. L. (1981). Post-high school experiences and college attrition. *Sociology of Education, 54*(1), 1–15.

Antonio, A. L. (2002). *College knowledge for successful K-16 transitions.* Paper presented at the annual meeting of the American Educational Research Association, New Orleans, LA.

Antonio, A. L. (1995). *Making social comparisons: Black and White peer group influence in college.* Paper presented at the annual meeting of the Association for the Study of Higher Education, Orlando, FL, November 2–5.

Arbuckle, D. S. (1976). The school counselor: Voice of society? *Personnel and Guidance Journal, 55*, 427–430.

Armor,D. J. (1971). *The American school counselor: A case study in the sociology of professions.* New York: Russell Sage Foundation.

Ascher, C. (1985). Helping students to complete high school and enter college. *Urban Review, 17*(1), 65–71.

Astin, A. (1993). *What matters in college: Four critical years revisited.* San Francisco: Jossey-Bass.

Atkinson, D. R., Jennings, R. G., & Liongson, L. (1990). Minority students' reasons for not seeking counseling and suggestions for improving services. *Journal of College Student Development, 31*(4), 342–350.

Attinasi, L. C., Jr. (1989). Getting in: Mexican Americans' perceptions of university attendance and the implications for freshman year persistence. *Journal of Higher Education, 60*(3), 247–277.

Aubrey, R. F. (1982). A house divided: Guidance and counseling in 20th-century America. *Personnel and Guidance Journal, 61*(4), 198–204.

Aubrey, R. F. (1969). Misapplication of therapy models to school counseling. *Personnel Guidance, 48*(4), 273–277.

Auerbach, S. (2002). *Exposing the rules of the game of college access: Making privileged information accessible in a family outreach program.* Paper presented at the annual meeting of the Sociology of Education Association, Asilomar, CA.

Auerbach, S. (2001). *Under co-construction: Parent roles in promoting college access for students of color.* Unpublished doctoral dissertation, UCLA Graduate School of Education and Information Sciences.

Avis, J. P. (1982). Counseling: Issues and challenges. *Education and Urban Society, 15*(1), 70–87.

Azmitia, M., & Cooper, C. R. (2001). Good or bad? Peer influences on Latino and European American adolescents' pathways through school. *Journal of Education for Students Placed at Risk, 61*(1 & 2), 45–71.

Azmitia, M., Cooper, C. R., Garcia, E. E., & Dunbar, N. D. (1996). The ecology of family guidance in low-income Mexican-American and European-American families. *Social Development, 5*(1), 1–23.

Baker, A. J. L., & Soden, L. M. (1998, April). The challenges of parent involvement research. *ERIC Clearinghouse on Urban Education Digest, 134*, 1–4.

Baker, D. P., & Stevenson, D. L. (1986). Mothers' strategies for children's school achievement: Managing the transition to high school. *Sociology of Education, 59*(July), 156–166.

Bandura, A. (1989). Regulation of cognitive processes through perceived self-efficacy. *Developmental Psychology, 25*(5), 729–735.

Bandura, A. (1977). *Social learning theory.* Englewood Cliffs, NJ: Prentice Hall.

Barela, E., Christie, C. A., & Alkin, M. C. (2001). *Assessing the impact of UCLA's student-centered academic outreach activities: A Delphi study.* Outreach Evaluation Project Occasional Report No. 8. Los Angeles: UCLA Graduate School of Education and Information Studies.

Barnett, W. S. (1993). The economic evaluation of home visiting programs. *The future of children: Home visiting, 3* (pp. 93–112). Center for the Future of Children. Los Altos, CA: David and Lucile Packard Foundation.

Bauch, P. A. (1993). Improving education for minority adolescents: Toward an ecological perspective on school choice and parent involvement. In N. F. Chavkin (Ed.), *Families and schools in a pluralistic society* (pp. 121–148). Albany: State University of New York Press.

Beale, A. V. (1986). Trivial pursuit: The history of guidance. *School Counselor, 34*(1), 14–17.

Beattle, I. R. (2002). Are all "adolescent econometricians" created equal? Racial, class, and gender differences in college enrollment. *Sociology of Education, 75*(January), 19–43.

Beck, L. G. (1994). *Reclaiming educational administration as a caring profession.* New York: Teachers College Press.

Berkner, L. K., & Chavez, L. (1997). *Access to postsecondary education for the 1992 high school graduates* (Report No. NCES 98-105). Washington, DC: U.S. Department of Education, National Center for Education Statistics.

Berndt, T. J., Hawkins, J. A., & Jiao, Z. (1999). Influences of friends and friendships on adjustment to junior high school. *Merrill-Palmer Quarterly, 45*(1), 13–41.

Berndt, T. J., Laychak, A. E., & Park, K. (1990). Friends' influence on adolescents' academic achievement motivation: An experimental study. *Journal of Educational Psychology, 82*(4), 664–670.

Bidwell, C. E., & Friedkin, N. E. (1988). The sociology of education. In N.J. Smelser (Ed.), *Handbook of Sociology* (pp. 449–471). Beverly Hills, CA: Sage.

Bishop, J. (1989). Why the apathy in American high schools? *Educational Researcher, 18*, 6–10.

Borman, G. D., & Hewes, G. M. (2001). *The long-term effects and cost-effectiveness of success for all.* Unpublished research paper. Baltimore, MD: Johns Hopkins University.

Borus, M. E., & Carpenter, S. A. (1984). Factors associated with college attendance of high-school seniors. *Economics of Education Review, 3*(3), 169–176.

Bourdieu, P. (1977). Cultural reproduction and social reproduction. In J. Karabel & A. H. Halsey (Eds.), *Power and ideology in education* (pp. 487–511). New York: Oxford University Press.

Bourdieu, P. (1986). The forms of capital. In J. Richardson (Ed.), *Handbook of theory and research for the sociology of education* (pp. 241–258). Westport, CT: Greenwood Press.

Bourdieu, P. & Passeron, J. (1977). *Reproduction in education, society and culture.* Beverly Hills, CA: Sage.

Bouse, G. A., & Hossler, D. (1991). Studying college choice: A progress report. *Journal of College Admissions, 130*, 11–15.

Bowen, H. R. (1980). *The costs of higher education: How much do colleges and universities spend per student and how much should they spend?* San Francisco, CA: Jossey-Bass.

Bowen, H. R. (1977). *Investment in learning: Individual and social value of American higher education.* San Francisco: Jossey-Bass.

Boyer, E. (1987). *College: The undergraduate experience in America.* New York: Harper and Row.

Braham, M. (1965). Peer group deterrents to intellectual development during adolescence. *Educational Theory, 15,* 248–258.

Bransford, J. D., Brown, A. L., & Cocking, R. R. (1999). *How people learn: Brain, mind, experience, and school.* Washington, DC: National Academy Press.

Broh, B. A. (2002). Linking extracurricular programming to academic achievement: Who benefits and why. *Sociology of Education, 75*(1), 69–91.

Brown, B. B. (1982). The extent and effects of peer pressure among high school students: A retrospective analysis. *Journal of Youth and Adolescence, 11*(2), 121–133.

Brown, B. B. (1989). The role of peer groups in adolescents' adjustment to secondary school. In T. J. Berndt & G. W. Ladd (Eds.), *Peer relationships in child development.* New York: John Wiley and Sons.

Brown, B. B. (1988, Spring). The vital agenda for research on extracurricular influences: A reply to Holland and Andre. *Review of Educational Research, 58,* 107–111.

Brown, B. B., Clasen, D. R., & Eicher, S. E. (1986). Perceptions of peer pressure, peer conformity dispositions, and self-reported behavior among adolescents. *Journal of Personality and Social Psychology, 22,* 521–530.

Brown, B. B., Kohrs, D. M., & Lazarro, C. (1991, April). *What price sports glory? Academic costs and consequences of extracurricular participation in high school.* Paper presented at the annual meeting of the American Educational Research Association, Chicago, IL.

Brown, B. B., Mounts, N., Lamborn, S., & Steinberg, L. (1993). Parenting practices and peer group affiliation in adolescence. *Child Development, 64*(2), 467–482.

Brown, B. B., & Theobald, W. (1998). Learning contexts beyond the classroom: Extracurricular activities, community organizations, and peer groups. In K. Borman & B. Schneider (Eds.), *The adolescent years: Social influences and educational challenges* (pp. 109–141). Chicago: University of Chicago Press.

Bryk, A., Lee, V., & Holland, P. (1993). *Catholic schools and the common good.* Cambridge: Harvard University Press.

Buckhalt, J. A., Halpin, G., Noel, R., & Meadows, M. E. (1992). Relationship of drug use to involvement in school, home, and community activities: Results of a large survey of adolescents. *Psychological Reports, 70,* 139–146.

Busch, J. (1985). Mentoring in graduate schools of education: Mentors' perception. *American Educational Research Journal, 22*(2), 257–265.

Cabrera, A. F., & La Nasa, S. M. (2001). On the path to college: Three critical tasks facing America's disadvantaged. *Research in Higher Education, 42*(2), 119–149.

Cabrera, A. F., & La Nasa, S. M. (2000a, Fall). Overcoming the tasks on the path to college for America's disadvantaged. *New Directions for Institutional Research, 107,* 31–44.

Cabrera, A. F., & La Nasa, S. M. (2000b, Fall). Three critical tasks America's disadvantaged face on their path to college. *New Directions for Institutional Research, 107,* 23–30.

Cabrera, A. F., & La Nasa, S. M. (Eds.) (2000c). Understanding the college choice of disadvantaged students. *New Directions for Institutional Research, 107.*

Cabrera, A. F., & La Nasa, S. M. (2000d, Fall). Understanding the college-choice process. *New Directions for Institutional Research, 107,* 5–22.

Cabrera, A. F., La Nasa, S. M., & Burkam, K. R. (2001). *Pathways to a four-year degree: The higher education story of one generation.* Unpublished report.

Calabrese, R. L., & Noboa, J. (1995). The choice for gang membership by Mexican-American adolescents. *The High School Journal, 78*(4), 226–235.

California Postsecondary Education Commission. (1992). *Eligibility of California's 1990 high school graduates for admission to the state's public universities.* Sacramento, CA: CPEC.

California Postsecondary Education Commission. (1997). *Eligibility of California's 1996 high school graduates for admission to the state's public universities.* Commission Report 97-9. Sacramento, CA: CPEC.

California Postsecondary Education Commission. (1996, June). *Progress report on the effectiveness of collaborative student academic development programs.* Sacramento, CA: CPEC.

Camp, W. G. (1990). Participation in student activities and achievement: A covariance structural analysis. *Journal of Educational Research, 83,* 272–278.

Caplan, C., Choy, M. H., & Whitmore, J. K. (1992). Indochinese refugees and academic achievement. *Scientific American, 266*(2), 36–42.

Carnegie Council on Adolescent Development. (1992). *A matter of time: Risk and opportunity in the nonschool hours.* Report of the Task Force on Youth Development and Community Programs. Washington, DC: Carnegie Council on Adolescent Development.

Carroll, M. R. (1985, December). School counseling: Dissolution or survival? *NASSP Bulletin,* 1–5.

Catsambis, S. (1998). *Expanding the knowledge of parental involvement in secondary education: Effects on high school academic success* (Report No. 27). Baltimore:

Johns Hopkins University, Center for Research on the Education of Students Placed at Risk.

Catsiapis, G. (1987). A model of educational investment decisions. *Review of Economics and Statistics, 69*, 33–41.

Center for Higher Education Policy Analysis. (2002). *Making the grade in college prep: A guide for improving college preparation programs*. Los Angeles: University of Southern California.

Chaney, B., Lewis, L., & Farris, E. (1995). *Programs at higher education institutions for disadvantaged students* (Report No. NCES 96-230). Washington, DC: U.S. Department of Education, Office of Educational Research and Improvement.

Chapman, D. W., & De Masi, M. E. (1984). College advising in the high school: Priority and problems. *Journal of College Admissions, 27*, 3–7.

Chen, X. (1997, June). *Students' peer groups in high school: The pattern and relationship to educational outcomes* (NCES 97-055). Washington, DC: U.S. Department of Education, Office of Educational Research and Improvement.

Chen, X., Chen, H., & Kaspar, V. (2001). Group social functioning and individual socioemotional and school adjustment in Chinese children. *Merrill-Palmer Quarterly, 47*(2), 264–99.

Cheng Gorman, J., & Balter, L. (1997). Culturally sensitive parent education: A critical review of quantitative research. *Review of Educational Research, 67*(3), 339–369.

Choy, S. P. (2002). *Access and persistence: Findings from 10 years of longitudinal research on students*. Washington, DC: American Council on Education.

Choy, S. P., Horn, L. J., Nuñez, A. M., & Chen, X. (2000, Fall). Transition to college: What helps at-risk students and students whose parents did not attend college. *New Directions for Institutional Research, 107*, 45–63.

Cicourel, A., & Kitsuse, J. (1963). *The educational decisionmakers*. Indianapolis, IN: Bobbs-Merrill.

Clark, R. (1983). *Family life and school achievement: Why poor Black children succeed or fail*. Chicago: University of Chicago Press.

Cochran, M., Larner, M., Riley, D., Gunnarsson, L., & Charles, R. H. (1990). *Extending families: The social networks of parents and their children*. New York: Cambridge University Press.

Cohen, J. M. (1983). Peer influence on college aspirations with initial aspirations controlled. *American Sociological Review, 48*, 728–734.

Cohen, J. M. (1977). Sources of peer group homogeneity. *Sociology of Education, 50*(October), 227–241.

Cole, C. G. (1991, April). Counselors and administrators: A comparison of roles. *NASSP Bulletin*, 5–13.

Coleman, J. C. (1980). Friendship and the peer group in adolescence. In J. Adelson (Ed.), *Handbook of adolescent psychology*. New York: John Wiley and Sons.

Coleman, J.S. (1966). *Equality of educational opportunity*. Washington, DC: U.S. Government Printing Office.

Coleman, J. S. (1987). *Public and private high schools: The impact of communities*. New York: Basic.

Coleman, J. S. (1988). Social capital in the creation of human capital. *American Journal of Sociology, 94*(Supplement), S95–S120.

Coleman, J. S. (1961). *The adolescent society*. New York: Free Press.

Coleman, J. S., Hoffer, T., & Kilgore, S. B. (1982). *High school achievement: Public, Catholic, and private schools compared*. New York: Basic.

Coles, A. S. (1999, Winter). Early education awareness activities: Interventions that make postsecondary education a viable goal. *Advances in Education Research, 4*, 20–30.

Coles, A. S. (1993). *School to college transition programs for low-income minority youth*. Washington, DC: Education Resources Institute.

College Board. (2000). *National survey of outreach programs directory*. Washington, DC: College Board.

College Board. (1999). *Reaching the top: A report of the National Task Force on Minority High Achievement*. New York: College Entrance Examination Board.

College Board. (2002). *Ten-year trend in SAT scores indicates increased emphasis on math is yielding results; reading and writing are causes for concern*. Press release. http://www.collegeboard.com/about/news_info/cbnews.html.

Collins, P. (1986). Learning from the outsider within: The sociological significance of black feminist thought. *Social Problems, 33*, S14–S32.

Conklin, M. E., & Dailey, A. R. (1981). Does consistency of parental educational encouragement matter for secondary school students? *Sociology of Education, 54*(4), 254–262.

Cookson, P. (1981). *Private secondary boarding school and public surburban high school graduates: An analysis of college attendance plans*. Dissertation submitted to the faculty of New York University.

Cookson, P., & Persell, C. H. (1985). *Preparing for power: America's elite boarding schools*. New York: Basic.

Cooper, C. R. (2000). *A family involvement checklist: Where experts agree. Isolating key spheres of elementary equity: Defining equal access to early learning opportunities*. San Francisco: U.S. Office for Civil Rights.

Cooper, C. R. (1999). *When diversity works: Formative evaluation of student outreach, UC system-regional partnerships, and student pathways through college*. Santa

Cruz, CA: University of California Office of the President Outreach Evaluation Advisory Committee.

Cooper, C. R., Azmitia, M., Garcia, E. E., Ittel, A., Lopez, E. M., Rivera, L., & Martínez-Chávez, R. (1994). Shifting aspirations of low-income Mexican American and European American parents. In F. A. Villaruel & R. M. Lerner (Eds.), *Environments for socialization and learning: New directions in child development.* San Francisco: Jossey-Bass.

Cooper, C. R., & Cooper, R. G. (1992). Links between adolescents' relationships with their parents and peers: Models, evidence, and mechanisms. In R. D. Parke & G. W. Ladd, *Family-peer relationships: Modes of linkage* (pp. 135–158). Hillsdale, NJ: Lawrence Erlbaum Associates.

Cooper, C. R., Jackson, J. F., Azmitia, M., Lopez, E. M., & Dunbar, N. (1995). Bridging students' multiple worlds: African American and Latino youth in academic outreach programs. In R. F. Macías & R. G. García Ramos (Eds.), *Changing schools for changing students: An anthology of research on language minorities* (pp. 211–234). Santa Barbara: University of California Linguistic Minority Research Institute.

Cota, I. (1997). The role of previous educational learning experiences on current academic performance and second language proficiency of intermediate school limited English proficient students. *Bilingual Research Journal, 21*(2 & 3), 147–162.

Coy, D. R. (1991, April). The role of the counselor in today's school. *NASSP Bulletin,* 15–19.

Crockett, L., Losoff, M., & Petersen, A. C. (1984). Perceptions of the peer group and friendship in early adolescence. *Journal of Early Adolescence, 4,* 155–181.

Csikzentmihalyi, M., & Schmidt, J. (1998). Stress and resilience in adolescence: An evolutionary perspective. In K. Borman & B. Schneider (Eds.), *The adolescent years: Social influences and educational challenges* (pp. 1–17). Chicago: University of Chicago Press.

Cummins, J. (1997). Minority status and schooling in Canada. *Anthropology and Education Quarterly, 28*(3), 411–430.

Currie, J., & Duncan, T. (2000, Fall). School quality and the longer-term effects of Head Start. *Journal of Human Resources, 35*(4), 755–774.

Cutler, W. W., III. (2000). *Parents and schools: The 150-year struggle for control in American education.* Chicago: University of Chicago Press.

D'Amico, S. (1975). The effects of clique membership upon academic achievement. *Adolescence, 10,* 93–100.

Dauber, S. L., & Esptein, J. L. (1993). Parents' attitudes and practices of involvement in inner-city elementary and middle schools. In N. Chavkin (Ed.), *Families and schools in a pluralistic society* (pp. 53–72). Albany: State University of New York Press.

Davies, D. (1996). *Family, community and school partnerships in the 1990's: The good news and the bad.* Boston: Institute for Responsive Education.

Davies, M., & Kandel, D. B. (1981). Parental and peer influences on adolescents' educational plans: Some further evidence. *American Journal of Sociology, 87*(2), 363–387.

Day, R. W., & Sparacio, R. T. (1980). *Impediments to the role and function of school counselors, School Counselor, 27*(4), 270–275.

De Lany, B. (1991). Allocation, choice, stratification within high schools: How the sorting machine copes. *American Journal of Education, 99*(February), 181–207.

Delgado-Gaitan, C. (1991). Involving parents in the schools: A process of empowerment. *American Journal of Education, 100*(1), 20–46.

Delgado-Gaitan, C. (1992). School matters in the Mexican-American home: Socializing children to education. *American Educational Research Journal, 29*(3), 495–513.

Delgado-Gaitan, C. (1994). Spanish-speaking families' involvement in schools. In C. L. Fagnano & B. Z. Werber (Eds.), *School, family, and community interaction: A view from the firing lines* (pp. 85–96). Boulder, CO: Westview Press.

Delgado-Gaitan, C., & Segura, D. A. (1989). The social context of Chicana women's role in their children's schooling. *Educational Foundations, 3*, 71–92.

Deyhle, D. (1995). Navajo youth and Anglo racism: Cultural integrity and resistance. *Harvard Educational Review, 65*, 403–444.

Dika, S., & Singh, K. (2002). Applications of social capital in educational literature: A critical synthesis. *Review of Educational Research, 72*(1), 31–60.

DiMaggio, P. (1982). Cultural capital and school success: The impact of status culture participation on the grades of U.S. high school students. *American Sociological Review, 47*, 189–201.

DiMaggio, P., & Mohr, J. (1985). Cultural capital, educational attainment, and marital selection. *American Journal of Sociology, 90*(6), 1231–1261.

Dodd, A. W., & Konzal, J. L. (1999). *Making our high schools better: How parents and teachers can work together.* New York: St. Martin's Press.

Dornbusch, S. M., & Ritter, P. L. (1988). Parents of high school students: A neglected resource. *Educational Horizons, 66*(2), 75–77.

Downs, W. R. (1985). Using panel data to examine same sex differences in causal relationships among adolescent alcohol use, norms, and peer alcohol use. *Journal of Youth and Adolescence, 14*, 469–486.

Duncan, O. T., Haller, A. O., & Portes, A. (1968). Peer influences on aspirations: A reinterpretation. *American Journal of Sociology, 74*(2), 119–137.

Dunphy, D. (1963). The social structure of urban adolescent peer groups. *Sociometry, 26*(2), 230–246.

Eccles, J. S., & Harold, R. D. (1993). Parent-school involvement during the early adolescent years. *Teachers College Record, 94*(3), 568–587.

Eckert, P. (2000). *Linguistic variation as social practice*. Malden, MA: Blackwell Publishers.

Eder, D., Evans, C. C., & Parker, S. (1995). *School talk: Gender and adolescent culture*. New Brunswick, NJ: Rutgers University Press.

Eisenberg, N., & Martin, G. (2001). *Survey of UCLA outreach programs*. Outreach Evaluation Report No. 3. Los Angeles: Graduate School of Education and Information Studies.

Eitle, T. M., & Eitle, D. J. (2002). Race, cultural capital, and the educational effects of participation in sports. *Sociology of Education, 75*, 123–146.

Elder, G.H., Jr. (1998). The life course as developmental theory. *Child Development, 69*(1), 1–12.

Elder, G.H., Jr. (1985). Perspectives on the life course. In E. H. Elder (Ed.), *Life course dynamics* (pp. 23–49). Ithaca, NY: Cornell University Press.

England, R. E., Meier, K. J., & Fraga, L. R. (1988). Barriers to equal opportunity: Educational practices and minority students. *Urban Affairs Quarterly, 23*(4), 635–646.

Epstein, J. L. (1995, May). School/family/community partnerships: Caring for the children we share. *Phi Delta Kappan,* 701–712.

Epstein, J. L. (1990). School and family connections: Theory, research and implications for integrating sociologies of education and family. In D. G. Unger & M. B. Sussman (Eds.), *Families in community settings: Interdisciplinary perspectives* (pp. 99–126). New York: Haworth Press.

Epstein, J. L. & Dauber, S. L. (1991). School programs and teacher practices of parent involvement in inner-city elementary and middle schools. *Elementary School Journal, 91*(3), 289–305.

Epstein, J. L., & Karweit, N. (Eds.). (1983). *Friends in school: Patterns of selection and influence in secondary schools*. New York: Academic Press.

Erikson, E. (1968). *Identity, youth and crisis*. New York: Norton.

Fallon, M. (1997). The school counselor's role in first generation students' college plans. *School Counselor, 44*, 384–394.

Falsey, B., & Heyns, B. (1984). The college channel: Private and public schools reconsidered. *Sociology of Education, 57*, 111–122.

Fashola, O. S., & Slavin, R. E. (1997). *Effective dropout prevention and college attendance programs for Latino students*. Washington, DC: U.S. Department of Education.

Fejgin, N. (1994). Participation in high school competitive sports: A subversion of school mission or contribution to academic goals? *Sociology of Sport Journal, 11*, 211–230.

Feldman, K. A., & Newcomb, T. M. (1969). *The impact of college on students*. San Francisco: Jossey-Bass.

Fenske, R. H., Geranios, C. A., Keller, J. E., & Moore, D. E. (1997). *Early intervention programs: Opening the door to higher education* (ASHE-ERIC Higher Education Report, Vol. 25, No. 6). Washington, DC: George Washington University, Graduate School of Education and Human Development.

Fenske, R. H., Irwin, G. F., & Keller, J. F. (1999, Winter). Toward a typology of early intervention programs. *Advances in Educational Research, 4*, 117–134.

Festinger, L. (1954). A theory of social comparison processes. *Human Relations, 7*, 117–140.

Fine, M. (1993). [Ap]parent involvement: Reflections on parents, power, and urban public schools. *Teachers College Record, 94*(4), 682–709.

Fine, M. (1991). *Framing dropouts: Notes on the politics of an urban public high school*. Albany: State University of New York Press.

Fitzsimmons, W. (1991, January/February). Risky business. *Harvard Magazine*, 23–29.

Flanders, J. R. (1987). How much of the content of math textbooks is new? *Arithmetic Teacher, 35*, 18–23.

Fleming, J. (1981). Special needs of blacks and other minorities. In A. W. Chickering & Associates (Eds.), *The modern American college* (pp. 393–410). San Francisco: Jossey-Bass.

Foley, D. (1997). Deficit thinking models based on culture: The anthropological protest. In R. Valencia (Ed.), *The evolution of deficit thinking: Educational thought and practice*. Stanford Series on Education and Public Policy. London: Falmer Press.

Foley, D. E. (1990). *Learning capitalist culture: Deep in the heart of Tejas*. Philadelphia: University of Pennsylvania Press.

Fordham, S. (1996). Blacked out: Dilemmas of race, identity, and success at Capital High. Chicago: University of Chicago Press.

Fordham, S. (1988). Racelessness as a factor in Black students' success: Pragmatic strategy or pyrrhic victory? *Harvard Educational Review, 58*(1), 54–83.

Fordham, S., & Ogbu, J. (1986). Black students' school success: Coping with the burden of "acting white." *Urban Review, 18*, 176–206.

Foster, L. (2001, March). *Effectiveness of mentor programs: Review of the literature from 1995–2000.* California Research Bureau CRB-01-004. Sacramento, CA: California State Library.

Fountain, D., & Arbreton, A. (1999). The cost of mentoring. In J. B. Grossman (Ed.), *Contemporary Issues in Mentoring.* Philadelphia: Public/Private Ventures.

Furman, W., & Gavin, L. A. (1989). Peers' influence on adjustment and development. In T. J. Berndt & G. W. Ladd (Eds.), *Peer relationships in child development* (pp. 319–340). New York: John Wiley and Sons.

Furstenberg, F. F., Jr., Cook., T. D., Eccles, J., Elder, G. H., Jr., & Sameroff, A. (1999). *Managing to make it: Urban families and adolescent success.* Chicago: University of Chicago Press.

Gamoran, A. (1993). Alternative uses of ability grouping in secondary schools: Can we bring high-quality instruction to low ability classes? *American Journal of Education, 102*, 1–22.

Gamoran, A. (1987). The stratification of high school learning opportunities. *Sociology of Education, 60*, 135–155.

Gamoran, A. (1992). The variable effects of high school tracking. *American Sociological Review, 57*, 812–828.

Gamoran, A., & Mare, R. D. (1989). Secondary school tracking and educational inequality: Compensation, reinforcement, or neutrality? *American Journal of Sociology, 94*(5), 1146–1183.

Gamoran, A., Porter, A. C., Smithson, J., & White, P. A. (1997). Upgrading high school mathematics instruction: Improving learning opportunities for low-achieving, low-income youth. *Educational Evaluation and Policy Analysis, 19*(4), 325–338.

Gándara, P. (2002b). A study of high school Puente: What we have learned about preparing Latino youth for postsecondary education. *Educational Policy, 16*(4), 474–495.

Gándara, P. (1998). Capturing Latino students in the academic pipeline. *California Policy Seminar Brief Series, 10*(3). Berkeley: University of California Latino/Latina Policy Research Program.

Gándara, P. (2002a). Meeting common goals: Linking K–12 and college interventions. In W. G. Tierney & L. S. Hagedorn (Eds.), *Increasing access to college: Extending possibilities for all students* (pp. 81–103). Albany: State University of New York Press.

Gándara, P. (1995). *Over the ivy walls: The educational mobility of low-income Chicanos.* Albany: State University of New York Press.

Gándara, P. (2001). *Paving the way to postsecondary education: K–12 intervention programs for underrepresented youth.* NCES 2001–205. Washington, DC: U.S. Government Printing Office.

Gándara, P. (1999). *Priming the pump: Strategies for increasing the achievement of underrepresented minority undergraduates* (College Board No. 987257). New York: College Board Publications.

Gándara, P., & Bial, D. (1999). *Paving the way to higher education: K–12 intervention programs for underrepresented youth* (draft). Washington, DC: National Postsecondary Education Cooperative, National Center for Education Statistics.

Gándara, P., & Bial, D. (2001). *Paving the way to postsecondary education: K–12 intervention programs for underrepresented youth* (NCES 2001–205r). Washington, DC: U.S. Department of Education, National Center for Education Statistics.

Gándara, P., Gutiérrez, D., & O'Hara, S. (2001). Planning for the future in rural and urban high schools. *Journal of education for Students Placed at Risk, 6*(1 & 2), 73–93.

Gándara, P., Larson, K., Mehan, H., & Rumberger, R. (1998). *Capturing Latino students in the academic pipeline.* Berkeley, CA: Chicano/Latino Policy Project.

Gándara, P., & Maxwell-Jolley, J. (1999). *Priming the pump: Strategies for increasing the achievement of underrepresented minority undergraduates* (College Board No. 987257). New York: College Board Publications.

Gándara, P., Mejorado, M., Molina, M., & Gutierrez, D. (1998). *High school Puente evaluation final report.* Davis: University of California.

Gándara, P., O'Hara, S., & Gutiérrez, D. (2004). The changing shape of aspirations: Peer influence on achievement behavior. In M. Gibson, P. Gándara, & J. Koyama (Eds.), *School Connections, U.S. Mexican Youth, Peers, and School Achievement* (pp. 39–65). New York: Teachers College Press.

Garet, M. S., & DeLany, B. (1988). Students, courses and stratification. *Sociology of Education, 61*(2), 61–77.

Garmezy, N. (1985). Stress-resistant children: The search for protective factors. In J. Stevenson (Ed.), *Recent research in developmental psychopathology,* (pp. 213–233). Oxford: Pergamon.

Gerber, S. B. (1996). Extracurricular activities and academic achievement. *Journal of Research and Development in Education, 30,* 42–50.

Gibson, R. (1986). *Critical theory and education.* London: Hodder and Stoughton.

Giroux, H. (1983). Theories of reproduction and resistance in the new sociology of education: A critical analysis. *Harvard Educational Review, 53,* 257–293.

Gladieux, L., & Swail, W. S. (1999). Financial aid is not enough: Improving the odds for minority and low-income students. In J. E. King (Ed.), *Financing a college education: How it works, how it's changing* (pp. 177–197). Phoenix, AZ: Oryx Press.

Gladieux, L., & Swail, W. S. (1998). *Financial aid is not enough: Improving the odds of college success for low-income minority students.* Washington, DC: College Board.

Glynn, T. (1981). From family to peer: A review of transitions of influence among drug-using youth. *Journal of Youth and Adolescence, 10,* 363–383.

Goddard, R. D., Sweetland, S. R., & Hoy, W. K. (2000). Academic emphasis of urban elementary schools and student achievement in reading and mathematics: A multilevel analysis. *Educational Administration Quarterly, 36*(5), 683–702.

Gonzales, N., Andrade, R., Civil, M., & Moll, L. (2001). Bridging funds of distributed knowledge: Creating zones of practices in mathematics. *Journal of Education for Students Placed at Risk, Vol. 6*(1–2), 115–132.

Goodenow, C., & Grady, K. (1993). The relationship of school belonging and friends' values among urban adolescent students. *Journal of Experimental Education, 62*(1), 60–71.

Goodlad, J. (1983). *A place called school.* New York: McGraw-Hill.

Gordon, T. (1995). Cultural politics of the African American male experience. In R. Valencia (Ed.), *The evolution of deficit thinking: Educational thought and practice.* Stanford Series on Education and Public Policy. London: Falmer Press.

Governor's Mentoring Partnership. (2001). Online, www.adp.ca.gov/cf/Governors Mentoring Partnership.default.htm. Downloaded May 11, 2002.

Grant Commission on Work, Family, and Citizenship, William T. (1988). *The forgotten half: Pathways to success for America's youth and young families.* Washington, DC: Author.

Grossman, J. B., & Garry, E. M. (1997). Mentoring—A proven delinquency strategy. *Juvenile Justice Bulletin.* Office of Juvenile Justice and Delinquency Prevention, U.S. Department of Justice.

Grossman, J. B., & Johnson, A. (1999). Assessing the effectiveness of mentoring programs. In J. B. Grossman (Ed.), *Contemporary issues in mentoring.* Philadelphia: Public/Private Ventures.

Grossman, J. B., & Tierney, J. P. (1998). Does mentoring work? An impact study of the Big Brothers/Big Sisters of America Program. *Evaluation Review, 22,* 403–426.

Grotevant, H. D., & Cooper, C. R. (1985). Patterns of interaction in family relationships and the development of identity formation in adolescence. *Child Development, 56,* 415–428.

Guest, A., & Schneider, B. (2003). Adolescents' extracurricular participation in context: The mediating effects of schools, communities, and identity. *Sociology of Education, 76,* 89–109.

Gunnings, B. B. (1982). Stress and the minority student on a predominately white campus. *Journal of Non-White Concerns, 11,* 11–16.

Hagedorn, L. S., & Fogel, S. (2002). Making school to college programs work: Academics, goals, and aspirations. In W. G. Tierney & L. S. Hagedorn (Eds.), *Increasing access to college: Extending possibilities for all students* (pp. 169–193). Albany: State University of New York Press.

Hagedorn, L. S., & Tierney, W. G. (2002). Cultural capital and the struggle for educational equity. In W. G. Tierney & L. S. Hagedorn (Eds.), *Increasing access to college: Extending possibilities for all students* (pp. 1–8). Albany: State University of New York Press.

Haller, A. O., & Butterworth, C. E. (1960). Peer influences on levels of occupational and educational aspiration. *Social Forces, 38*, 289–295.

Hallinan, M. T. (1979). Structural effects on children's friendship cliques. *Social Psychology Quarterly, 42*, 43–54.

Hallinan, M. T. (1996). Track mobility in secondary school. *Social Forces, 74*(3), 983–1002.

Hallinan, M. T., & Williams, R.A. (1990). Students' characteristics and the peer-influence process. *Sociology of Education, 63*, 122–132.

Hanford, G. H. (1991). *Life with the SAT: Assessing our young people and our times.* New York: College Board.

Hanks, M. P., & Eckland, B. K. (1976). Athletics and social participation in the educational attainment process. *Sociology of Education, 49*, 271–294.

Hart, D. H., & Prince, D. J. (1970). Role conflict for school counselors: Training versus job demands. *Personnel and Guidance Journal, 48*(5), 374–380.

Hartup, W. W. (1992). Social relationships and their developmental significance. *American Psychologist, 44*, 120–126.

Hayward, G. C., Brandes, B. G., Kirst, M. W., & Mazzeo, C. (1997). *Higher education outreach programs: A synthesis of evaluations.* Sacramento, CA: Policy Analysis for California Education. Available: http://www.ucop.edu/sas/publish/pace/index.html.

Hearn, J. C. (1991). Academic and nonacademic influences on the college destinations of 1980 high school graduates. *Sociology of Education, 64*, 158–171.

Hearn, J. C. (2002). Access to postsecondary education: Financing equity in an evolving context. In M. B. Paulsen & J. C. Smart (Eds.), *The finance of higher education: theory, research, policy, and practice* (pp. 439–460). New York: Agathon Press.

Hearn, J. C. (1987). Pathways to attendance at the elite colleges. In P. W. Kingston & L. S. Lewis (Eds.), *The high status track: Studies of elite schools and stratification* (pp. 121–145). Albany: State University of New York Press.

Hearn, J. C. (1984). The relative roles of academic, ascribed, and socioeconomic characteristics in college destinations. *Sociology of Education, 57*(1), 22–30.

Hebert, T. P., & Reis, S. M. (1999). Culturally diverse high-achieving students in an urban high school. *Urban Education, 34*(4), 428–457.

Heller, D. E. (2001). *The states and public higher education policy: Affordability, access, and accountability.* Baltimore, MD: Johns Hopkins University Press.

Henderson, A. T., & Berla, N. (1997). *A new generation of evidence: The family is critical to student achievement.* Washington, DC: Center for Law in Education.

Herriot, R. E. (1963). Some social determinants of educational aspiration. *Harvard Educational Review, 33,* 157–177.

Hersch, P. (1998). *A tribe apart: A journey into the heart of American adolescence.* New York: Fawcett Columbine.

Hinde, R. A. (1987). *Individuals, relationships and culture.* Cambridge: Cambridge University Press.

Hoffer, T. B. (1992). Middle school ability grouping and student achievement in science and mathematics. *Educational Evaluation and Policy Analysis, 14*(3), 205–227.

Hogarth, C. P. (1987). *Quality control in higher education.* Lanham, MD: University Press of America.

Holland, A., & Andre, T. (1991). Is the extracurriculum an extra curriculum? *American Secondary Education, 19,* 6–12.

hooks, b. (1990). Choosing the margin as a space of radical openness. In b. hooks (Ed.), *Yearnings: Race, gender, and cultural politics* (pp. 145–154). Boston, MA: South End Press.

Hoover-Dempsey, K., & Sandler, H. (1997). Why do parents become involved in their children's education? *Review of Higher Education, 67*(1), 3–42.

Horn, L. J. (1997). *Confronting the odds: Students at risk and the pipeline to higher education* (Report No. NCES 98-094). Washington, DC: U.S. Department of Education, Office of Educational Research and Improvement.

Horn, L., & Chen, X. (1998). *Toward resiliency: At-risk students who make it to college.* Washington, DC: U.S. Department of Education, Office of Educational Research and Improvement.

Horn, L., & Kojaku, L. (2001). *High school academic curriculum and the persistence path through college* (Report No. NCES 2001-163). Washington, DC: U.S. Department of Education, Office of Educational Research and Improvement.

Horn, L., & Nuñez, A.-M. (2000). *Mapping the road to college: First-generation students' math* track, planning strategies, and context of support. Washington, DC: U.S. Department of Education, Office of Education, Research and Improvement.

Horvat, E. M. (1996). *African-American student and college choice decisionmaking in social context.* Unpublished doctoral dissertation, University of California at Los Angeles, Graduate School of Education and Information Studies.

Hossler, D., Braxton, J., & Coopersmith, G. (1989). Understanding student college choice. In J. Smart (Ed.), *Higher education: Handbook of theory and research* Vol. 5, pp. 231–238. New York: Agathon Press.

Hossler, D., & Gallagher, K. S. (1987). Studying student college choice: A three phase model and the implications for policy makers. *College and University, 2*(3), 207–221.

Hossler, D., Schmit, J., & Vesper, N. (1999). *Going to college: How social, economic, and educational factors influence the decisions students make.* Baltimore: Johns Hopkins University Press.

Hossler, D., & Vesper, N. (1993). An exploratory study of the factors associated with parental savings for postsecondary education. *Journal of Higher Education, 64*(2), 140–165.

Hotchkiss, L., & Vetter, L. (1987). *Outcomes of career guidance and counseling.* Columbus, OH: National Center for Research in Vocational Education.

Hrabowski, F. A., III, Maton, K. I., & Greif, G. L. (1998). *Beating the odds: Raising academically successful African American males.* New York: Oxford University Press.

Huey, W. C. (1987, May). The principal-counselor partnership: A winning combination. *NASSP Bulletin*, 14–18.

Hull, B. J. (1979). The way we were and are: The changing roles of the high school counselor and the college admissions officer. *National ACAC Journal, 23*(2), 25–27.

Hultsman, W. Z. (1992). Constraints to activity participation in early adolescence. *Journal of Early Adolescence, 12*, 280–299.

Hummel-Rossi, B., & Ashdown, J. (2002). The state of cost-benefit and cost-effectiveness analyses in education. *Review of Educational Research, 72*(1), 1–30.

Hurtado, A. (1989). Relating to privilege: Seduction and rejection in the subordination of white women and women of color. *Signs: Journal of Women in Culture and Society, 14*, 833–855.

Hutchinson, R. L., & Bottorff, R. L. (1986). Selected high school counseling services: Student assessment. *School Counselor, 33*, 350–354.

Hutchinson, R. L., & Reagan, C. A. (1989). Problems for which seniors would seek help from school counselors. *School Counselor, 36*, 271–280.

Hyman, H. H. (1942). The psychology of status. *Archives of Psychology*, 269–361.

Ide, J. K., Parkerson, J., Haertel, G. D., & Walberg, H. J. (1981). Peer group influence on educational outcomes: A quantitative synthesis. *Journal of Educational Psychology, 73*(4), 472–484.

Institute for Higher Education Policy. (1997). *Missed opportunities: A new look at disadvantaged college aspirants*. Boston: Education Resources Institute.

Jackson, G. A. (1990). Financial aid, college entry, and affirmative action. *American Journal of Education,* (August), 523–550.

Jackson, G. A. (1982). Public efficiency and private choice in higher education. *Educational Evaluation and Policy Analysis, 4,* 237–247.

James, D. W., Jurich, S., & Estes, S. (2002). *Raising minority academic achievement: A compendium of educational programs and practices*. Washington, DC: American Youth Policy Forum.

Johnson, A. (1998). *An evaluation of long term impacts of the Sponsor-a-Scholar Program on student performance. Final Report to the Commonwealth Fund*. Princeton, NJ: Mathematica Policy Research.

Johnsrud, L. (1990). Mentor relationships: Those that help and those that hinder. *New Directions for Higher Education, 18,* 57–66.

Jordan, C., Orozco, E., & Averett, A. (2002). *Emerging issues in school, family and community connections: Annual synthesis 2001*. Austin, TX: Southwest Educational Development Laboratory.

Jordan, W. J., & Nettles, S. M. (1999, January). How students invest their time out of school: Effects on school engagement, perceptions of life chances, and achievement. (Report 29). Baltimore, MD: Johns Hopkins University, Center for Research on the Education of Students Placed at Risk.

Jun, A., & Colyar, J. (2002). Parental guidance suggested: Family involvement in college preparation programs. In W. G. Tierney & L. S. Hagedorn (Eds.), *Increasing access to college: Extending possibilities for all students* (pp. 195–215). Albany: State University of New York Press.

Jun, A., & Tierney, W. G. (1999). At-risk students and college success: A framework for effective preparation. *Metropolitan Universities,* (Spring), 49–60.

Kahne, J., & Bailey, K. (1999). The role of social capital in youth development: The case of "I Have a Dream" programs. *Educational Evaluation and Policy Analysis, 21*(3), 321–343.

Kandel, D. B. (1973). Adolescent marihuana use: Role of parents and peers. *Science, 181,* 1067–1069.

Kandel, D. B., & Lesser, G. S. (1969). Parental and peer influences on educational plans of adolescents. *American Sociological Review, 34*(2), 213–223.

Kandel, D. B., & Lesser, G. S. (1970a). Relative influence of parents and peers on the educational plans of adolescents in the United States and Denmark. In M. B. Miles, W. W. Charters, Jr., & N. L. Gage (Eds.), *Learning in social settings: New readings in the social psychology of education*. Boston: Allyn and Bacon.

Kandel, D. B., & Lesser, G. S. (1970b). School, family, and peer influences on educational plans of adolescents in the United States and Denmark. *Sociology of Education, 43*(Summer), 270–287.

Kane, T. J. (1999). *The price of admission: Rethinking how Americans pay for college.* Washington, DC: Brookings Institution Press.

Kane, T., & Spizman, L. M. (1994). Race, financial aid awards, and college attendance: Parents and geography matter. *American Journal of Economics and Sociology, 53*(1), 73–97.

Kanter, R. M. (1977). *Men and women of the corporation.* New York: Basic Books.

Kao, G., & Tienda, M. (1998). Educational aspirations of minority youth. *American Journal of Education, 106,* 349–384.

Karen, D. (1988). *Who applies where to college?* Paper presented at the annual meeting of the American Educational Research Association, New Orleans, LA.

Karoly, L. A., Greenwood, P. W., Everingham, S. S., Houbé, J., Kilburn, M. R., Rydell, C. P., Sanders, M., & Chiesa, J. (1998). *Investing in our children: What we know and don't know about the costs and benefits of early childhood interventions.* MR-898. Santa Monica, CA: RAND.

Karoly, L. A., Kilburn, M. R., Bigelow, J. H., Caulkins, J. P., Cannon, J. S., & Chiesa, J. (2001). *Assessing costs and benefits of early childhood interventions.* Santa Monica, CA: RAND.

Karweit, N. (1983). Extracurricular activities and friendship selection. In J. L. Epstein & N. Karweit (Eds.), *Friends in school: Patterns of selection and influence in secondary schools.* New York: Academic Press.

Kehas, C. (1975). What research says about counselor role. In H. Peters, & R. Aubrey (Eds.), *Guidance: Strategies and techniques: Essays from Focus on Guidance Education series.* Denver: Love Publishing.

Kemper, T. (1968). Reference groups, socialization and achievement. *American Sociological Review, 33*(1), 31–45.

Kettner, P. M., Moroney, R. M., & Martin, L. L. (1990). *Designing and managing programs: An effectiveness-based approach.* Newbury Park, CA: Sage Publications.

Kezar, A. (2000a). College summit. *The ERIC Review: Early Intervention: Expanding Access to Higher Education: A Class Act, 8*(1), 27–28.

Kezar, A. (2000b). Does it work? Research on early intervention. *The ERIC Review: Early Intervention: Expanding Access to Higher Education: A Class Act, 8*(1), 15–19.

King, J. (1996). *The decision to go to college: Attitudes and experiences associated with college attendance among low-income students.* Washington, DC: College Board.

Knight, M. G., Newton, R., & Oesterreich, H. (2000, April). *It doesn't happen by accident: Creating successful cultures of college preparation for urban youth.* Paper presented at the annual meeting of the American Educational Research Association, New Orleans, LA.

Kozol, J. (1991). *Savage inequalities: Children in America's schools.* New York: Crown Publishers.

Krauss, I. (1964). Sources of educational aspirations among working-class youth. *American Sociological Review, 29*(6), 867–879.

Krei, M. S., & Rosenblaum, J. E. (2001). Career and college advice to the forgotten half: What do counselors and vocational teachers advise? *Teachers College Record, 103,* 823–842.

Kroll, A. M. (1973). Computer-based systems for career guidance and information: A status report. *Focus on Guidance, 10*(10), 1–15.

Kulik, C. C., & Kulik, J. A. (1982). Effects of ability grouping on secondary school students: A meta-analysis of evaluation findings. *American Educational Research Journal, 19*(3), 415–428.

Laguardia, A. (1998). A survey of school/college partnerships for minority and disadvantaged students. *Urban Review, 30*(2), 167–185.

Lake, S. (1988). *Equal access to education: Alternatives to tracking and ability grouping.* Practitioner's Monograph #2. EDRS Clearinghouse #UD026638. Sacramento: California League of Middle Schools.

Lambert, N. M., & McCombs, B. L. (1998). *How students learn: Reforming schools through learner-centered education.* Washington, DC: American Psychological Association.

Lamont, M. & Lareau A. (1986). Cultural capitalist: Allusions, gaps, and glissandos in recent theoretical developments. *Sociological Theory, 6,* 153–168.

Lapan, R. T., Gysbers, N. C., Multon, K. D. & Pike, G. R. (1997). Developing guidance competency self-efficacy scales for high school and middle school students. *Measurement and Evaluation in Counseling and Development, 30*(1), 4–16.

Lareau, A. (1989). *Home advantage: Social class and parental intervention in elementary education.* London: Falmer Press.

Lareau, A., & Horvat, E. M. (1999). Moments of social inclusion: Race, class and cultural capital in family-school relationships. *Sociology of Education, 71,* 39–56.

Lawrence-Lightfoot, S. (1978). *Worlds apart: Relationships between families and schools.* New York: Basic Books.

Lee, V. E., & Ekstrom, R. B. (1987). Student access to guidance counseling in high school. *American Educational Research Journal, 24*(2), 287–309.

Lemann, N. (1999). *The big test: The secret history of the American meritocracy.* New York: Farrar, Straus and Giroux.

Leslie, L. L., & Brinkman, P. T. (1988). *The economic value of higher education.* New York: American Council on Education, Macmillan.

Levin, H. M., & Belfield, C. R. (2002). Families as contractual partners in education. *UCLA Law Review, 49*(6), 1799–1824.

Levin, H. M., & McEwan, P. J. (2001). *Cost-effectiveness analysis: Methods and applications* (2nd ed.). Thousand Oaks, CA: Sage Publications.

Levine, A., & Nidiffer, J. (1996). *Beating the odds: How the poor get to college.* San Francisco: Jossey-Bass.

Lindsay, P. (1984). High school size, participation in activities, and young adult social participation: Some enduring effects of schooling. *Education Evaluation and Policy Analysis, 6,* 73–83.

Lisella, L. C., & Serwatka, T. S. (1996). Extracurricular participation and academic achievement in minority students in urban schools. *Urban Review, 28,* 63–80.

Lockwood, A. T., & Secada, W. G. (1999). Transforming education for Hispanic youth: Exemplary practices, programs, and schools. *NCBE Resource Collection Series, 12.*

Lombana, J. H. (1985). Guidance accountability: A new look at an old problem. *School Counselor, 32,* 340–346.

Lucas, S. R. (1999). *Tracking inequality: Stratification and mobility in American high schools.* New York: Teachers College Press.

MacLeod, J. (1995). *Ain't no makin' it: Aspirations and attainment in a low-income neighborhood.* Boulder, CO: Westview Press.

Mahoney, J. L., & Cairns, R. B. (1997). Do extracurricular activities protect against early school dropout? *Developmental Psychology, 33,* 241–253.

Manski, C., & Wise, D. A. (1983). *College choice in America.* Cambridge: Harvard University Press.

Marcia, J. (1980). Identity in adolescence. In J. Adelson (Ed.), *The handbook of adolescent psychology* (pp. 159–187). New York: Wiley.

Markus, H., & Nurius, P. (1986, September). Possible selves. *American Psychologist,* 954–969.

Marsh, H. W. (1993). The effects of participation in sport during the last two years of high school. *Sociology of Sport Journal, 10,* 18–43.

Marsh, H. W. (1992). Extracurricular activities: Beneficial extension of the traditional curriculum or subversion of academic goals? *Journal of Educational Psychology, 84,* 553–562.

Martinez, G. (2000). *Making a difference: The effects of an undergraduate research mentorship program on the production of minority scholars.* Unpublished doctoral dissertation, University of California, Davis.

Matthay, E. R. (1989). A critical study of the college selection process. *School Counselor, 36,* 359–370.

Matthews, J. (2002, July 21). Success for some. *The Washington Post Magazine,* p. 33.

Matute-Bianchi, M. E. (1986). Ethnic identities and patterns of school success and failure among Mexican-descent and Japanese-American students in a California high school: An ethnographic analysis. *American Journal of Education, 95*(1), 233–255.

Mayeroff, M. (1971). *On caring.* New York: Harper and Row.

McClafferty, K. A., & McDonough, P. M. (2000). *Creating a K-16 environment: Reflections on the process of establishing a college culture in secondary schools.* Paper presented at the annual meeting of the Association for the Study of Higher Education, Sacramento, CA.

McClafferty, K. A., McDonough, P., & Fann, A. (2001). *Parent involvement in the college planning process.* Paper presented at the annual conference of the Association for the Study of Higher Education, Richmond, VA.

McDill, E. L., & Coleman, J.S. (1965). Family and peer influences in college plans of high school students. *Sociology of Education, 38,* 112–126.

McDonough, P. M. (1998). *African American and Latino perceptions of college access in California after affirmative action: UCOP preliminary report, emergent findings.* Oakland, CA: University of California Office of the President.

McDonough, P. M. (1994). Buying and selling higher education: The social construction of the college applicant. *Journal of Higher Education, 65,* 427–446.

McDonough, P. (1997). *Choosing colleges: How social class and schools structure opportunity.* Albany: State University of New York Press.

McDonough, P. M. (1999). *Doing whatever it takes: Conflict-based college admissions in the post-affirmative action era.* Paper presented at the annual meeting of the American Educational Research Association, Montreal, Canada.

McDonough, P. M. (2002). *High school counseling and college access: A report and reconceptualization.* Oakland: University of California, Office of the President, Outreach Evaluation Task Force.

McDonough, P. M., & McClafferty, K. A. (2000). Creating a K-16 environment: reflections on the process of establishing a college culture in secondary schools. Paper presented at the annual meeting of the Association for the Study of Higher Education, Sacramento, CA.

McDonough, P. M., Korn, J., & Yamasaki, E. (1997). Access, equity, and the privatization of college counseling. *Review of Higher Education, 20,* 297–317.

McDonough, P. M., & McClafferty, K. (2001). *Rural college opportunity: A Shasta and Siskiyou county perspective.* Reading, CA: University of California, Office of the President and McConnell Foundation.

McDonough, P. M., Perez, L., Fann, A., Tobolowsky, B., Smith, M., Teranishi, R., & Auerbach, S. (2000). *Parent involvement programs in education: Best research and practices.* Los Angeles: GEAR-UP State Support Systems for Families Implementation Committee, UCLA.

McDonough, P. M., Ventresca, M., & Outcalt, C. (2000). Field of dreams: Organizational field approaches to understanding the transformation of college access, 1965–1995. *Higher Education: Handbook of Theory and Research, 14,* 371–405.

McLaughlin, M. W. (2000). *Community counts: How youth organizations matter for youth development.* Washington, DC: Public Education Network.

McLaughlin, M., Irby, M. A., & Langman, J. (1994). *Urban sanctuaries: Neighborhood organizations in the lives and futures of inner-city youth.* San Francisco: Jossey-Bass.

McLearn, K. T., Colasanto, D., Schoen, C., & Shapiro, M. Y. (1999). In J. B. Grossman (Ed.), *Contemporary issues in mentoring* (pp. 66–83). Philadelphia: Public/Private Ventures.

McNeal, R. B. (1998). High school extracurricular activities: Closed structures and stratifying patterns of participation. *Journal of Educational Research, 91,* 183–191.

McNeal, R. B. (1995). Extracurricular activity participation and dropping out of high school. *Sociology of Education, 68,* 62–80.

McPartland, J. M., & Nettles, S. M. (1991, August). Using community adults as advocates or mentors for at-risk middle school students: A two-year evaluation of Project RAISE. *American Journal of Education, 99,* 568–586.

McPherson, M. S. (1993). How can we tell if financial aid is working? In M. S. McPherson, M. O. Shapiro, & G. C. Winston (Eds.), *Paying the piper: Productivity, incentives, and financing in U.S. higher education* (Chapter 6). Ann Arbor: University of Michigan Press.

Mehan, H., Villanueva, I., Hubbard, L., & Lintz, A. (1996). *Constructing school success: The consequences of untracking low-achieving students.* New York: Cambridge University Press.

Mejorado, M. (2000). *Navigating complex issues in a California statewide mentoring program for Mexican American high school students.* Unpublished doctoral dissertation, University of California, Davis.

Melnick, M. J., Sabo, D. F., & Vanfossen, B. (1992, Summer). Educational effects of interscholastic athletic participation on African-American and Hispanic youth. *Adolescence, 27,* 295–308.

Milem, J. (1998). Attitude change in college students. *The Journal of Higher Education, 69*(2), 117–140.

Miller, G., & Boller, J. (1975). *Closing the gaps: A study of four counselor education programs and efforts to facilitate role implementation and counselor effectiveness in the school.* St. Paul: Minnesota Department of Education.

Miller, T. K. (1998). *Secondary school counselor survey report: A report on the work environment and characteristics of secondary school counselors.* Alexandria, VA: National Association for College Admission Counseling.

Mills, R. (1998). *Grouping students for instruction in middle schools.* Washington, DC: Office of Educational Research and Improvement.

Mitchell, J. C. (1969). The concept and use of social networks. In J. C. Mitchell (Ed.), *Social networks in urban situations* (pp. 1–50). Manchester, U.K.: Manchester University Press.

Moles, O. C. (1993). Collaboration between schools and disadvantaged parents: Obstacles and openings. In N. Chavkin (Ed.), *Families and schools in a pluralistic society* (pp. 21–49). Albany: State University of New York Press.

Moles, O. (1991). Guidance programs in American high schools: A descriptive portrait. *School Counselor, 38,* 163–177.

Moll, L., Amanti, C., Neff, D., & Gonzalez, N. (1992). Funds of knowledge for teaching: Using a qualitative approach to connect homes and classrooms. *Theory Into Practice, 31*(2), 132–141.

Monson, R., & Brown, D. (1985, December). Secondary school counseling: A time for reassessment and revitalization. *NASSP Bulletin,* 32–35.

Morrow, K., & Styles, M. (1995). *Building relationships with youth in program settings: A study of Big Brothers/Big Sisters.* Philadelphia: Public/Private Ventures.

Mortenson, T. (2002, February 15). *Higher education as private and social investment.* A presentation to the Key Bank Financing Conference 2002, Orlando, FL.

Mounts, N. S., & Steinberg, L. (1995). An ecological analysis of peer influence on adolescent grade point average and drug use. *Developmental Psychology, 31*(6), 915–922.

Muro, J. (1965). In defense of the counselor-educator. *ACAC Journal, 11,* 20–22.

Murray, E., & Mosidi, R. (1993, Autumn). Career development counseling for African Americans: An appraisal of the obstacles and intervention strategies. *Journal of Negro Education, 62*(4), 441–447.

Myers, D., & Schirm, A. (1999, April). *The impacts of Upward Bound: Final report for phase I of the national evaluation final report.* (MPR Reference No. 8046-515). Washington, DC: U.S. Department of Education.

National Assessment of Educational Progress. (2001). *The nation's report card: Mathematics 2000.* Washington, DC: National Center for Education Statistics. (http://nces.ed.gov/nationsreportcard/pdf/main2000/2001517a.pdf)

National Association of College Admission Counselors. (1986). *Frontiers of possibility: Report of the national college counseling project.* Alexandria, VA: Author.

National Association of College Admission Counselors. (2000). *Statement on counselor competencies.* Alexandria, VA: Author.

National Center for Education Statistics. (2002). *The condition of education, 2002.* (NCES 2002-025). Washington, DC: U.S. Government Printing Office.

National Center for Education Statistics. (2001). *Digest of education statistics: 2000.* (NCES 2001-034). Washington, DC: U.S. Department of Education.

National Center for Public Policy and Higher Education. (2000). *Measuring Up 2000.* Washington, DC: Author.

National Commission on Children. (1991). *Speaking of kids: A national survey of children and parents.* Washington, DC: Author.

National Education Association. (2002). Per pupil expenditure data from the NEA Web site (http://nea.org/publiced/edstats/rankings/#h11).

National Research Council. (1993). *Losing generations: Adolescents in high-risk settings.* Washington, DC: National Research Council Panel on High Risk Youth. National Academy of Sciences.

Nettles, S. M. (1991, Fall). Community involvement and disadvantaged students: A review. *Review of Educational Research, 61,* 379–406.

Newcomb, T. M. (1943). *Personality and social change: Attitude formation in a student community.* New York: Dryden Press.

Newman, P. R., & Newman, B. M. (1976). Early adolescence and its conflict: Group identity versus alienation. *Adolescence, 11*(42), 261–274.

Noddings, N. (1984). *Caring: A feminine approach to ethics and moral education.* Berkeley: University of California Press.

Noeth, R. J., & Wimberly, G. L. (2002). *Creating seamless educational transitions for urban African American and Hispanic students.* Iowa City, IA: ACT Office of Policy Research.

Nora, A. (2002). A theoretical and practical view of student adjustment and academic achievement. In W. G. Tierney & L. S. Hagedorn (Eds.), *Increasing access to college: Extending possibilities for all students* (pp. 65–77). Albany: State University of New York Press.

Oakes, J. (1985). *Keeping track: How schools structure inequality.* New Haven, CT: Yale University Press.

Oakes, J. (1994). More than misapplied technology: A normative and political response to Hallinan on tracking. *Sociology of Education, 67*(2), 84–89.

Oakes, J. (1995). Two cities' tracking and within-school segregation. *Teachers College Record, 96*(4), 681–690.

Oakes, J. (1982). The reproduction of inequity: The content of secondary school tracking. *Urban Review, 14,* 107–120.

Oakes, J., & Guiton, G. (1995). Matchmaking: The dynamics of high school tracking decisions. *American Educational Research Journal, 32*(1), 3–33.

Oakes, J., Quartz, K. H., Ryan, S., & Lipton, M. (2000). *Becoming good American schools: The struggle for civic virtue in education reform.* San Francisco: Jossey-Bass.

Oakes, J., Rogers, J., Lipton, M., & Morrell, E. (2002). The social construction of college access: Confronting the technical, cultural, and political barriers to low-income students of color. In W. G. Tierney & L. S. Hagedorn (Eds.), *Increasing access to college: Extending possibilities for all students* (pp. 105–121). Albany: State University of New York Press.

O'Connor, C. (1997). Dispositions toward (collective) struggle and educational resilience in the inner city: A case analysis of six African-American high school students. *American Educational Research Journal, 34*(4), 593–629.

Oesterreich, H. (2000a). Characteristics of effective urban college preparation programs. *ERIC Digest Number 159,* ED448244.

Oesterreich, H. (2000b). The technical, cultural, and political factors in college preparation programs for urban and minority youth. *ERIC Digest Number 158,* ED448243.

Ogbu, J. U. (1991). Immigrant and involuntary minorities in comparative perspective. In M. Gibson & J. Ogbu (Eds.), *Minority status and schooling* (pp. 3–33). New York: Garland.

Ogbu, J. U. (1978). *Minority education and caste: The American system in cross-cultural perspective.* New York: Academic Press.

Ogbu, J. U. (1984). *Understanding community forces affecting minority students' academic effort.* Paper prepared for the Achievement Council, Oakland, CA.

Okagaki, L., & Frensch, P. A. (1998). Parenting and children's school achievement: A multiethnic perspective. *American Educational Research Journal, 35*(1), 123–144.

Oliver, M., & Shapiro, H. (1995). *Black wealth/white wealth: New perspectives on racial inequality.* New York: Routledge.

Olson, L., & Rosenfeld, R. A. (1984). Parents and the process of gaining access to student financial aid. *Journal of Higher Education, 55*(4), 455–480.

Orfield, G., & Paul, F. (1993). *High hopes, long odds: A major report on Hoosier teens and the American dream.* Indianapolis: Indiana Youth Institute.

Osterman, K. (2000). Students' need for belonging in the school community. *Review of Educational Research, 70*(3), 323367.

Otto, L. B. (1975). Extracurricular activities in the educational attainment process. *Rural Sociology, 40,* 162–176.

Pascarella, E., & Terenzini, P. (1991). *How college affects students.* San Francisco: Jossey-Bass.

Pascarella, E. T., & Terenzini, P. T. (1983). Predicting voluntary freshman year persistence/withdrawal behavior in a residential university: A path analytic validation of Tinto's model. *Journal of Educational Psychology, 75,* 215–226.

Pascarella, E. T., & Terenzini, P. T. (1980). Predicting freshman persistence and voluntary dropout decisions from a theoretical model. *Journal of Higher Education, 51,* 60–75.

Paul, F. G. (2002). *Bridging paradigms: A profession in transition.* Oakland, CA: University of California Office of the President Educational Outreach and K–12 Improvement Research and Evaluation Unit.

Paulsen, M. B. (1998). Recent research on the economics of attending college: Returns on investment and responsiveness to price. *Research in Higher Education, 39,* 471–489.

Paulsen, M. B. (1990). *College choice: Understanding student enrollment behavior.* (ASHE-ERIC Higher Education Report #6). Washington, DC: George Washington University, School of Education and Human Development.

Pearl, R., Bryan, T., & Herzog, A. (1990). Resisting or acquiescing to peer pressure to engage in misconduct: Adolescents' expectations of probable consequences. *Journal of Youth and Adolescence, 19*(1), 43–55.

Pérez, L. X. (1999). *The interface of individual, structural, and cultural constructs in Latino parents' effort to support their children in planning for college.* Unpublished doctoral dissertation, UCLA Graduate School of Education and Information Studies.

Perna, L. W. (2002). Early intervention programs: An approach to achieving equal educational opportunity for low-income students (pp. 97–112). In D. Heller (Ed), *Condition of access: Higher education for lower income students.* Phoenix, AZ: Oryx Press.

Perna, L. W. (2000a). Differences in the decision to attend college among African Americans, Hispanics, and whites. *Journal of Higher Education, 71*(2), 117–141.

Perna, L. W. (1995). *Early intervention programs: A new approach to increasing college access.* Paper presented at the NASSGP/NCHELP Research Network Conference, Minneapolis: MN.

Perna, L. W. (1999). Early intervention programs: A new approach to increasing college access. *Advances in Education Research, 4* (Winter).

Perna, L. W. (2002). Pre-college outreach programs: Characteristics of programs serving historically underrepresented groups of students. *Journal of College Student Development, 43*(1), 64–83.

Perna, L. W. (2000b). Promoting college enrollment through early intervention. *The ERIC Review: Early Intervention: Expanding Access to Higher Education: A Class Act, 8*(1), 8–14.

Perna, L. W., Fenske, R. H., & Swail, W. S. (2000). Sponsors of early intervention programs. *The ERIC Review: Early intervention: Expanding Access to Higher Education, 8*(1), 15–18.

Perna, L. W., & Swail, W. S. (1998). *Early intervention programs: How effective are they at increasing access to college?* Paper presented at the annual meeting of the Association for the Study of Higher Education, Miami, FL.

Perna, L. W., & Swail, W. S. (2001). Pre-college outreach and early intervention programs: An approach to achieving equal educational opportunity. *Thought and Action, 17*(1), 99–110.

Perna, L. W., & Titus, M. (2001, November). *The role of social capital in understanding racial/ethnic group differences in the realization of educational plans.* Paper presented as part of a symposium, Parental Guidance Suggested: Family Involvement in College Preparation Programs, at the annual conference of the Association for the Study of Higher Education, Richmond, VA.

Phelan, P., Davidson, A., & Yu, H. C. (1998). *Adolescents' worlds: Negotiating family, peers, and schools.* New York: Teachers College Press.

Phinney, J., (1990). Ethnic identity in adolescents and adults: A review of research. *Psychological Bulletin, 180,* 499–514.

Piaget, J. (1991). Advances in child and adolescent psychology. In P. Light, S. Sheldon & M. Woodhead (Eds.), *Learning to think: Child development in social context* Vol. 2, pp. 5–15. New York: Routledge.

Piaget, J. (1932). *The moral judgment of the child.* Glencoe, IL: Free Press.

Picou, J. S., & Carter, T. M. (1976). Significant-other influence and aspirations. *Sociology of Education, 49*(1), 12–22.

Plank, S. B., & Jordan, W. J. (2001). Effects of information, guidance, and actions on postsecondary destinations: A study of talent loss. *American Educational Research Journal, 38*(4), 947–980.

Plank, S. B., & Jordan, W. J. (1997). *Reducing talent loss: The impact of information, guidance, and actions on postsecondary enrollment.* (Center for Research on the Education of Students Placed at Risk Report #9). Baltimore: Johns Hopkins University.

Pombeni, M. L., Kirchler, E., & Palmonari, A. (1990). Identification with peers as a strategy to muddle through the troubles of adolescent years. *Journal of Adolescence, 13*, 351–369.

Post, D. (1990). College-going decision by Chicanos: The politics of misinformation. *Educational Evaluation and Policy Analysis, 12*(2), 174–187.

Powell, A. G. (1996). *Lessons from privilege: The American prep school tradition.* Cambridge: Harvard University Press.

Praport, H. (1993, March). Reducing high school attrition: Group counseling can help. *School Counselor, 40,* 309–311.

Quiroz, P. A., Gonzalez, N. F., & Frank, K. A. (1996). Carving a niche in the high school social structure: Formal and informal constraints on participation in the extra curriculum. *Research in Sociology of Education and Socialization, 11,* 93–120.

Rehberg, R. A., & Schafer, W. E. (1968). Participation in interscholastic athletics and college expectations. *American Journal of Dociology, 73*, 732–740.

Rhodes, J., Grossman, J., & Resch, N. (2000). Agents of change: Pathways through which mentoring relationships influence adolescents' academic adjustment. *Child Development, 71*, 1662–1671.

Rice, J. K. (1993). Cost analysis as a tool for education reform. In S. L. Jacobson & R. Berne (Eds.), *Reforming education: The emerging systemic approach* (pp. 131–150). Thousand Oaks, CA: Corwin Press.

Rice, J. K. (1997, Winter). Cost analysis in education: Paradox and possibility. *Educational Evaluation and Policy Analysis, 19*(4), 309–317.

Rice, J. K. (1996). Cost-effectiveness as a basic concept. In R. Berne (Ed.), *New York State Board of Regents study on cost-effectiveness in education: Final report.* New York: University of the State of New York.

Roberts, A., & Cotton, L. (1994). Note on assessing a mentor program. *Psychological Reports, 75*, 1369–1370.

Roche, G. (1979). Much ado about mentors. *Harvard Business Review, 57,* 14–28.

Roffman, J. G., Pagano, M. E., & Hirsch, B. J. (2001). Youth functioning and experiences in inner-city after-school programs among age, gender, and race groups. *Journal of Child and Family Studies, 10*, 85–100.

Rogoff, B. (1994). Developing understanding of the idea of communities of learners. *Mind, Culture, and Activity, 1*, 209–229.

Rogoff, B. (1995). Observing sociocultural activity on three planes: Participatory appropriation, guided participation, and apprenticeship. In J. V. Wertsch, P. Del Rio, & A. Alvarez (Eds.), *Sociocultural studies of mind* (pp. 139–164). Cambridge, U.K.: Cambridge University Press.

Rogoff, B., Baker-Sennett, J., Lacasa, P., & Goldsmith, D. (1995). Development through participation in sociocultural activity. In J. Goodnow, P. Miller, & F. Kessel (Eds.), *Cultural practices as contexts for development* (pp. 45–65). San Francisco: Jossey-Bass.

Romo, H. D., & Falbo, T. (1996). *Latino high school graduation: Defying the odds.* Austin: University of Texas Press.

Rosenbaum, J. (1976) . *Making inequality.* New York: Wiley.

Rosenbaum, J., Miller, S. R., & Krei, M. S. (1996). Gatekeeping in an era of more open gates: High school counselors' views of their influence on students' college plans. *American Journal of Education, 104*(4), 257–279.

Rosenthal, D. A., Moore, S. M., & Taylor, M. J. (1983). Ethnicity and adjustment: A study of the self-image of Anglo-, Greek-, and Italian-Australian working class adolescents. *Journal of Youth and Adolescence, 12*(2), 117–135.

Rossi, P. H., & Freeman, H. E. (1993). *Evaluation: A systematic approach* (5th ed.). Newbury Park, CA: Sage Publications.

Roth, J., Brooks-Gunn, J., Murray, L., & Foster, W. (1998). Promoting healthy adolescents: Synthesis of youth development program evaluations. *Journal of Research on Adolescence, 8*(4), 423–459.

Rouse, C. E. (1994). What to do after high school: The two-year versus four-year college enrollment decision. In R. G. Ehrenberg (Ed.), *Choices and consequences: Contemporary policy issues in education* (pp. 59–88). New York: IRL Press.

Rowe, F. A. (1989). College students' perceptions of high school counselors. *School Counselor, 36*, 260–264.

Royse, D. (1998). Mentoring high risk minority youth. Evaluation of the Brothers Project. *Adolescence, 33*, 145–159.

Rubin, K. H., Bukowski, W., & Parker, J. G. (1998). Peer interactions, relationships, and groups. In N. Eisenberg (Ed.), *Handbook of child psychology* Vol. 3 (pp. 619–700). New York: Wiley.

Rueda, R., Monzó, L., & Arzubiaga, A. (2003). Academic instrumental knowledge: Deconstructing cultural capital theory for strategic intervention approaches. *Current Issues in Education, 6*(14), 1–18. Available: http://cie.ed.asu.edu/volume6/number14/

Rumberger, R. (1991). Chicano dropouts: A review of research and policy issues. In R. Valencia (Ed.), *Chicano school failure and success* (pp. 64–89). New York: Falmer Press.

Rumberger, R., & Brenner, M. (2000, April 25). *Can mentoring improve academic achievement? Results from a 3-year evaluation of an early adolescent program.* Paper presented at the American Educational Research Association Conference, New Orleans, LA.

Rutter, M. (1987). Psychosocial resilience and protective mechanisms. *American Journal of Orthopsychiatry, 57*, 316–331.

Sacerdote, B. (2001). Peer effects with random assignment: Result for Dartmouth roommates. *Quarterly Journal of Economics, 116*(2), 681–704.

Salchak, S. (2002). Engaging families and communities in supporting the college access and success. *Pathways to College Network Clearinghouse PathNotes, 1*(2).

Sanders, M. G., Epstein, J. L., & Connors-Tadros, L. (1999). *Family partnerships with high schools: The parents' perspective* (Report no. 32). Baltimore: Johns Hopkins University, Center for Research on the Education of Students Placed at Risk.

Santor, D. A., Messervey, D., & Kusumakar, V. (2000). Measuring peer pressure, popularity, and conformity in adolescent boys and girls. *Journal of Youth and Adolescence, 29*(2), 163–182.

Sax, L., Lindholm, J., Astin, A., Korn, W. S., & Mahoney, K. (2001). *The American freshman: National norms for fall 2001*. Los Angeles: Higher Education Research Institute, University of California.

Schafer, W. E., & Reber, R. A. (1970). Athletic participation, college aspirations, and college encouragement. *Pacific Sociological Review, 13*, 182–186.

Scheidlinger, S. (1984). The adolescent peer group revisited: Turbulence or adaptation? *Small Group Behavior, 15*(3), 387–397.

Schneider, B., & Stevenson, D. (1999). *The ambitious generation: America's teenagers, motivated but directionless*. New Haven, CT: Yale University Press.

Schweinhart, L. J., Barnes, H. V., & Weikart, D. P. (1993). *Significant benefits: The High/Scope Perry Preschool Study through age 27*. Monographs of the High/Scope Educational Research Foundation, No. 10. Ypsilanti, MI: High/Scope Educational Research Foundation.

Scott, W. R. (1998). *Organizations: Rational, natural, open systems* (4th ed.). Upper Saddle River, NJ: Prentice Hall.

Scott-Jones, D. (1995). Parent-child interactions and school achievement. In B. Ryan, G. Adams, T. Gullotta, R. Weissberg, & R. Hampton (Eds.), *The family-school connection: Theory, research, and practice* (pp. 75–107). Thousand Oaks, CA: Sage.

Serna, I., & Collatos, T. (2001). *Achieving from the margins: Students of color in AP classes*. Paper presented at the annual meeting of the American Educational Research Association, Seattle, WA.

Sewell, M., & Marczak, M. (2002). *Using cost analysis in evaluation*. Unpublished paper, University of Arizona (http://ag.arizona.edu/fcr/fs/cyfar/Costben2.htm).

Sewell, W. H. (1971). Inequality of opportunity for higher education. *American Sociological Review, 36*, 793–809.

Sewell, W. H., Haller, A. O., & Ohlendorf, G. W. (1970a). The educational and early occupational attainment process. *American Sociological Review, 34*, 82–92.

Sewell, W. H., Haller, A. O., & Ohlendorf, G. W. (1970b). The educational and early occupational status attainment process: Replication and revision. *American Sociological Review, 35,* 1014–1027.

Sewell, W. H., & Shah, V. P. (1968). Social class, parental encouragement, and educational aspirations. *American Journal of Sociology, 73*(5), 559–572.

Shieh, Y. (2002, April 2). *Relationship between high school extracurricular activities and postsecondary educational attainment.* Paper presented at the annual meeting of the American Educational Research Association in New Orleans, LA.

Shirley, D. (1997). *Laboratories of democracy: Community organizing for school reform.* Austin: University of Texas Press.

Shonkoff, J. P., & Phillips, D. A. (2000). *From neurons to neighborhoods: The science of early childhood development.* Washington, DC: National Academy Press.

Shumow, L., & Lomax, R. (2002). Parental efficacy: Predictor of parenting behavior and adolescent outcomes. *Parenting: Science and practice, 2*(2), 127–150.

Simon, B. (2001). *High school-family partnerships: Effects of school outreach on family involvement practices.* Paper presented at the annual meeting of the American Educational Research Association, Seattle, WA.

Simpson, R. L. (1962). Parental influence, anticipatory socialization, and social mobility. *American Sociological Review, 27,* 517–522.

Singer, D. G., & Revenson, T. A. (1996). *A Piaget primer: How a child thinks.* New York: Plume Printing.

Sipe, C. (1999). Mentoring adolescents: What have we learned? In J. B. Grossman (Ed.), *Contemporary issues in mentoring.* Philadelphia: Public/Private Ventures.

Sipe, C. L. (1996). *Mentoring: A synthesis of P/PV's research: 1988–1995.* Philadelphia: Public/Private Ventures.

Smith, M.J . (2002). *Using sociological forms of capital and black feminist epistemology to understand African American parent participation in college choice.* Unpublished doctoral dissertation, UCLA Graduate School of Education and Information Studies.

Snyder, E. E., & Spreitzer, E. (1990). High school athletic participation as related to college attendance among black, Hispanic, and white males: A research note. *Youth and Society, 21,* 390–398.

Snyder, E. E., & Spreitzer, E. A. (1977). Participation in sports as related to educational expectations among high school girls. *Sociology of Education, 50,* 47–55.

Snyder, J., Dishion, T. J., & Patterson, G. R. (1986). Determinants and consequences of associating with deviant peers during preadolescence and adolescence. *Journal of Early Adolescence 6,* 23.

Solorzano, D.G. (1997). Images and words that wound: Critical race theory, racial stereotyping and teacher education. *Teacher Education Quarterly, 24,* 5–19.

Solorzano, D. G. (1992a). Chicano mobility aspirations: A theoretical and empirical note. *Latino Studies Journal, 3*(1), 48–66.

Solorzano, D. G. (1992b). An exploratory analysis of the effects of race, class, and gender on student and parent mobility aspirations. *Journal of Negro Education, 61*(1), 30–44.

Solorzano, D. G., & Solórzano, R. W. (1995). The Chicano education experience: A framework for effective schools in Chicano communities. *Educational Policy, 9*(3), 293–314.

Solorzano, D. G., & Villalpando, O. (1998). Critical race theory, marginality, and the experiences of students of color in higher education. In C. A Torres & T. R. Mitchell (Eds.), *Sociology of education: Emerging perspectives* (pp. 299–319). New York: SUNY Press.

Spade, J. Z., Columbda, L., & Vanfossen, B. E. (1997). Tracking in mathematics and science: Courses and course-selection procedures. *Sociology of Education, 70*, 108–127.

Spady, W. G. (1970). Lament for the letterman: Effects of peer status and extracurricular activities on goals and achievement. *American Journal of Sociology, 75*(4), 680–702.

Spencer, M. B., Brookins, G. K., & Allen, W. R. (1985). *Beginnings: The social and affective development of black children*. Hillsdale, NJ: Erlbaum.

St. John, E. P. (1991). What really influences minority attendance? Sequential analysis of the High School and beyond sophomore cohort. *Research in Higher Education, 32*(2), 141–158.

St. John, E. P., & Asker, E. H. (2003). *Refinancing the college dream: Access, equal opportunity, and justice for taxpayers*. Baltimore, MD: Johns Hopkins University Press.

St. John, E. P., & Noell, J. (1989). The effects of student financial aid on access to higher education: An analysis of progress with special consideration of minority enrollments. *Research in Higher Education, 30*(6), 563–581.

Stader, D., & Gagnepain, F. G. (2000). Mentoring: The power of peers. *American Secondary Education, 28*(3), 28–32.

Stage, F., & Hossler, D. (1989). Differences in family influences on college attendance plans for male and female ninth graders. *Research in Higher Education, 30*(3), 301–315.

Stanton-Salazar, R. (1997). A social capital framework for understanding the socialization of racial minority children and youths. *Harvard Educational Review, 67*(1), 1–40.

Stanton-Salazar, R. (2001). *Manufacturing hope and despair: The school and kin support networks of U.S.-Mexican youth*. New York: Teachers College Press.

Stanton-Salazar, R. D., & Dornbusch, S. M. (1995). Social capital and the reproduction of inequality: Information, networks among Mexican-origin high school students. *Sociology of Education, 68*, 116–135.

Steele, C. (1997, June). A threat in the air. *American Psychologist*, 613–628.

Steinberg, L. (1996). *Beyond the classroom: Why school reform has failed and what parents need to do.* New York: Simon and Schuster.

Steinberg, L., Brown, B., Cider, M., Kaczmarek, N., & Lazzaro, C. (1988). *Non-instructional influences on high school achievement: The contributions of parents, peers, extracurricular activities, and part time work.* Madison: National Center on Effective Secondary Schools, University of Wisconsin, Wisconsin Center for Educational Research.

Steinberg, L., Dornbusch, S. M., & Brown, B. B. (1992). Ethnic differences in adolescent achievement: An ecological perspective. *American Psychologist, 47*(6), 723–729.

Stevenson, D. L., Schiller, K. S., & Schneider, B. (1994). Sequences of opportunities for learning. *Sociology of Education, 67*, 184–198.

Sullivan, H. S. (1953). *The interpersonal theory of psychiatry.* New York: Norton.

Sutton, J. M., & Fall, M. (1995, January/February). The relationship of school climate factors to counselor self-efficacy. *Journal of Counseling and Development, 73*, 331–336.

Swail, W. S. (2001b). Engaging a nation: Expanding the role of TRIO and other outreach programs. *The Council Journal*, November, 5–10.

Swail, W. S. (2000, Fall). Preparing America's disadvantaged for college: Programs that increase college opportunity. *New Directions for Institutional Research, 107*, 85–101.

Swail, W. S. (2001a). *The College Board outreach program handbook.* Arlington, VA: SRI International.

Swail, W. S., & Perna, L. W. (2000). A view of the landscape: Results of the national survey of outreach programs. In *2001 Outreach Program Handbook* (pp. xvii–xxxvi). New York: College Board.

Swail, W. S., & Perna, L. W. (2002). Pre-college outreach programs: A national perspective. In W. G. Tierney & L. S. Hagedorn (Eds.), *Increasing access to college: Extending possibilities for all students* (pp. 15–34). Albany: State University of New York Press.

Swanson, M. C. (1993). *The AVID classroom: A system of academic and social supports for low-achieving students.* East Lansing, MI: National Center for Research on Teacher Learning. (ERIC Document Reproduction Service No. ED368832)

Swap, S. M. (1993). *Developing home-school partnerships: From concepts to practice.* New York: Teachers College Press.

Szasz, M. C. (1977). *Education and the American Indian: The road to self-determination since 1928.* Albuquerque: University of New Mexico Press.

Terenzini, P. T., Cabrera, A. F., & Bernal, E. M. (2001). *Swimming against the tide: The poor in American higher education.* (Research Report No. 2001-1). New York: College Board.

Terenzini, P. T., Rendon, L. I., Upcraft, M. L., Millar, S. B., Allison, K. W., Gregg, P. L., & Jalomo, R. (1994). The transition to college: Diverse students, diverse stories. *Research in Higher Education, 35*(1), 57–73.

Thomas, G. E. (1980). Race and sex differences and similarities in the process of college entry. *Higher Education, 9,* 179–202.

Thomas, G. E. (1979). The influence of ascription, achievement, and educational expectations on black-white postsecondary enrollment. *Sociological Quarterly. 20,* 209–222.

Tibby, E. R. (1965). Let's educate the educators. *ACAC Journal, 11,* 35–38.

Tiedeman, D. V. (1968). *Economic, educational and personal implications of implementing computerized guidance information systems* (Information Systems for Vocational Decisions. Project report No. 13). Cambridge: Harvard Graduate School of Education.

Tierney, W. G. (1993). *Building communities of difference: Higher education in the twenty-first century.* Westport, CT: Greenwood.

Tierney, W. G. (1999). Models of minority college-going and retention: Cultural integrity versus cultural suicide. *Journal of Negro Education, 68*(1), 80–91.

Tierney, W. G. (1992). *Official encouragement, institutional discouragement: Minorities in academe—The Native American experience.* Norwood, NJ: Ablex.

Tierney, W. G. (2002a). Parents and families in precollege preparation: The lack of connection between research and practice. *Educational Policy, 16*(4), 588–606.

Tierney, W. G. (2002). Reflective evaluation: Improving practice in college preparation programs. In W. G. Tierney & L. S. Hagedorn (Eds.), *Increasing access to college: Extending possibilities for all students* (pp. 217–230). Albany: State University of New York Press.

Tierney, W. G., & Colyar, J. (2001). Students of college preparation programs in postsecondary institutions: Improving program effectiveness and student achievement. Los Angeles: Center for Higher Education Policy Analysis.

Tierney, W. G., & Hagedorn, L. (2002). *Making the grade.* Los Angeles: Center for Higher Education Policy Analysis, University of Southern California.

Tierney, W. G., & Jun, A. (2001, March/April). A university helps prepare low income youths for college: Tracking school success. *Journal of Higher Education, 72*(2), 205–225.

Tierney, W. G., & Jun, A. (1999). At-risk students and college success: A framework for effective preparation. *Metropolitan Universities, 9*(4), 49–60.

Tornatsky, L., Cutler, R., & Lee, J. (2002). College knowledge: What Latino parents need to know and why. Claremont, CA: Tomas Rivera Policy Institute.

Treisman, U. (1992). Studying students studying calculus: A look at the lives of minority mathematics students in college. *College Mathematics Journal, 25*(5), 362–372.

Ungar, M. (2000). The myth of peer pressure. *Adolescence, 35*(137), 167–180.

University of Missouri--Kansas City. (1997). *Financial impact of supplemental instruction through higher student persistence and graduation rates.* A research document from the Supplemental Instruction Web site (www.Umkc.Edue/centers/cad/si/sidocs/dacost97.htm).

Urberg, K. A., Degirmencioglu, S. M., Tolson, J. M., & Halliday-Sher, K. (1995). The structure of adolescent peer networks. *Developmental Psychology, 31*(4), 540–547.

USA Weekend. (1997, April 25–27). A meeting of minds. p. 5.

U.S. Department of Education. (1994, September). *Strong families, strong schools: Building community partnerships for learning.* Washington, DC: Author.

U.S. Department of Education, National Center for Education Statistics. (2001). *The Condition of Education 2001.* Washington, DC: Author.

Useem, E. L. (1992). Middle schools and math groups: Parents' involvement in children's placement. *Sociology of Education, 65*(October), 263–279.

Valdés, G. (1996). *Con respeto: Bridging the distances between culturally diverse families and schools: An ethnographic portrait.* New York: Teachers College Press.

Valencia, R. (Ed.) (1997). *The evolution of deficit thinking: Educational thought and practice.* The Stanford Series on Education and Public Policy. London: Falmer Press.

Valenzuela, A. (1999). *Subtracting schooling: U.S.-Mexican youth and the politics of caring.* Albany, NY: SUNY Press.

Van Acker, R., & Wehby, J. (2000). Exploring the social contexts influencing student success or failure: Introduction. *Preventing School Failure, 44*(3), 93–96.

Vandell, D., & Posner, J. (1999). Conceptualization and measurement of children's after-school environments. In S. L. Friedman, & T. D. Wachs (Eds.), *Measuring environment across the life span* (pp. 167–198). Washington, DC: American Psychological Association Press.

Velez-Ibanez, C., & Greenberg, J. B. (1992). Formation and transformation of funds of knowledge among US-Mexican households. *Anthropology and Education Quarterly, 23*, 313–333.

Vigil, J. D. (1993). Gangs, social control, and ethnicity: Ways to redirect. In S. B. Heath & M. W. McLaughlin (Eds.), *Identity and inner-city youth: Beyond ethnicity and gender* (pp. 94–119). New York: Teachers College Press.

Vigil, J. D. (1999). Streets and schools: How educators can help Chicano marginalized gang youth. *Harvard Educational Review, 69*(3), 270–288.

Villanueva, I. (1996). Change in the educational life of Chicano families across three generations. *Education and Urban Society, 29*(1), 13–34.

Villanueva, I., & Hubbard, L. (1994). *Toward redefining parent involvement: Making parents' invisible strategies and cultural practices visible.* Paper presented at the annual meeting of the American Educational Research Association, New Orleans, LA.

Vriend, J. (1971). Computer power for guidance and counseling. In D. R. Cook (Ed.), *Guidance for education in revolution* (pp. 415–452). Boston: Allyn and Bacon.

Wallace, W. (1964). Institutional and life-cycle socialization of college freshmen. *American Journal of Sociology, 70*(3), 303–318.

Wallace, W. (1965). Peer influences and undergraduates' aspirations for graduate study. *Sociology of Education, 38*(5), 375–392.

Weinstein, R. S. (1996). High standards in a tracked system of schooling: For which students and with what educational supports? *Educational Researcher, 25*(8), 16–19.

Weisner, T. R., Gallimore, R., & Jordan, C. (1988). Unpackaging cultural effects on classroom learning: Native Hawaiian peer assistance and child-generated activity. *Anthropology and Education Quarterly, 19*, 327–353.

Wells, A. S., & Serna, I. (1996). The politics of culture: Understanding local political resistance to detracking in racially mixed schools. *Harvard Educational Review, 66*(1), 93–118.

Werner, E., & Smith, C. (1982). *Vulnerable but invincible: A longitudinal study of resilient children and youth.* New York: McGraw Hill.

West, C. (1993). The new cultural politics of difference. In B. Thompson, & S. Tyagi (Eds.), *Beyond a dream deferred: Multicultural education and the politics of excellence* (pp. 18–40). Minneapolis: University of Minnesota Press.

White, P. A., Gamoran, A., Smithson, J., & Porter, A. C. (1996). Upgrading the high school math curriculum: Math course-taking patterns in seven high schools in California and New York. *Educational Evaluation and Policy Analysis, 18*(4), 285–307.

Wilds, D. (2000). *Minorities in higher education: 17th annual status report.* Washington, DC: American Council on Education.

Wilmouth, D. (1991). *Should the SAT be a factor in college admissions?* (ERIC Clearinghouse #ED345592).U.S. Virginia.

Wilson, B., & Rossman, G. (1993). *Mandating academic excellence: High school responses to state curriculum reform.* New York: Teachers College Press.

Wilson, W. J. (1996). *When work disappears: The world of the new urban poor.* New York: Vintage Books.

Wright, B., & Tierney, W. G. (1991). American Indians in higher education: A history of cultural conflict. *Change, 23*(2), 11–18.

Yonezawa, S. S. (1997). *Making decisions about students' lives: An interactive study of secondary school students' academic program selection.* Unpublished doctoral dissertation, UCLA Graduate School of Education and Information Studies.

Yonezawa, S., & Oakes, J. (1999, April). Making parents partners in the placement process. *Educational Leadership,* 33–36.

Yonezawa, S., Wells, A., & Serna, I. (2002). Choosing tracks: "Freedom of choice" in detracking schools. *American Educational Research Journal, 39*(1), 37–67.

Youniss, J., & Smollar, J. (1985). *Adolescent relations with mothers, fathers, and friends.* Chicago: University of Chicago Press.

Zey, M. G. (1984). *The mentor connection.* Homewood, IL: Dow Jones-Irwin.

Contributors

WALTER R. ALLEN is currently Professor of Sociology at the University of California, Los Angeles. He is also codirector of CHOICES, a longitudinal study of college attendance among African Americans and Latinos in California. His research and teaching focuses on family patterns, socialization and personality development, race and ethnic relations, African American males, health inequality, and higher education. His writings appear in the *Harvard Educational Review, Journal of Marriage and Family, Phylon, Sociological Quarterly, Journal of Negro Education, Signs, Social Science and Medicine, Journal of General Internal Medicine,* and *Research in Higher Education,* among others. He has coauthored (with R. Farley) *The Color Line and the Quality of Life in America;* coedited *Beginnings: The Social and Affective Development of Black Children* (with G. Brookins and M. Spencer) and *Black American Families, 1965–84* (with R. English and J. Hall); and coauthored (with E. Epps and N. Haniff) *College in Black and White: African American Students in Predominantly White and Historically Black Public Universities* and (with S. Hurtado, J. Milem and A. Clayton-Pedersen) *Enacting Diverse Learning Environments and Improving the Climate for Racial/Ethnic Diversity in Higher Education.*

SUSAN AUERBACH is Assistant Professor in the Department of Educational Leadership and Policy Studies at California State University, Northridge. Formerly a Senior Research Associate at the Center for Higher Education Policy Analysis at the University of Southern California, she received her PhD from UCLA's Graduate School of Education and Information Studies Division of Urban Schooling. Her dissertation, an ethnographic case study of the role of working-class Latino and African American parents in promoting their children's college access, received the Outstanding Dissertation Award for 2001 from the AERA Family-School-Community Partnerships Special Interest Group. Her research interests relating to the social context of education and education policy include parent and community engagement, college access,

Latino education, and public engagement in reform and accountability. She recently published an article on Latino parents' narratives of schooling in *Teachers College Record* (November, 2002).

MARGUERITE BONOUS-HAMMARTH is Research Project Director of CHOICES: Access, Equity and Diversity in Higher Education, based at the Institute for Social Science Research at the University of California, Los Angeles. Her research examines the influence of value congruence in outcomes for students and faculty in higher education, student development in science, mathematics, and engineering careers, and factors related to organizational transformation at postsecondary institutions. Her publications include "Pathways to Success: Creating Opportunities for Science, Mathematics and Engineering Majors" (*Journal of Negro Education*) and "Value Congruence and Organizational Climates for Undergraduate Persistence" (*Higher Education Handbook on Theory and Research*), among others.

JULIA E. COLYAR is a Postdoctoral Research Associate at the Center for Higher Education Policy Analysis at the University of Southern California. At USC, she has also served as an undergraduate advisor, research assistant, and assistant lecturer in the general education program. Funded by the U.S. Department of Education, her current research involves cultural biography and college access. She is also interested in college preparation programs, transitions to college, and innovations in qualitative research.

ZOË B. CORWIN brings seven years of high school teaching experience to her graduate work in pursuit of a PhD in sociology at the University of Southern California. Her theoretical and research interests pertain to race, gender, and urban education. Corwin is currently a research assistant in the Center for Higher Education Policy Analysis at USC, where she is working on a three-year grant from the U.S. Department of Education that investigates access to college for students of color/low SES. Corwin earned a BA in sociology from the University of California, Los Angeles, and a master's degree in Spanish from the Madrid campus of St. Louis University.

PATRICIA GÁNDARA is Professor of Education in the School of Education at the University of California at Davis. She is also Associate to the Vice President of the University of California for Outreach. Her research interests include peer group influences, college-going behavior of low-income Latino and other ethnic minority students, bilingual education policy, high academic achievement of low-income Mexican Americans, Chicanos and educational mobility, and mathematics instruction in multicultural classrooms. Her recent publications include "Putting the Cart Before the Horse: Latinos and Higher Education" (with Lisa Chavez), in Lopez and Jimenez (Eds.), *Latinos in Cali-*

fornia, Assets at Risk (forthcoming); and *Paving the Way to Postsecondary Education* (Deborah Bial), published by the National Center for Education Statistics (2001). Her publication *Over the Ivy Walls: The Educational Mobility of Low-Income Chicanos* (1995) is a pivotal work in the area of college access.

JAMES C. HEARN is Professor of Public Policy and Higher Education at Vanderbilt University. Prior to entering his academic career, he worked as a policy researcher on issues relating to postsecondary student financial aid and access for the American College Testing program and for a consulting firm in Washington, DC. Professor Hearn currently focuses his research on higher education policy and organization, with particular attention to state-level policy and the role of student aid and other factors in students' college enrollment. His work has been published in sociology, economics, and education journals as well as in several edited books.

JANET M. HOLDSWORTH recently completed her PhD in Higher Education at the University of Minnesota. She is currently Director of Policy Research at the Midwestern Higher Education Compact and a research affiliate of the University of Minnesota's Postsecondary Education Research Institute. Her previous degrees are in history, political science, and public administration. Holdsworth's research interests include state-level postsecondary education policies related to equity and access, institution-level policy making and governance issues, conflict theory, and social responsiveness of universities and faculty.

PATRICIA M. MCDONOUGH is Associate Professor in the Higher Education and Organizational Change Division, Graduate School of Education and Information Studies, University of California, Los Angeles. Her research is in the areas of college access, organizational culture, and equity. Dr. McDonough has conducted research on students' college choice decision making, high school counseling, the impact of college rankings of students' college choices, access for African American and Latino students, rural college access, access in historically Black colleges, private college counselors, affirmative action, and college admissions officers. Dr. McDonough's book, *Choosing Colleges: How Social Class and Schools Structure Opportunity*, studies how students choose colleges and the influence of parents, schools, and colleges on that decision-making process.

MARIA MEJORADO is Assistant Professor in the Bilingual/Multicultural Education Department in the College of Education at California State University, Sacramento. She teaches in the area of bilingual and multicultural education. Between 1997 and 2001, she worked as an evaluator of the high school Puente project. She received her doctorate from the University of California, Davis.

LAURA W. PERNA is Assistant Professor of Higher Education at the University of Maryland. Her research explores the individual and structural factors that limit the ability of women, racial/ethnic minorities, and individuals of lower socioeconomic status to realize the economic, political, and social opportunities that are associated with two aspects of higher education: access as a student and employment as a faculty member. Her research also explores the effects of such public policies as precollege outreach programs, student financial aid, and affirmative action on the college enrollment of traditionally underrepresented groups. She serves on the editorial boards of the *Review of Higher Education* and the *Journal of College Student Development* and is a consulting editor for *Research in Higher Education*. Her research has been published as chapters in books, technical reports, and articles in such journals as *Journal of Higher Education, Review of Higher Education, Research in Higher Education, Journal of College Student Development*, and *Journal of Student Financial Aid*. She holds a BA in psychology and BS in economics from the University of Pennsylvania, and a master's in public policy and PhD in education from the University of Michigan.

ROBERT RUEDA is Professor in the Division of Learning and Instruction in the Rossier School of Education at the University of Southern California. His research has focused on the sociocultural basis of learning as mediated by instruction, with a focus on reading and literacy in English learners, students in at-risk conditions, and students with mild learning handicaps. His most recent work has focused on how paraeducators mediate instruction and provide cultural scaffolding to English learners and on issues of reading engagement among inner-city immigrant students in a central city community. He has consulted with a variety of professional, educational, and government organizations, has spoken at a wide range of professional meetings, and has published widely in the previously mentioned areas.

DANIEL G. SOLORZANO is a Professor in Social Science and Comparative Education and Chair of the Department of Education at UCLA. Dr. Solorzano's current research applies critical race theory to examine educational access, persistence, and graduation of underrepresented minority undergraduate and graduate students in the United States, with an emphasis on the college admissions process and access to Gifted and Talented in Education programs and advanced placement courses for African American and Chicano/Latino students. His scholarly publications include: *A Critical Race Analysis of Advance Placement Classes: A Case of Educational Inequalities* (with Armida Ornelas); *Affirmative Action, Educational Equity and Campus Racial Climate: A Case Study of the University of Michigan Law School* (with Walter Allen); *Critical Race Theory, Marginality, and the Experience of Minority Students in*

Higher Education (with Octavio Villalpando); *Critical Race Theory, Racial Microaggressions and Campus Racial Climate: The Experiences of African American College Students* (with Miguel Ceja and Tara Yosso); *The Chicano Educational Experience: A Proposed Framework for Effective Schools in Chicano Communities* (with Ronald Solorzano); *Critical Race Theory: Counterstorytelling the Chicana and Chicano Graduate School Experience* (with Tara Yosso); *Critical Race Theory, Transformational Resistance, and Social Justice: Chicana and Chicano Students in an Urban Context* (with Dolores Delgado Bernal).

WATSON SCOTT SWAIL is President of the Educational Policy Institute in Washington, DC, a nonprofit, nongovernmental organization dedicated to policy-based research on educational opportunity for all students. Dr. Swail has published extensively in national journals and publications. His most recent publications include "Higher Education and the New Demographics" in *Change* (2002), "Pre-College Outreach Programs: A National Perspective" in Tierney and Hagedorn's *Increasing Access to College,* and "Beyond Access: Increasing the Odds of College Success" (*Phi Delta Kappan,* May 2000). Dr. Swail directed and authored the College Board's Outreach Program Handbook 2001 and chaired the ConnectED 2000 National Summit on College Preparation and Opportunity. He also serves on a number of national advisory committees, including technical review panels for the major U.S. longitudinal and cross-sectional surveys sponsored by the U.S. Department of Education National Center for Education Statistics and has recently conducted projects for the Canada Millennium Scholarship Program related to postsecondary access in Canada.

WILLIAM G. TIERNEY is the Wilbur-Kieffer Professor of Higher Education and Director of the Center for Higher Education Policy Analysis at the University of Southern California. His research interests pertain to organizational performance, equity, and faculty roles and rewards. Dr. Tierney teaches courses on the administration and governance of higher education and on qualitative methods. His recent publications include *Increasing Access to College: Extending Possibilities for All Students* (with Linda Hagedorn); *Reflective Evaluation: Improving Practice in College Preparation Programs* (with Linda Hagedorn); *Building the Responsive Campus: Creating High Performance Colleges and Universities;* and *Representation and the Text: Reframing the Narrative Voice* (with Yvonna Lincoln). Professor Tierney is currently involved in a variety of funded projects that pertain to two broad areas: equity and access and governance and decision making. Specifically, he is studying the effectiveness of programs that prepare low-income youth for college and is involved in projects geared toward improving governance and decision making in colleges and universities.

OCTAVIO VILLALPANDO is currently Assistant Professor of Educational Leadership and Policy and Associate Director of the Center for the Study of Race and Diversity in Higher Education at the University of Utah. He is a former National Research Council/Ford Foundation Postdoctoral Fellow, as well as a Spencer Foundation/American Educational Research Association (AERA) Fellow. His research contributes to the field of higher education around questions of how structural and racial inequality in universities shapes the experiences of students of color and faculty of color, particularly among Chicano/as. He teaches courses in critical race theory, diversity and multiculturalism in higher education, and college students.

Index

Note: Page numbers in *italics* indicate tables or figures.

SUNY series: Frontiers in Education
Philip G. Altbach, Editor

List of Titles

Critical Perspectives on Early Childhood Education—Lois Weis, Philip G. Altbach, Gail P. Kelly, and Hugh G. Petrie (eds.)

Textbooks in American Society: Politics, Policy, and Pedagogy—Philip G. Altbach, Gail P. Kelly, Hugh G. Petrie, and Lois Weis (eds.)

Black Resistance in High School: Forging a Separatist Culture—R. Patrick Solomon

Emergent Issues in Education: Comparative Perspectives—Robert F. Arnove, Philip G. Altbach, and Gail P. Kelly (eds.)

Creating Community on College Campuses—Irving J. Spitzberg, Jr. and Virginia V. Thorndike

Teacher Education Policy: Narratives, Stories, and Cases—Hendrik D. Gideonse (ed.)

Beyond Silenced Voices: Class, Race, and Gender in United States Schools—Lois Weis and Michelle Fine (eds.)

The Cold War and Academic Governance: The Lattimore Case at Johns Hopkins—Lionel S. Lewis

Troubled Times for American Higher Education: The 1990s and Beyond—Clark Kerr

Higher Education Cannot Escape History: Issues for the Twenty-first Century—Clark Kerr

Multiculturalism and Education: Diversity and Its Impact on Schools and Society—Thomas J. LaBelle and Christopher R. Ward

The Contradictory College: The Conflicting Origins, Impacts, and Futures of the Community College—Kevin J. Dougherty

Race and Educational Reform in the American Metropolis: A Study of School Decentralization—Dan A. Lewis and Kathryn Nakagawa

Professionalization, Partnership, and Power: Building Professional Development Schools—Hugh G. Petrie (ed.)

Ethnic Studies and Multiculturalism—Thomas J. LaBelle and Christopher R. Ward

Promotion and Tenure: Community and Socialization in Academe—William G. Tierney and Estela Mara Bensimon

Sailing Against the Wind: African Americans and Women in U.S. Education—Kofi Lomotey (ed.)

The Challenge of Eastern Asian Education: Implications for America—William K. Cummings and Philip G. Altbach (eds.)

Conversations with Educational Leaders: Contemporary Viewpoints on Education in America—Anne Turnbaugh Lockwood

Managed Professionals: Unionized Faculty and Restructuring Academic Labor—Gary Rhoades

The Curriculum (Second Edition): Problems, Politics, and Possibilities—Landon E. Beyer and Michael W. Apple (eds.)

Education / Technology / Power: Educational Computing as a Social Practice—Hank Bromley and Michael W. Apple (eds.)

Capitalizing Knowledge: New Intersections of Industry and Academia—Henry Etzkowitz, Andrew Webster, and Peter Healey (eds.)

The Academic Kitchen: A Social History of Gender Stratification at the University of California, Berkeley—Maresi Nerad

Grass Roots and Glass Ceilings: African American Administrators in Predominantly White Colleges and Universities—William B. Harvey (ed.)

Community Colleges as Cultural Texts: Qualitative Explorations of Organizational and Student Culture—Kathleen M. Shaw, James R. Valadez, and Robert A. Rhoads (eds.)

Educational Knowledge: Changing Relationships between the State, Civil Society, and the Educational Community—Thomas S. Popkewitz (ed.)

Transnational Competence: Rethinking the U.S.-Japan Educational Relationship—John N. Hawkins and William K. Cummings (eds.)

Women Administrators in Higher Education: Historical and Contemporary Perspectives—Jana Nidiffer and Carolyn Terry Bashaw (eds.)

Faculty Work in Schools of Education: Rethinking Roles and Rewards for the Twenty-first Century—William G. Tierney (ed.)

The Quest for Equity in Higher Education: Towards New Paradigms in an Evolving Affirmative Action Era—Beverly Lindsay and Manuel J. Justiz (eds.)

The Racial Crisis in American Higher Education (Revised Edition): Continuing Challenges for the Twenty-first Century—William A. Smith, Philip G. Altbach, and Kofi Lomotey (eds.)

Increasing Access to College: Extending Possibilities for All Students—William G. Tierney and Linda Serra Hagedorn (eds.)

Burning Down the House: Politics, Governance, and Affirmative Action at the University of California—Brian Pusser

Mixed Race Students in College: The Ecology of Race, Identity, and Community on Campus—Kristen A. Renn

Preparing for College: Nine Elements of Effective Outreach—William G. Tierney, Zoë B. Corwin, and Julia E. Colyar (eds.)